Resolving Regional Conflicts

Resolving Regional Conflicts

Edited by Roger E. Kanet

University of Illinois Press

Urbana and Chicago

©1998 by the Board of Trustees of the University of Illinois
Manufactured in the United States of America
1 2 3 4 5 C P 5 4 3 2 1

This book is printed on acid-free paper.

Library of Congress Cataloging-in-Publication Data
Resolving regional conflicts / edited by Roger E. Kanet.
p.   cm.
Includes bibliographical references and index.
ISBN 0-252-06671-5 (pbk. : acid-free paper). —
ISBN 0-252-02368-4 (cloth : acid-free paper)
1. Security, International. 2. Civil war.
3. Intervention (International law)
I. Kanet, Roger E., 1936– .
JX1952.R384 1998
327.1'7—dc21   97-4802
CIP

Contents

Preface

The authors of the essays in this volume have all been members of the interdisciplinary program in Arms Control, Disarmament, and International Security (ACDIS) and either have held faculty appointments in various academic departments at the University of Illinois at Urbana-Champaign (UIUC) or, in two cases, were graduate students in the Department of Political Science. The essays brought together within the covers of this volume deal with regional and local conflict, the most important challenge to international security in the period after the cold war and the reduced danger of superpower confrontation. Moreover, these essays highlight the research being carried out at the University of Illinois in the general field of international security studies and conflict resolution. In addition to highlighting the research of UIUC faculty, the contributors also wish to demonstrate their appreciation to Jeremiah D. Sullivan, the director of ACDIS from 1986 to 1994, for his major contributions to the development and maturation of the ACDIS program.

ACDIS was founded in 1978 by a group of UIUC faculty concerned about the lack of communication across academic disciplines on issues of crucial importance to human survival. Arthur Chilton in nuclear engineering and Stephen P. Cohen and Edward A. Kolodziej, both in political science, were the cofounders and codirectors of the fledgling program. Under Kolodziej's leadership as the first director ACDIS acquired official campus status and refurbished space, developed the beginnings of a library, and began to host visiting scholars. Kolodziej also played the central role in obtaining the first major grant from the John D. and Catherine T. MacArthur Foundation, which allowed ACDIS to begin supporting both graduate and undergraduate programs in arms control and security. It was also during this time that Stephen P. Cohen obtained the funding from the Ford Foundation and elsewhere to initiate what is now the premier South Asian security program in the world and that Jeremiah D. Sullivan became increasingly involved in the activities of ACDIS.

When Kolodziej stepped down as director of ACDIS in 1986, Sullivan was the unanimous choice among ACDIS members to replace him as director. Under Sullivan's leadership the program developed many new activities and expanded existing ones. It promoted and encouraged interdisciplinary activity among students and faculty at UIUC by providing financial backing for faculty to develop interdisciplinary courses; support for workshops, conferences, and speakers from a mix of disciplines; and funds for departments to facilitate faculty recruitment. It also served as a source of both intellectual stimulation and financial aid for graduate students. Under Sullivan's leadership the ACDIS Undergraduate Honors Seminar, established in 1984 for juniors and seniors with serious interests in international cooperation and security, became even more prominent at the University of Illinois.

When Sullivan assumed the directorship in 1986, one of his first priorities was to establish an ACDIS bulletin. The result was *Swords and Ploughshares,* a quarterly journal of short, timely articles on issues relevant to arms control, international conflict and security, and peace for both a scholarly and general audience. The majority of the contributors to *Swords and Ploughshares* are ACDIS faculty, research associates, and graduate students. Without any special effort to advertise the publication, the number of requests—including requests from numerous foreign international affairs centers and the general public—has steadily increased since 1986. *Swords and Ploughshares* is currently distributed to more than 400 UIUC faculty and students and to 150 national and international individuals and institutions and is available on the World Wide Web, along with much other information, on the ACDIS homepage at http://acdisweb.acdis.uiuc.edu/.

The other major publication of the program, the ACDIS Occasional Paper Series, was established in 1978 to circulate research and analytical results of faculty, research associates, and students. During the years Sullivan was director ACDIS increased the number and distribution of ACDIS occasional papers. The series is now distributed to U.S. and foreign academic arms control and security centers; nonacademic research units; governmental offices, including the U.S. Arms Control and Disarmament Agency; the Department of the Air Force; congressional committees; and individuals.

Sullivan was also instrumental in organizing a diverse speakers' and visitors' program over the years. Because the program's events are not discipline-specific, most events are cosponsored with one or more departments or colleges. Some events are aimed at a general campus audience; others address small, specialized audiences. In addition, the program has always made an effort to give undergraduate and graduate students an opportunity to interact with its speakers and visitors. ACDIS also provides numerous opportunities for UIUC faculty and students to speak to campus and specialized audiences through panel discussions, seminars, workshops, and lectures.

ACDIS was established to create a permanent academic unit at UIUC engaged in the teaching, research, and policy analysis of issues relevant to cooperation, peace, arms control, disarmament, and security in regional and international contexts. Bringing together faculty and students from the social sciences, the physical and engineering sciences, and the humanities, as well as area specialists, ACDIS has also aimed to be interdisciplinary and multidisciplinary, working closely with the established disciplines and programs of UIUC to use existing expertise and resources and to overcome traditional barriers to interdisciplinary interactions. Under Sullivan's leadership ACDIS fulfilled these goals.

In the spring of 1994, after Jeremiah Sullivan made clear his intention to step down from his administrative responsibilities, ACDIS faculty members began to discuss the most appropriate form of recognition they might offer Sullivan for his pivotal service to ACDIS and to the university. We finally settled on a volume of essays written by ACDIS faculty members that focus on issues of current analytic and policy relevance, showcase the research activities of ACDIS faculty, and also honor an administrative leader who has made such important contributions to teaching, research, and analysis on peace, arms control, and security matters. That collection, which was broader in content than the current volume and included essays by several other UIUC faculty members, appeared in 1995 in a modest ACDIS publication entitled *Regional Conflicts and Conflict Resolution: Essays in Honor of Jeremiah D. Sullivan.*

As editor of the present volume, I wish to thank the authors for the timely completion of the initial drafts of their manuscripts, as well as for their acceptance of editorial suggestions and requests for revisions. Moreover, the authors and I want to express our appreciation to the anonymous readers for the University of Illinois Press, whose advice has contributed to a more focused volume. I also wish to express heartfelt gratitude to members of the staff at ACDIS, particularly Merrily Shaw, who served as critic, production editor, and publisher of the original ACDIS publication. Without her major contributions this project could not have come to fruition. I also want to thank Susanne M. Birgerson for her editorial assistance and Jerrie M. Merridith of the staff of International Programs and Studies for ensuring that incompatible computer programs did eventually result in a readable manuscript. Finally, I thank Stephen P. Cohen, current director of ACDIS, for financial and staff support that has made this volume possible.

Resolving Regional Conflicts

Introduction:
International Security after the Cold War

Roger E. Kanet

The end of the global confrontation between the United States and the Soviet Union was widely expected to bring with it a "new world order" based on principles of the peaceful resolution of conflict, the expansion of human welfare, and increased democratic participation of formerly subject peoples.[1] The primary threat to international security for the previous four decades had been the danger of nuclear war between the two superpowers. With the key areas of dispute between them resolved and the decision reached to pursue foreign policy based more on cooperation than conflict, the emergence of a peaceful and collaborative world order was expected. Yet in the period since the end of the cold war the security threat represented by possible nuclear warfare between the superpowers has been replaced by an explosion of regional conflicts across much of the former communist world and throughout Asia and Africa. Although the end of the superpower confrontation was important in resolving or bringing closer to resolution a number of major local and regional conflicts in which the United States and the Soviet Union had been deeply involved—for example, those in Angola, Cambodia, Ethiopia, the Middle East, Mozambique, Nicaragua, and South Africa—other conflicts either were not affected by the end of the cold war or were actually unleashed after 1989, when the superpowers reduced their involvement in local and regional affairs.

We now understand that the superpower confrontation and the division of the world into two dominant military blocs had, in effect, a dampening effect on much regional conflict.[2] For example, even though the United States and the Soviet Union were deeply involved in the Middle East conflict and actually contributed to the level of hostility by sending massive weapons shipments to the region, they also placed serious restraints on the use of that weaponry.[3] Once the Soviet Union and the United States withdrew from direct involvement in many of these conflicts, the restraints inherent in past dependency relationships disappeared. Moreover, during the cold war years the superpowers and their major allies had provided massive shipments of sophisticated weaponry to clients throughout the developing world, thereby raising the level of lethality in local or regional conflicts and enhancing the role of the military in domestic politics. With the loosening of the constraints associated with the reduction, even withdrawal, of superpower involvement in much of the developing world this weaponry was instrumental in attempts of various regional actors to gain objectives that had long been beyond their reach. In the Gulf region, for example, President Saddam Hussein of Iraq decided to resolve, once and for all, the longstanding confrontation with Iran over dominance in this oil-rich region by forcibly conquering and integrating Kuwait and its massive oil reserves into Iraq; in Somalia various clan leaders escalated their competition for dominance to the point that the very structures of the state disappeared. Ethnically based claims have been at the root of explosive civil wars in Rwanda, Sri Lanka, Afghanistan, the Caucasus, former Yugoslavia, and elsewhere. Instead of ushering in a period of peace, security, and human welfare as envisaged in President George Bush's "new world order," the end of the cold war in many regions of the world was but a prelude to the eruption of local and regional conflict at levels of destruction unimagined in the past.[4]

This development should not have been unexpected. Even though international relations after World War II were dominated by the competition between the United States and the Soviet Union as advocates of very different ways of organizing global society, most of the wars that occurred were not wars between established states. They have mainly been wars for national liberation and self-determination.[5] With the creation of more than a hundred new independent states out of the former European colonial empires, civil strife posed the most serious threat to international security even before the end of the cold war. Since the historical, national, ethnic, and religious factors at work in the drive for independence did not stop at the artificial territorial boundaries of the old empires, it should have been expected that many of the newly established states would face new demands for self-determination or for territorial changes from among their ethnically diverse populations.[6]

The collapse of the European Marxist-Leninist states during 1989–91—particularly the Soviet Union—brought to an end the global superpower confrontation and reduced the threat of global nuclear war. Even before the demise of the old system, however, emerging ethnically based conflict was already evident in Yugoslavia and the Soviet Union. With the end of the authoritarian pressures in both countries repressed demands and revived ethnic animosities began to play themselves out. These new outbreaks of local and regional conflict in Europe have been added to the already long list of similar conflicts in Asia, Africa, and Latin America. Edward A. Kolodziej has summarized the current global security situation as follows:

> Interstate war and conflict remain serious problems, although receding in saliency and import relative to the recent past; the prospects of global war appear remote; regional security appears now to be more central and urgent; at this level, internal strife, civil war and state implosion are clear and present dangers; and it may be that, as universal norms of human rights take root in the thinking and values of the diverse populations of the world, the protection of these rights and the processes of democratization with which they are associated may properly rank as central international security concerns. They are certainly more important than they were only a half century ago; and they loom larger as shared security concerns within and across state boundaries in the future.[7]

The essays in this volume examine various aspects of the current international security environment—particularly regional conflict and ways in which the international community has dealt with specific conflicts or might deal with them in the future. In the first part Edward E. Kolodziej maintains that since the end of the global superpower confrontation international security has been increasingly regionalized. The withdrawal of the major powers from involvement in local conflicts has actually made the resolution of these conflicts more problematic. Part 2 includes four articles that examine the way in which religious and ethnic conflict have played themselves out in Northern Ireland and in Southwest and South Asia. Although they concern only a few of the plethora of ethically and religiously based conflicts currently plaguing the international community, the conflicts described and proposals considered are in many ways representative of a large number of conflicts in other countries and regions of the world.[8]

In the first essay of this section William F. Kelleher traces the background of the current conflict in Northern Ireland and explores the factors that contribute to the sense of Irish identity and to the competing identities of the people of Northern Ireland. He argues that social and economic change must be taken into account in analyzing conflicts in states undergoing the transition between the collapse of an old political order and the construction of a new one. To maximize the prospects for the ultimate success of the peace process in Northern Ireland, democratization must accompany peace efforts, and social and cultural divisions need to be addressed. Kelleher employs an ethnographic method to examine the everyday cultural practices that he thinks are essential in the study of conflict resolution.

In the second essay Robert J. McKim also treats the issue of the Irish conflict, but he focuses on the philosophical and legal underpinnings of the claims for self-determination and the need for outsiders to take an impartial approach in their attempts to help resolve the conflict. Impartiality refers to an evenhanded application of the logic underlying rival claims for self-identification. In effect, any proposal for settling ethnic or religious disputes should recognize that both sides usually have equally strong cases for self-determination. McKim does not assume that self-determination refers to independent statehood. Rather, it should be a way of guaranteeing that a group's future will be determined by its members, not by outside groups. In the same vein the future of the two factions in Ireland should be determined by their respective members.

The other two essays in this section deal explicitly with the conflicts in Southwest and South Asia. Marvin G. Weinbaum examines the complexities of the foreign policy of Pakistan as it faces the ongoing chaos in Afghanistan, its place in the often conflictual relationships among Muslim states in West Asia, and its role in newly independent Muslim Central Asia. He argues that Pakistan has managed its relations with a reasonable degree of success, thereby making it a major actor in the region. For a variety of reasons, from the stalemate with India to the end of the cold war and U.S. patronage, Pakistan has refocused its energies on strategic states in the region. It has positioned itself as the mediator between the Islamic states and the West, including the Russian Federation. It has also striven to present itself as a moderate state, so that it would not alienate the West while retaining its links to the Islamic world.

In the fourth and final essay in part 2, Stephen P. Cohen uses a theory of regional conflict to explore the origins of war and the conditions for peace in South Asia. He argues that regional conflict is not inevitable and that it is possible to formulate strategies designed to mitigate or manage conflict, if the causes of conflict can be positively identified. In the case of South Asia the primary cause of conflict stems from a minority complex felt by two important states in the region, each of which sees itself as a minority threatened by the other and its proclaimed allies—for India Pakistan is part of the Muslim world that, along with the West, destroyed India's former greatness, while Pakistan sees India as a much larger and potentially dominant regional state. Any regional peace initiative must account for the self-perceptions of these two states.

The essays in part 3 assess the place of third parties in regional conflict and in efforts to ameliorate such conflict. Once again the essays treat only a part of the broad set of issues, but they contribute to the growing literature on the role of external actors in facilitating conflict resolution.[9] Paul W. Schroeder argues that the liberal institutionalist (or idealistic) view of international politics is ultimately more applicable to international politics than is the competing view, realism, for the very same reason cited in favor of the realist approach: very diverse communities compete with one another for the same resources. Schroeder maintains that communities can learn to cooperate in the same manner that they previously learned to hate each other. In essence communities can learn, and have learned, over time that cooperation can be more fruitful than conflict. To support of this argument, Schroeder draws on the history of Europe and finds many instances of cooperation that could—and did—form the basis of a more lasting peace.

Turning to the potential of United Nations' peacekeeping operations in the post–cold war era, Paul F. Diehl surveys its peacekeeping operations in former Yugoslavia, Somalia, and Cambodia. He concludes that the relative success or failure of these missions provides some insight concerning the likely direction of U.N. peacekeeping operations. He notes two major trends. First, peacekeeping forces are deployed in areas of civil conflict, precisely the most problematic area of peacekeeping. Second, peacekeeping operations have taken on new roles, specifically election supervision and humanitarian assistance. New strategies must, however, be developed in response to the new challenges facing the post–cold war world order, if future peacekeeping attempts are to be successful.

Gerardo L. Munck and Chetan Kumar explain that similar conflict resolution efforts in El Salvador and Cambodia had dissimilar outcomes because of differences in the implementation process. They argue that the cases share several similarities regarding the nature of conflict and the circumstances that brought about a resolution. The different outcomes stem from a combination of domestic and external factors significant in the successful implementation of a peace accord.

The final two essays in part 3 examine conflict in the postcommunist world. Carol Skalnik Leff discusses the disintegration of the cold war security regime in Europe that unleashed long suppressed ethnic conflicts in Eastern Europe, conflicts from which Western Europe had previously been insulated. In the aftermath of the collapse of the cold war framework, Western European international organizations, such as the European Union and its affiliates, have by default emerged as the arbiters of conflicts in Eastern Europe. The primary reason for this, she argues, lies in the universal desire of the Eastern European states for integration into the political, security, and economic structures of Western Europe. Although the transition process in postcommunist Europe promises to be slow, protracted, and filled with potential conflicts, the network of European institutions may provide some guidelines by which to survive the transition process without reverting to an authoritarian system or turning to armed conflict.

Alexander V. Kozhemiakin and Roger E. Kanet maintain that Russia is pursuing an assertive foreign policy in the former republics of the Soviet Union, especially in the realm of "peacekeeping." The goals of Russian foreign policy stem from the desire to stabilize the areas bordering Russia—even to reincorporate much of the territory into a new "Union." Obstacles include domestic pressure against the cost, both human and economic, of peacekeeping missions and pressure from the countries of the "near abroad," which have appealed to the West and to various international organizations for protection against Russian intervention. With the exception of the Baltics, the West has not positively refuted Russia's claims to a dominant role in the "near abroad." Given the current international climate, Russian involvement in the "near abroad" is likely to expand, partly under the guise of peacekeeping operations.

Taken together the essays that follow outline the degree to which international conflict has been regionalized in the 1990s and examine a cross section of the types of issues associated with contemporary regional conflict. They also discuss the ways in which external actors, including foreign governments and international organizations, have attempted to deal with these and related conflicts, and they note that at times external "peacekeepers" may actually be part of the problem or may exacerbate existing problems.

Notes

1. For a discussion of the place of a "new world order" in U.S. foreign policy during the Bush administration, see Terry L. Diebel, "Bush's Foreign Policy: Mastery and Inaction," *Foreign Policy,* no. 84 (1991): 3–23. See also Roger E. Kanet and James T. Alexander, "The End of the Cold War and the 'New World Order': Implications for the Developing World," in *Russia and the Third World in the Post-Soviet Era,* ed. Mohiaddin Mesbahi (Gainesville: University Press of Florida, 1994), 192–222.

2. An extensive literature has emerged that deals with both the mitigating effect of the superpower conflict on regional conflict and the expansion of conflict

after the cold war. See, for example, John L. Gaddis, "Threat Illusions, the Long Peace, and the Future of the International System," in *The Long Postwar Peace,* ed. Charles W. Kegley Jr. (New York: HarperCollins, 1991), 25–55; and Edward A. Kolodziej and Roger E. Kanet, eds., *Coping with Conflict after the Cold War* (Baltimore: Johns Hopkins University Press, 1996).

3. See, for example, Galia Golan, "Superpower Cooperation in the Middle East," in *The Cold War as Cooperation: Superpower Cooperation in Regional Conflict Management,* ed. Roger E. Kanet and Edward A. Kolodziej (London: Macmillan, 1991), 121–46.

4. Members of the ACDIS faculty at the University of Illinois have long been involved in analyzing the sources of regional conflict and the role of the superpowers in those conflicts. For example, the following books, all sponsored by ACDIS, deal explicitly with regional conflict: Kanti P. Bajpai, and Stephen P. Cohen, eds., *South Asia after the Cold War: International Perspectives* (Boulder, Colo.: Westview, 1993); Kanti P. Bajpai, P. R. Chari, Pervaiz I. Cheema, Stephen P. Cohen, and Sumit Ganguly, *Brasstacks and Beyond: Perception and Management of Crisis in South Asia* (New Delhi, India: Manohar, 1995); Stephen P. Cohen, ed., *The Security of South Asia: American and Asian Perspectives* (Urbana: University of Illinois Press, 1987; reprint, New Delhi, India: Vistaar, 1988); Paul F. Diehl, *International Peacekeeping* (Baltimore: Johns Hopkins University Press, 1993); Shivaji Ganguly, *U.S. Policy toward South Asia* (Boulder, Colo.: Westview, 1990); Sumit Ganguly, *The Origins of War in South Asia: The Indo-Pakistani Conflicts since 1947* (Boulder, Colo.: Westview, 1986); Kanet and Kolodziej, eds., *The Cold War as Cooperation;* Roger E. Kanet and Alexander V. Kozhemiakin, eds., *The Foreign Policy of the Russian Federation* (London: Macmillan, 1997); Edward A. Kolodziej, ed., *Making and Marketing Arms: The French Experience and Its Implications for the International System* (Princeton, N.J.: Princeton University Press, 1987); Kolodziej and Kanet, eds., *Coping with Conflict after the Cold War;* Edward A. Kolodziej and Roger E. Kanet, eds., *The Limits of Soviet Power in the Developing World: Thermidor in the Revolutionary Struggle* (Baltimore: Johns Hopkins University Press, 1989).

5. On the preponderance of wars for independence or self-determination, see, for example, K. J. Holsti, *Peace and War: Armed Conflicts and International Order, 1648–1989* (Cambridge: Cambridge University Press, 1991), 274–78.

6. On the issue of ethnically based conflict two especially valuable collections are Joseph V. Montville, ed., *Conflict and Peacemaking in Multiethnic Societies* (Lexington, Mass.: Lexington Books, 1990); and Michael E. Brown, ed., *Ethnic Conflict and International Security* (Princeton, N.J.: Princeton University Press, 1993).

7. Edward A. Kolodziej, "International Security after the Cold War: From Globalization to Regionalization" (Unpublished manuscript, spring 1996).

8. For recent discussions of conflict resolution in situations of local or regional conflict, see Timothy D. Sisk, *Power Sharing and International Mediation in Ethnic Conflicts* (Washington, D.C.: United States Institute of Peace, for the Carnegie Corporation of New York, 1996); Andrew Gamble and Anthony Payne, eds., *Regionalism and World Order* (New York: St. Martin's, 1996); and Commission on

Global Governance, *Our Global Neighborhood: The Report of the Commission on Global Governance* (Oxford: Oxford University Press, 1995), especially chapter 3, "Promoting Security," 77–134.

9. See, for example, Lori Fisler Damrosch, ed., *Enforcing Restraint: Collective Intervention in Internal Conflicts* (New York: Council on Foreign Relations, 1993); and Kolodziej and Kanet, eds., *Coping with Conflict after the Cold War.*

Part One

The Regionalization of
International Security

1

Modeling International Security

Edward A. Kolodziej

Several converging factors at play in the post–cold war environment suggest that in the immediate future most of the security problems confronting the world society will be at the regional level. First and foremost the end of the cold war and bipolar competition between the United States and the former Soviet Union has dissolved the incentives for Washington and Moscow to globalize regional security systems. On the one hand, each antagonist sought clients in its struggle to gain regional and global ascendancy or to deny its rival the support of a newly emerging state or the switch of an alliance partner, such as in the African Horn or Eastern Europe. Intervention in support of client states or revolutionary groups encouraged both to send arms and even troops to assist its allies. Moscow and Washington accounted for most of the arms and military technology transferred to other states during the cold war.[1] On the other hand, as the cold war evolved and as the excesses of clients threatened to engulf the superpowers in a direct clash that might trigger an escalation of hostilities and a nuclear exchange, both global rivals intervened to restrain regional conflict. The result was a very complex game of conflict and cooperation that tended toward a series of regional balances shaped in ways congenial to the security interests of one or the other or both of these global antagonists.[2] Neither of these two sets of conflicting incentives, either to seek and save allies or to constrain them, works today. An imploded Soviet Union has left a weakened Russian Federation in its wake—a state burdened by internal revolt, economic collapse, social upheaval, political corruption, and a broken and dispirited military.

Second, although this global interventionist proclivity, while hardly eliminated—witness U.S. interventions in Panama, Haiti, and Bosnia—is now less pronounced, regional security questions are increasingly framed by local self-help efforts. Regional rivals now have less cause to worry that outside powers will preempt their efforts to pursue their security interests. Slobodan Milosevic could destroy the Yugoslav state in the name of Serbian nationalism. Fear of Serbian domination prompted Slovenia, Croatia, and, later, Bosnia to secede and to ignite yet another round of Balkan wars at untold cost in human life and material damage to all the rivals. Belgrade's support of the breakaway Bosnia Serbs has been costly, too, because of U.N. economic sanctions, but its intransigence has not incurred Western responses sufficiently grave at any time to threaten the survival of this rump inheritor of the Yugoslav state. Nor, until the signing of the Dayton agreement and the arrival of large NATO forces in 1995, have the Bosnian Serbs confronted a serious threat to their security, territorial, and statehood aims. However, NATO's intervention promises to be less decisive in resolving the Bosnian conflict politically than the countervailing power that regional opponents, principally Croatian and Bosnian Muslim forces, can dispose to check Bosnia Serb pretensions—and each other.

If aggressive regional rivals can now reckon that outside armed intervention will very likely either not occur or be ineffective in blocking their efforts to reach their security and political aims through force, the targets of their aggression must also count on receiving less support to prevail against their local antagonists than they might have during the cold war. The Bosnian Muslims have had to learn this lesson the hard way after repeated hints and veiled promises of Western help did not materialize. The arms embargo, purportedly aimed at all parties to the conflict, in reality hurt the Bosnian Muslims most; Bosnian Serbs could still rely on Belgrade or the Yugoslav army for arms, heavy weapons, and supplies despite U.N. sanctions. The United States similarly refused to intervene on behalf of Shi'ite and Kurd opponents of the Baghdad regime, defeated in Desert Storm. While encouraging them to revolt, it did nothing to spare them from the ruthless reprisals of the Hussein government as compensation for their misplaced confidence in American and Western promises of assistance. Nor did the United States do much to protect its Kurdish agents and families from reprisals by opponents in the Kurdish civil war or from Iraqi forces that sided with one of the factions. Contrast, too, the lengths to which the United States was prepared to go—using the United Nations as well as American military forces and CIA agents—to ensure Colonel Mobutu's takeover of Zaire and its indifference to his plight in the face of the rebellion launched by the forces of Laurent Kabila.[3]

Third, the sheer diminution of the threat of global war reduces Western interest in controlling the outcomes of regional conflicts, however lamentable their human and material tragedy. The Yugoslavia tragedy, the

Chechnyan disaster, and the mindless slaughter in Rwanda and Burundi illustrate the point. As some authors suggest,[4] the outcomes of these local struggles would appear to have no decisive impact on the vital security interests of the Western powers. Their cold war victory and their security gains with the passing of the Soviet threat remain essentially intact. The incompetence displayed by the Russian military in their attempts to squelch the Chechnyan uprising, not to mention the political corruption and Moscow's failure to provide effective leadership for Russian forces, strengthens Western confidence that Russia will be unable to project its depleted and divided power abroad, whatever its nationalist blusterings may otherwise suggest. The Russian military lacks the adequate arms, morale, competent leadership, coherent and incorruptible political direction, and public support to pose a clear and present danger to the West. Even if a nationalist and expansionist government were to assume power in Moscow, by the ballot box or bullets, it would lack the means, nuclear weapons as caveat to this line of reasoning notwithstanding, to gravely threaten Western security interests.

China might challenge the Westcentric system—at least in Northeast Asia—but not anytime soon as it embarks on economic development and market reforms, whose success depends more on detente than on inciting geopolitical conflict and tensions. Moreover, its armed forces remain at a low level of technological sophistication and operational preparedness. Their ability to project military power is limited; their internal coherence and unity are suspect in the wake of Tiananmen Square; and important military leadership cadres are reportedly more preoccupied with economic development and lining their own pockets than with military efficiency and modernization. All these constraints may be surmounted— and for the worse for the West. Samuel P. Huntington's ominous warnings about coming cultural struggles between Confucian and Christian civilizations (not to mention underlying racial antagonism) may come to pass,[5] but that prospect is no less problematic and speculative than those associated with narrower concerns over the expansion of Chinese military capabilities and the mischief they might cause.

Fourth, there is a heightened sense of pessimism among the members of the prevailing Westcentric system that member efforts would come to naught, even if they had the will and used the superior military and economic capabilities at their disposal to intervene in a regional conflicts. The intractability of enduring rivalries cautions against quick outside fixes— or against undertaking fixes at all. Massive military intervention on the scale of Desert Storm might well end the fighting in Bosnia once and for all; but, absent a political settlement reached by the regional rivals, it would hardly bring peace unless foreign troops were stationed there permanently, which democratic constraints and unacceptable high material and human costs to implement would rule out. Greek-Turkish antagonism within NATO evidences the formidable difficulties of containing, much less resolving, conflicts even among ostensible allies. The renewed outbreak of communal violence in Cyprus in the summer of 1996 indicates just how tenuous any cease-fire accord can be when age-old animosities and accumulated grievances, real or imagined, remain firmly fixed in the minds of the regional antagonists. These forces lurk below the surface, threatening to reerupt to shatter a temporary lull in hostilities or to frustrate efforts at rapprochement between Greeks and Turks.

Fifth, de Tocqueville's observation about democracies also has relevance in explaining the renewed reluctance of the big powers of the Western coalition to intervene and thereby to globalize regional conflicts in attempts to contain them. Western democratic populations, relieved of half a century of cold war burdens and preoccupied with serious economic and social problems at home, are not keen on expending their blood and treasure to help others whose conflicts do not appear to bear directly on either their security interests and survival or their economic well-being. The Kuwait crisis illustrates this new rule of Western engagement. Only the threat of Iraq's control of the West's oil lifeline and its acquisition of nuclear weapons could marshal the diffuse economic and military power of the Western coalition to roll back the Kuwaiti seizure. There is also a decided asymmetry in measuring the political costs and benefits of intervention abroad for democratic political leaders. As George Bush painfully learned in 1992, even huge foreign policy successes are short-lived electoral assets. Elections are still won and lost over local issues and short-term political concerns, all the more so now that foreign threats appear to be less clear and certainly less pressing.

Finally, prevailing military strategic doctrine, particularly in the United States, conspires with these political, economic, and psychological constraints to caution against entry into a regional conflict. As a consequence of the Vietnam experience, the U.S. military resists sending in U.S. armed forces unless several hard-to-fill preconditions are met. First, a plan for exit—an endgame—must be delineated to warrant the use of U.S. military assets and to justify the inevitable losses of material and personnel. Second, the American public must be fully enlisted in support of the military intervention. Third, overwhelming military force must be employed to ensure American control of the local terrain and the conflicting factions at war. Fourth, the command of U.S. forces must be under tight national control, political and military.

These conditions are so taxing that they inhibit exercising a military option. Most international security problems, notably those arising from civil war, are surrounded with so much uncertainty that these conditions essentially argue against most proposals for intervention, however urgent. This is true even in cases like Somalia, where a brief can be made that the introduction of U.S. military power had a positive effect on reducing the misery of the Somalian population suffering from widespread starvation and civil war. Endgames are hard to devise when meeting urgent cries for immediate relief—witness the massacre of hundreds of thousands of civilians in Rwanda. Public support, absent strong leadership, cannot easily be mobilized given prevailing democratic electoral constraints and domestic socioeconomic preoccupations; proposals to intervene from governmental officials are likely to occasion bitter partisan debate; controlling local terrain exclusively by force is often difficult since, as in Somalia or Yugoslavia, foreign military forces are likely to be engaged in reaching political compromises with local factions even as they attempt to impose a solution on them to end the fighting. NATO forces were reluctant to apprehend war criminals, notably Bosnian Serb president Radovan Karadzic and General Ratko Mladic. They resisted any widening of the scope of their mission that might make them participants in the Yugoslav civil war and that might jeopardize their roles as mediators and conciliators between the warring parties.

Interventions also imply, as often as not, multilateral efforts and the need to compromise with supportive allies over the terms of the military control of operations and of political endgames. Such compromises are not easily orchestrated or, once achieved, of long duration. U.S. support of U.N. peacekeeping operations offers a sobering illustration of these limitations. Rather than herald these interventions as a contribution to regional and global peace in keeping with Security Council obligations under the United Nations Charter and, incidentally, as a cost-effective way to address threats to international security in lieu of unilateral national efforts, both major candidates for the presidency in 1996 opposed the reelection of Boutros Boutros-Ghali as U.N. secretary-general as a way to curry votes by repudiating his resourceful efforts to discharge U.N. peacekeeping responsibilities. Russia and China are hardly alone in being moved by national sentiment in the conduct of foreign policy.

Regional Security Systems

If the regionalization of security appears to be the wave of the future, how is that future likely to unfold? The first and most overarching observation that might be made is that each region is different. In other words, the security problems of each region are shaped by different historical, geographic, and environmental factors, divergent security interests, radically varying actors (with a wide range of military capabilities at their disposal), region-specific axes of conflict defining the structure of the local security complex, and uniquely constructed security systems to address the problems of the rivals at interstate and intrastate levels. This emphasis on differentiation does not imply that regions cannot be compared or that common modes of analysis cannot be used to define security problems while engineering solutions tailored to address the unique needs of each region. If tools of analysis are potentially comparable, solutions are not. A tour d'horizon of regional security complexes suggests these possibilities.

There are at least six kinds of security arrangements that can be identified, singly or in combination, to address the emerging security problems confronting regionally interacting states (see figure 1). These may be roughly differentiated, hierarchically, by the degree to which the states and peoples of a region are willing to resolve their differences and govern their interdependent affairs through peaceful bargaining and negotiations rather than through coercive threats and force. These include (1) a security community, (2) hegemonic consensual leadership, (3) a pluralistic security community, (4) a concert of states (especially of big powers), (5) a concert based on spheres of influence with hegemonic coercive leadership, and (6) multiple balance of power arrangements.

The European Security Complex

These six security models can perhaps be best understood by examining figure 2, which suggests that each of these approaches is currently in play in the ladder that constitutes the European security complex. The latter comprises the diverse and contentious peoples populating the area from the British Isles in the west to the Russian Federation in the east and includes in these security arrangements the active—many would contend indispensable—participation of the United States, a geopolitical external actor. European security systems have also been supplemented by universal systems (primarily the United Nations) and by critically important nonmilitary means and mechanisms, notably the European Union. Europe is easily the most advanced region of the world in the number of solutions that are being tested to manage and resolve the security problems of the peoples and states of the region.

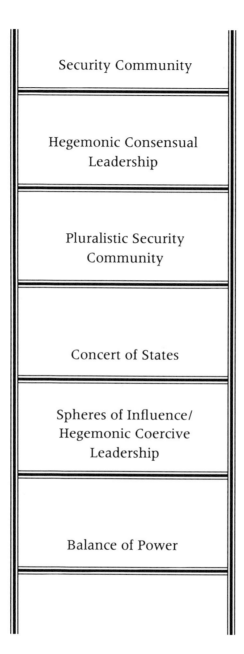

Figure 1. Regional Security Systems

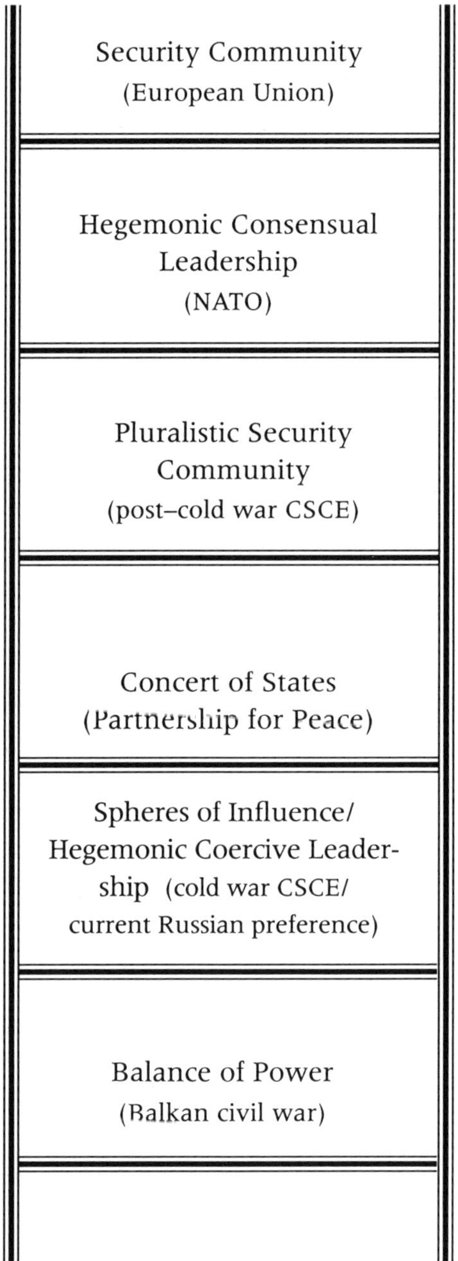

Security Community
(European Union)

Hegemonic Consensual
Leadership
(NATO)

Pluralistic Security
Community
(post–cold war CSCE)

Concert of States
(Partnership for Peace)

Spheres of Influence/
Hegemonic Coercive Leadership (cold war CSCE/
current Russian preference)

Balance of Power
(Balkan civil war)

Figure 2. European Security Complex

Security Community

Karl Deutsch defines a security community as one whose members share fundamental values and conform their behavior to common principles, norms, institutions, and joint processes of decision in the service of peaceful change.[6] If we follow Deutsch, the European Union (EU) qualifies as an emerging security community. With the passage of the Maastricht Treaty, member states are dedicated to the development of not only an integrated economy for its 350 million members, soon to be enlarged by the entry of several neutrals into the community, but also a single monetary policy, banking system, and currency, as well as a common security and foreign policy. The EU has been the principal European vehicle for resolving the Franco-German rivalry that plunged Europe and the globe into two world wars. The proposal for a European army to be built around the now evolving Eurocorps symbolizes and putatively institutionalizes the commitment of the member states to renounce force in resolving their differences and to seek a common position, in tandem with their commercial policies, to address their relations with the outside world.

The European Union, however, falls well short of a collective security organization.[7] The member states are at odds over their policies toward the conflict in Yugoslavia. The British and French maintain peacekeeping troops under U.N. command. Germany, whose recognition of Bosnia-Herzegovina precipitated Serbian and Croatian declarations of independence, is all but precluded from assuming a major military role in these operations because of the lingering animosities over the Nazi occupation of Yugoslavia during World War II. Greece is in incipient conflict with Macedonia over claims to independence. Italy still harbors claims against Yugoslavia over Trieste. The smaller states and neutrals, such as Ireland (soon to be joined by Sweden, Finland, and Austria), have little appetite for military interventions inside Europe, much less outside. As the EU enlarges, extending quite likely to Eastern Europe by the end of the century, the prospects of developing a common defense and foreign policy will become more daunting and the likelihood ever dimmer.

Hegemonic Consensual Leadership

NATO supplements the European security community and enlarges the pacific union of democratic states to include the United States. It falls short of meeting the test of a security community itself since it includes at least two members, Greece and Turkey, that have already engaged in armed hostilities within the alliance. Indeed, one of the implicit functions of NATO, under U.S. leadership, is to monitor its southern tier and to inter-

cede in or head off conflicts between allies. This same function is directed, soto voce, toward Germany, a security imperative that has become
more important with the passing of the cold war. In these capacities, the
United States acts as a reluctant hegemon—present at the behest of its
allies but nonplused by the inability of the European states, materially
endowed and even more populous than the United States, to cope with
their regional security problems.

The Bush administration initially acceded to European entreaties to stay
clear of the Yugoslav debacle, only to be slowly drawn into the conflict
by the impotence of the Europeans to contain or resolve the civil war. The
intervention of British and French forces under the aegis of the United
Nations proved ineffectual. Their announced aims—to minimize the loss
of lives, to create safe havens for the civilian population, and to end ethnic cleansing—were frustrated at every turn. U.N. peacekeeping efforts
were also discredited as Anglo-French elements, as often as not, were
outmanned and outgunned by Serbian and Croatian forces and, to add
to their humiliation, were often used as hostages to shield Serbian and
Croatian forces.

Pluralistic Security Community

From yet another perspective Europeans are also relying on a pluralistic
security community (PSC) to address their several security dilemmas. A
PSC is essentially a group of states dedicated to peaceful relations in their
mutual dealings. In principle they have no fundamental differences dividing them, although they may not have the same form of political regimes or share the same values. They are agreed, however, on settling their
differences peacefully. Toward other parties outside the PSC, members
may well assume a different stance, even hostility. Insulating the PSC from
this disruption is not always easy. The weak institutional vehicle of this
approach in Europe is the Organization for Security and Cooperation in
Europe (OSCE), which grew out of the Conference on Security and Cooperation in Europe, initially created to stabilize and legitimate Europe's
division in the Helsinki Accords of 1975. What began as a mechanism to
stabilize the cold war balance of power between NATO and the Warsaw
Pact has since evolved, with the implosion of the Soviet Union, into a PSC.
In 1990 the OSCE was given slightly more organizational profile as a
mechanism to articulate pan-European security concerns by adding a
secretariat and modest crisis and conflict resolution functions.

Ideally, no elaborate organization structure is needed to make a PSC
work since the member states have no intention of attacking one another and have confidence in one another's expression of peaceful intent. The

underlying assumption of peaceful intent and good behavior of all members is highly tenuous in the light of the Yugoslav crisis, however. Lacking NATO's military capabilities and composed of all of the states of Europe, the OSCE mirrors rather than addresses the underlying security dilemmas besetting the continent. It can offer no real response to a state that defects and abandons its promise to renounce force in settling its differences with rivals. This concern is very much on the mind of the Eastern European states faced with a resurgent nationalist Russia. This pervasive worry traces the limits of this security arrangement and explains the determination of the former Eastern European satellites of the Soviet Union to seek NATO protection. These real and perceived concerns and the inability of the OSCE to resolve them should not obscure those useful, if only supplementary, security functions that the organization can play. It is principally a forum for stating their differences. The OSCE can also serve as a vehicle for confidence-building measures and arms control and disarmament, as the 1990 conventional force reductions accord suggests. The OSCE also helped monitor elections in Bosnia under the Dayton Peace Accords. Like the United Nations, it may evolve into a useful peacekeeping, if not peacemaking, organization.

Concert of States

OSCE shortcomings prompt the search for a security framework somewhere between a security community and a PSC, on the one hand, and discredited balance of power systems, on the other. These efforts are largely aimed at reintegrating Russia into a more stable and peaceful European security complex. One approach, resting on the assumption of a democratizing market-oriented Russian Federation, is to return to the Vienna solution of a concert of states.[8] Several serious problems arise in attempting to apply this formula. The problems of economic and political reform among the states of the former Soviet Union have not been surmounted and are not likely to be solved anytime soon despite progress, albeit uneven, throughout the region. Worse, in this transition period internal nationalist sentiment has become shriller and more intransigent in its opposition to any hint of Russian subordination to Western and, specifically, American hegemony, however much the West and Washington may insist on their peaceful intentions. Reflecting this national mood, Moscow has agreed to participate in Partnership for Peace discussions but has resisted, however ineffectually, NATO's determination to expand eastward to embrace several former Warsaw Pact states. Its extension is interpreted by Moscow as an alliance against Russia, not as a move to integrate Russia into a concert. Similarly, there is little sentiment within NATO to accord membership to Russia anytime soon. If the proposition of a pacific union of democratic states approaches a "scientific law"—and many would dispute this claim—much of the concern about reintegrating Russia into such a union revolves around the problems associated with the transition from an authoritarian political and a directed economic system to an open democracy and a market economy. This period of lengthy upheaval and turmoil breeds the conditions for misdirected nationalism and xenophobia as well as internally rapacious politics among warring groups seeking control of the coercive powers of the Russian state and its bureaucracies—an extremely volatile mix that encourages tensions with other states and the possibility of armed hostilities.[9]

Spheres of Influence and Balances of Power

The failure, thus far, to reintegrate Russia as a satisfied power within an all-European security complex raises the prospect of a return to a policy of spheres of influence, gravitating toward a classic balance of power system. On the surface the European peoples and their ruling elites, including members of the former Warsaw Pact, are strongly opposed to this solution. The Russian government, however, appears attached to the idea of having the Western states recognize its "special interests and responsibilities" among its former sister republics and in Eastern Europe. Moscow has also tried, unsuccessfully, to get the United Nations or the OSCE to recognize its interventions in Georgia, in Tajikistan, and in areas of its former Eastern European domain as peacekeeping operations. These overtures assume a somewhat hollow ring for many former allies and former subject peoples in the region, most notably in the Baltic states, particularly in the light of Moscow's brutal and botched suppression of the Chechnyan uprising.

The resistance of many Europeans and the United States to accept a "spheres of influence" solution as they did, however conditionally, in signing the Helsinki Accords suggests a more pronounced and shared aversion to reverting to the self-defeating past practices of the balance of power in addressing Europe's pressing security problems. Angst and antipathy do not equate to complete abandonment of this approach, however. Russian opposition to NATO and its extension to Eastern Europe, as noted earlier, is still cast in classic balance of power terms. It would also be misleading to suggest that German ensnarement in a set of entangling multilateral organizations and commitments, economic and military, is the only hedge on which Western states rely to check the possibility of renewed German expansionism. There is still an implicit, and unstated, accord among the former World War II allies that their national military capabilities are insurance policies against the possible resurgence of German (and Russian) militarism. British and French retention of nuclear forces suggests that neither is prepared to relinquish, any more than the United States or Russia, national means of ensuring their security interests. France still assigns high value to its nuclear forces, whatever the claims of some analysts about their diminishing importance.[10] Paris risked the ire of world public opinion and the sanctions of the states bordering the test sites in the South Pacific in resuming underground nuclear tests (since suspended) to perfect its arsenal. French nuclear weapons implicitly respond to lingering French fears of a resurgent and nuclear-armed Germany. This scenario, however remote at this time, is posited by some as likely to reemerge as an inevitable consequence of interstate conflict and an anarchic nation-state system that promotes self-help security policies by the member states.[11] In any event, peace in the Balkans is likely to rest more on a balance of power among the contending opponents of this subregion than on a definitive political solution to the ethnic conflicts.

In sum, Europe can be seen as a vast testing ground—a laboratory— for security systems tailored to its specialized, yet diverse, needs. There are clear problems with this proliferation of ideas and systems. Balances of power cannot be squared with a security community. The institutional requirements of the security community are also at odds with the relaxed and satisfying assumptions about the automaticity of security implied by a pluralistic security community. Institutional guarantees and joint decision making in developing security policies are not consistent with a PSC system. A concert possesses the flexibility and attractiveness of the kind of "equilibrium" that brought a "long peace" to Europe in the nineteenth century,[12] but if it resolves itself into "spheres of influence" and potential conflict over the boundaries of these spheres among the big powers, can balance of power politics be far behind? Big-power spheres of influence as solutions for regional security problems have had a tattered history. Aside from their dubious past, they would also immediately run against prevailing notions of legitimacy, as the Soviet Union discovered in its relations with the Baltic states. An attempt to define spheres of influence would also inhibit the free flow of ideas, people, and goods across state boundaries. Movements downward on the security ladder, depicted in figure 1, toward spheres of influence and balances of power, would clearly be a step in the direction of a primitive security order. It would be several rungs lower than the progress already made toward developing increasingly more complex and mature security arrangements associated with consensual over coercive solutions to the diverse and conflicting security needs of Europe's peoples.

The Middle East Security Complex

The Middle East would appear to conform primarily to balance of power arrangements. These are not easy to summarize in brief compass. There is little or no inclination of the contesting parties in the region, again including the United States, to rely on the promise of peaceful intent associated with members of a security community or a pluralistic security community. Yet the balance of power arrangements that exist today in the Middle East—particularly between Israel and the Palestinian Liberation Front (PLO), the central axis of conflict in the region—have been essentially transformed over the past half century. The maturity of the Middle East system does not approach the level of peaceful accord among the members of the European Union, principally France and Germany, but bilateral peace accords between Israel, Egypt, and Jordan and the agreements to extend greater autonomy to the Palestinians in the West Bank, most notably over Hebron, suggest that at least selected parts of the Middle East security complex are more subtle and complex than those associated simply with pure balance of power politics, the kind that best describe Iraqi-Israeli and to an appreciable degree Syrian-Israeli relations.

The long process of consolidating and institutionalizing consensual cooperation in coping with conflict in the Middle East on a par with the success of the European Union, a process spanning almost half a century, has only just begun. The security complex of the region is still at a low level of maturity. Only two rungs of the ladder are marked out (see figure 3). More mature security frameworks do not appear because there are no rungs on which they can be hooked. These are more visionary than real possibilities in the near future.

For almost half a century Israelis and Palestinians have been unable to move much beyond the routinization—some might even contend ritualization—of their conflict. Until recently, third parties, principally the United States, have been frustrated in their efforts to move the conflict up the security ladder. Except for the Israeli-Egyptian accord of the late 1970s, these efforts were primarily focused, not unexpectedly, on containing the rivalry rather than resolving it. The complex accord reached in Oslo on Palestinian autonomy in the West Bank, containing over four hundred pages of detailed specifications to implement this changeover, is a crude measure of the modest progress that has been made to surmount a politics of mutual denial on the surface—each opponent denying the moral existence of the other and its legitimacy—and a death struggle below.

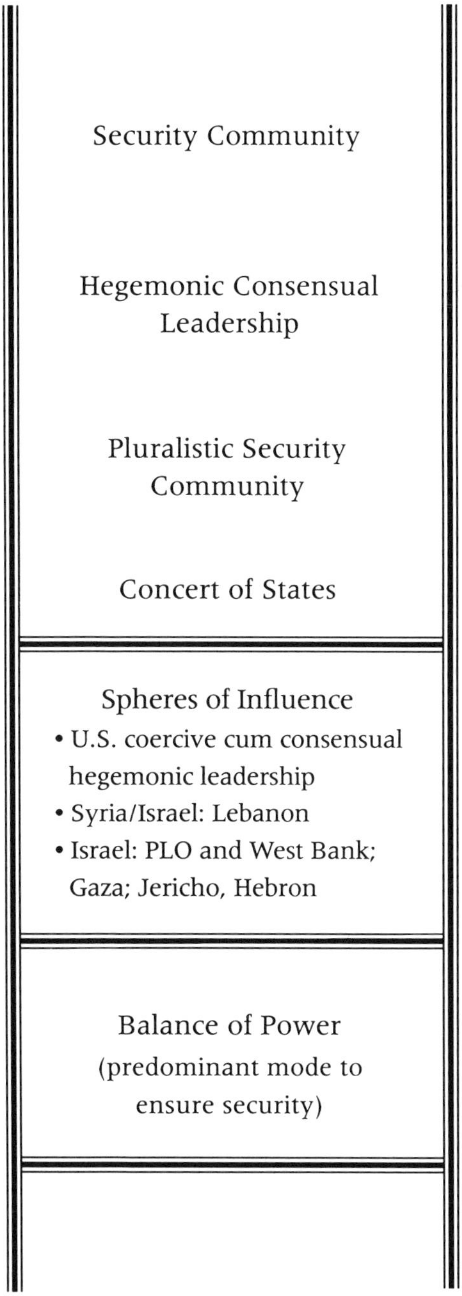

Security Community

Hegemonic Consensual
Leadership

Pluralistic Security
Community

Concert of States

Spheres of Influence
- U.S. coercive cum consensual
  hegemonic leadership
- Syria/Israel: Lebanon
- Israel: PLO and West Bank;
  Gaza; Jericho, Hebron

Balance of Power
(predominant mode to
ensure security)

Figure 3. Middle East Security Complex

The marked differences between Europe and the Middle East with respect to the impact of systemic factors promoting peace should be noted. The contrast underlines the difficulty of developing a single, coherent theory of security that can be applied to all regions of the world. Whereas the cold war and the Soviet threat created some of the necessary conditions for Franco-German reconciliation, the superpower conflict had the opposite effect on the Israeli-Arab conflict. The cold war and the U.S.-Soviet competition served to reinforce the existing structure of hostilities between local powers in the region. Now, in place of the superpower axis of conflict in the region, U.S. hegemony is ascendant. The United States assumes the role of, alternately, a consensual and coercive hegemon. Its coercive role is chiseled in its crushing of Iraqi military forces, by some estimates the fourth largest military in the world on the eve of the Gulf War, and its partial success in isolating Iran and Libya.

Yet the United States is also an indispensable consensual hegemon in the region. It provides crucial material resources to support the peace process. Egypt and Israel, for example, are the principal recipients of American foreign assistance, accessing approximately half of all transfers. Washington has also established a measure of credibility as an evenhanded mediator between the warring parties. This has been no mean feat. The United States has earned a reputation for equity and trust despite its position as an interested mediator, which is by no means indifferent to the kinds of security regimes that are being constructed in the region. It continues to oppose the expansion of Iraqi, Syrian, and Iranian power, and it resists the rise of Muslim fundamentalism and terrorism. It is also determined to maintain the free flow of oil to the West. Yet these obvious geopolitical and economic interests have not precluded Israeli-PLO accord, however tenuous and unstable. Quite the contrary, they have worked to foster Israeli-PLO agreement, as explained below, and to encourage them to assume principal responsibility for resolving their differences.

How did this state of affairs come about? The end of the cold war and the collapse of the Soviet Union deprived the PLO of Moscow's arms, aid, and diplomatic support. By extension it narrowed PLO access to the leverage afforded by Moscow's surrogates in the Middle East, principally Syria and Iraq. Even before the disintegration of the Soviet Union, Moscow had already joined the Western powers against Iraq and the PLO, which had badly miscalculated in supporting Saddam Hussein in his grab for Kuwait. The creation of the Russia Federation, its manifest internal political and economic weaknesses, and its dependence on the West foreclosed any reasonable expectation that the PLO, in an isolated political and increasingly vulnerable security and economic position, could persist in its refusal to negotiate with the Israeli state, much less to insist on its destruction.

The PLO's monumental blunders during the Kuwait crisis also severely weakened its bargaining position vis-à-vis Israel and undermined its regional stance. It lost the extensive financial and economic support of the conservative oil states, principally Saudi Arabia. No longer shielded on its right flank by the Arab sheikdoms, it was exposed to the full force of U.S. and Western pressures in the peace process revived by the Bush administration. These could no longer be mediated and muted through Riyadh to bolster PLO resistance to Western insistence that it recognize Israel and enter into direct negotiations with the Israeli government. The cross-pressured pillars of the PLO strategic position—Soviet military support, conservative Arab financial assistance, and their implicit diplomatic convergence in support of PLO claims and bargaining position—had collapsed almost overnight. Its remaining Arab allies, principally Iraq and Syria, were shaky and unreliable reeds upon which to lean. Iraq was a defeated and discredited power. Syria was preoccupied with shoring up its own eroding influence in the Middle East in the wake of the Iraqi debacle. In this recovery effort the PLO—a Syrian ally of convenience, not of necessity—was more a burden than a boon.

The end of the cold war also compelled a rethinking of Israeli strategy and intransigence toward the PLO. If the collapse of Soviet influence and the defeat of PLO allies enhanced Israel's power position, sustained exterior support, mainly from the United States, could not be confidently expected over the long run. The United States was increasingly concerned with domestic issues—budget, crime, welfare demands, and foreign economic challenges. Even if U.S. support were not in immediate question, Washington's ability to make economic and military resources available to bolster Israel's security and bargaining position was clearly in doubt. These concerns did little to relieve worries about the health of the Israeli economy. Its prospects for growth depend on expanding exports, notably those available in the Middle East, where it enjoys a comparative advantage if the political and security obstacles to trade and investment can be surmounted or at least neutralized.

The Iraqi missile attack on Israel also exposed the limits of relying primarily on conventional and nuclear deterrence to ensure Israeli security and survival. The mounting costs of maintaining Israeli rule in the West Bank and Gaza made more acute these pessimistic appraisals of Israel's receding power base. The Intifada was a constant drain on Israeli resources and a persistent security preoccupation. The growing strength of radical Palestinian groups, such as Hamas, and Iranian fundamentalist support for Israel's opponents within the Palestinian and Islamic communities created an implicit convergence of interest between the then ruling Labor coalition in Israel and an isolated and weakened PLO. The PLO was driven to a moderate position in the Arab camp, pushed from above by the collapse of the Soviet Union and the end of the cold war, and from below by the rise of Muslim fundamentalism.

These global and regional structural changes in power relations essentially transformed the Israeli-Palestinian calculus of conflict. They were further reinforced by the self-help efforts of the parties, the crucial role that third parties played in fostering the peace process, and the incentives of shared economic growth and development for both rivals if peace could be achieved. Each of these dimensions of the coping process warrants brief comment to identify the several actors, diverse resources, tangible and intangible, and divergent strategies that ultimately had to converge, however provisionally and not altogether by design, to move the conflict off dead center.

Neither side in the conflict could move toward negotiations in the absence of a long process of "de-demonization" of the images held by the elites and populations on both sides. This process did not begin with the end of Desert Storm. It commenced much earlier, at least as far back as Egyptian president Anwar Sadat's visit to Jerusalem in 1977.[13] The Camp David accords between Israel and Egypt, reached a year later through U.S. mediation and its willingness to bear the heavy cost of guaranteeing the agreement, solidified the psychological breakthrough achieved in the Sadat visit. These events and accords demonstrated that five wars in twenty-five years between seemingly implacable foes did not have to stand in the way of creating a process of peaceful engagement if the leaders of both camps were prepared to assume the risks of fundamentally revising their previous security relationship, even at the expense of the assassination of the Egyptian president and, later, of an Israeli prime minister. The bitter experience of a generation of flawed efforts to resolve the conflict by imposing a solution on one or the other of the parties to the rivalry slowly and indiscernibly prepared, as William Zartman suggests in his notion of the "hurting stalemate," the psychological and political ground for reversing the hostile perceptions, fueled by unrelieved hatreds, each held of the other.[14]

There is also evidence that both sides, at least those in control of the negotiation process, perceived their mutual entrapment and the need to escape the damaging effects of continued stalemate. Prospects that one or the other side would prevail appeared to be receding, particularly because each was confronted, although for different reasons, with an erosion of its long-term bargaining position. The intervention of a neutral party (Norway), the guarded secrecy of direct bilateral talks between the principals, the willingness of each negotiator to assume the risks of exposure and attack from supporters at home and abroad, and, finally, a recognition of their alignment of interests regarding opponents in their own camps essentially fulfilled Zartman's conditions for successful bargaining to end an enduring rivalry.

The incentives of greater economic development for the Israeli and Palestinian peoples should also not be underestimated as a major contributor to peace, once imposing a preferred outcome on the opponent was perceived as unfeasible. Moving from a zero-sum to a mixed- or positive-sum relationship did not come easy, nor should this transition be considered inevitable or irreversible. The Israeli-PLO process of constructing a security community that inches toward the Deutschian ideal has come about only after a long and difficult period of mutual learning in the wake of a century—some might argue several millennia—of costly trial and error by force of arms. Israel and the PLO also create a new process of security bargaining in which they pool their risks of failure while testing whether self-rule will work and whether the process between them, based on a record of tangible achievements, can conceivably be extended to other areas of dispute. These range from complete Israeli return of Arab lands—and PLO independence—to water rights in the region.

The peace process also opens the way for the expansion of Israeli markets in the region, where Israel's advanced economic and technological development bolsters its comparative advantage. Peace also provides Palestinian access to Arab and Western economic assistance that has been withheld since Desert Storm, with the promise of more support in the future. The leadership of the United States in gaining assurances for financial support of the peace process from other states in the Western coalition, including Japan, reinforces Arafat's leadership of the PLO and his claim that he can deliver important economic benefits and advance PLO political interests in achieving limited self-rule in Gaza, Jericho, and Hebron.

It is by no means certain that the modest progress up the Deutschian ladder toward a security community, jointly defined by the contending parties to their mutual satisfaction, will not be reversed. The assassination of Yitzhak Rabin, the chief architect of the Oslo accord, the subsequent election of a right-of-center coalition composed of elements opposed to further concessions to Palestinian autonomy, the renewal of terrorist attacks against the Israeli population, and the withering of Arab support for the peace process have dampened optimism that the Middle

East security system will progress beyond the level depicted in figure 3. The possibility of interstate war is still possible, as the military exchanges between Iraq and Israel during the Gulf War demonstrate. These are likely to be overshadowed by internal threats to regional security, such as the possibility of political upheaval in Jordan, where the Palestinian population's loyalty to the Hashemite Kingdom is always in doubt. Or, nationally based Muslim fundamentalism, whose influence is felt throughout the region and is growing in such key states as Egypt and Algeria and among the Palestinian populations, particularly the younger generation, may diminish Israeli willingness to negotiate with its Arab rivals or concede land for security, a reluctance already present in the wake of the narrow victory of the conservative Likud party in the Israeli parliamentary elections of 1996.

Other Regional Security Complexes

The contrasting experience of the European and Middle East cases underscores the point that coping strategies have to be fine-tuned to the special requirements of each region. These respond to the special needs of local inhabitants and to the unique historical evolution of their security relations. Moreover, the process of adjustment is ongoing and dynamic. Even long-established peaceful relations between neighbors, say the United States and Canada, are not without frictions, as can be seen in Washington-Ottawa disagreements over such issues as the superpower arms race and U.S. arms transfers, U.S. intervention in Vietnam, and political ties with the Communist regime of Fidel Castro or the imposition of U.S. economic sanctions on Canadian companies investing in Cuba.

Northeast Asia

Northeast Asia may be said to conform to a balance of power model, but it differs radically from the Middle East version. Here four big powers—the United States, Japan, China, and a weakened Russia are engaged, as well as a divided Korea and a flawed Taiwan, whose fate as an independent state or as a province of China has yet to be settled after half a century. China and a divided Korea, for different reasons, appear to pose the most immediate threats to region's security.

China continues to modernize its military forces, nuclear and conventional, and insists on its sovereignty over much of the Spratly Islands in counterpoint to the claims of most of its neighbors. Periodically, threatening military moves are aimed at Taiwan, and reminders issue from official Beijing sources of its determination to reintegrate the island into

China, by force if necessary. U.S.-Chinese differences over human rights are also sore points, straining relations between Beijing and Washington and impeding accord on other geopolitical and economic matters. China's occupation of Tibet recalls the sometimes forgotten point that self-determination is not simply a Chinese claim; rather, China and rising Chinese geopolitical and economic power are a threat to other states and peoples in the region. These serious problems, not to mention the possibility of heightened domestic turmoil in the wake of Deng Xaoping's death, suggest that Northeast Asia will not soon surmount balance of power arrangements, however much muted or deflected they may be by economic development as well as trade or investment issues. Trade and investment may themselves become sources of geopolitical conflict. China's violation of private patents and copyrights and U.S. opposition to its entry into the World Trade Organization until these and other alleged trade issues are resolved illustrate some of the sources of conflict between Beijing and its economic partners.

Tensions between North and South Korea also continue to divide the region. These have been moderated by the U.S. brokered agreement to provide nuclear expertise and electrical generating facilities as well as economic aid to the North Korean regime in exchange for its promise to abandon a military nuclear program. The American-sponsored package included significant financial and technical support from Seoul and Tokyo and the tacit approval of Beijing and Moscow. None of the major powers relished the prospect of an isolated, embattled, and xenophobic Pyongyang with nuclear weapons. In return for its promise to forego nuclear weapons, the North Korean regime received desperately sought international recognition, a modest measure of political legitimacy, vital (if modest) economic assistance, and nuclear know-how. Whether the accord with North Korea will stick remains, however, an open question. Cheating is always a possibility. The open sore of a divided Korea and a vulnerable North Korea also prompt incentives for Seoul and Pyongyang to intervene in each other's internal affairs to unsettle its competitor.

Just below the surface of these security issues lie increased tensions between the United States and Japan over trade, investment, and burden sharing to maintain an open international economic regime. Some see in these conflicts the seeds of growing security differences between Japan and the United States.[15] Japan no longer needs the United States to protect itself against Moscow. It is quite capable of pressing its outstanding territorial claims against Moscow, including Russian occupation of the Sakhalin Islands, without U.S. intervention or protection. Its economic power—either in blocking or denying aid, investment, or trade conces-

sions or in making these carrots readily available as positive sanctions—
is a formidable weapon. The United States has had to urge caution in Japan
to mollify heightened nationalist sentiment in Russia in the wake of the
precipitous decline of Russian power. Tensions between China and the
United States are also incentives for Japan to adopt a unilateral course in
pursuing its geopolitical and economic interests in China rather than work
through Washington; these could be at risk if Washington and Beijing are
not able to manage their differences peacefully.

These disquieting changes in the post–cold war environment in Northeast Asia have not induced Japan to abandon the U.S.-Japanese alliance
and its security ties to the United States. Rising nationalist sentiment in
Japan has been contained, although its influence appears to be increasing in policy-making circles. The cold war system provided for half a century of peace, rising prosperity, and democratic government at home;
these benefits will not be risked by precipitously abandoning the cold war
system before something as reliable can be put in its place. Conversely, if
American reliability as a security guarantor is undermined for some reason or if the United States is again seen as a threat to Japanese economic
and political aims in the region, as was the case in the interwar period,
then the precarious balances of power that currently underwrite peace
in Northeast Asia might well be upset, and in their wake pressures may
build that elicit greater friction, higher spending on arms, and heightened
conflict.

ASEAN and Latin America

The prospects for reduced conflict appear brighter for the member states
of Southeast Asia and Latin America, but only reservedly so. Both may
be said to be pluralistic security communities. Both also have regional
organizations that institutionalize this commitment. The Association of
South East Asian Nations (ASEAN) was originally organized to insulate
the region from superpower penetration and, less explicitly, to limit the
damaging effects of the Vietnam War and overall Chinese influence. Limiting Chinese influence was of particular interest to Indonesia, ASEAN's
largest state, because of the bitter rivalry between its indigenous peoples
and the Chinese minority. The recent addition of Vietnam to ASEAN has
enlarged the organization's security reach. The states of the system are
pledged to peace and economic development. The mix of regimes, largely authoritarian states, suggests that the democratic pacific union, much
touted today, can conceivably extend to other regimes and states. ASEAN
has also attempted to enlarge its multilateral consultative mechanisms
through the Post-Ministerial Conference, which acts as a forum on secu-

rity issues.[16] The growing economic power of these states and their progressively denser economic and cultural ties would seem to ensure a zone of relative peace, despite the lack of strong institutional arrangements to guarantee their security relations.

Threats to the security of this region, as in other regions of the developing world, are likely to be more internal than external in their initial impact. Indonesia, as the most populous and militarily most powerful member, is vulnerable to domestic political strife, civil unrest, and even armed uprisings. The nepotism and corruption of the Soharto regime, its determined authoritarian rule, and its reflexive crackdown on the smallest stirrings of political dissent isolate Indonesia internationally. Its suppression of the separatist movement in East Timor has been condemned by human rights organizations and states around the globe. Its civil and human rights violations widen dissent and spark demands for greater participation in the political process and protection of minority rights. Like all military authoritarian systems, it has not solved the problem of representation—an imperative all the more acute in a multilingual and multicommunal society.[17]

The Indonesian case raises questions about ASEAN's success in developing a working pluralistic security community. The bloody civil war that brought the Soharto regime to power, ostensibly aimed at Communist party members but disproportionately concentrated against the Chinese minority, has had long-lasting effects on Chinese-Indonesian relations. Internal upheavals in other ASEAN nations could also have similar disturbing interstate security implications. In contrast the Malaysian social compact between the Malay majority and Chinese minority has apparently resolved—or better managed—the conflict between these communities. There is also some basis for optimism that the agreement between Manila and its Muslim community, principally centered on the island of Mindanao, will finally end the long civil war.

Latin America would seem to parallel the success of the ASEAN states in developing a pluralistic security community. The region was relatively free of superpower competition. The United States followed a policy of restricting arms to the region; the surprise sale of Soviet jets to Peru never seriously upset this pattern of arms restraint in the region. Brazil's export of arms, while disquieting to Washington, affected other regions more than Latin America, principally the Middle East. The weapons production programs and arms sales of Argentina and Brazil never kindled either a conventional or a nuclear arms race between them. The principal powers—Argentina, Brazil, and Chile—enjoy peaceful and increasingly confident relations. Democratization has grown apace throughout the region. The military forces are back in their barracks, chastised by their failure to solve their country's political problems or to make much headway in spurring economic development (except perhaps in Chile). Most Latin American states are now pursuing sobering economic market policies, which enjoy varying degrees of public support. They are also abandoning previous protectionist measures, inefficient import substitution policies, and restrictions on investment and the free flow of capital. In the past these have hobbled economic development, encouraged corporate and public economic mismanagement, and fostered official corruption.

The Organization of American States (OAS), while certainly no collective security organization, reassures most members of one another's peaceful intentions, while containing somewhat the power and influence of the United States. Washington has never been able to count on the organization to do its bidding. It prefers to work outside the OAS, as the Panamanian intervention suggests, to maintain a free hand in the Western Hemisphere, while it attempts to solicit support when needed, as in the case of the Cuban missile crisis or in efforts to topple the military dictatorship in Haiti. Security problems in the region are largely internal. They have to do more with surging populations, economic underdevelopment, wide disparities in income, the breakdown of civic culture and public order, and drug trafficking, notably in Colombia and Peru, than with threats of invasion by neighbors.

Central America and the Caribbean

This region presents a different picture than Latin America or ASEAN do. U.S. military intervention in the region remains a constant threat. The imbalance of power between the United States and the states of the region enhances the incentives for intervention in this region because on the surface the risks of failure appear lower. Propinquity and historical pronouncements of the region's insulation from outside intervention, dating from the Monroe Doctrine, strengthen the inclination of Washington, whoever is in office or whatever party is in control, to intervene when American interests and preferences, broadly interpreted, appear at risk. Examples abound, ranging from threats to investments (the Roosevelt Corollary) to direct military challenges (the Zimmermann note and the Cuban missile crisis) or humanitarian and human rights abuses (Spanish depredations in Cuba or Haitian military atrocities).

The post–cold war interventions in Panama and more recently in Haiti suggest that, despite domestic opposition to intervention almost anywhere in the world today, Washington policymakers will still be tempted to intervene in Caribbean and Central American affairs. This is a pattern that well precedes the cold war era. Political leaders and parties continue to vie with each other for the title of who can be tougher on Caribbean and Central American opponents of U.S. policies in the region. For over thirty years Cuba has been the central target of this competition. The presence of a large number of Cuban refugees in key electoral states, notably Florida, fuels this competition. Congressional passage of increased economic sanctions against Cuba in the wake of its downing of aircraft flown by harassing Cuban refugees illustrates the complexity of bettering regional relations when the hegemon has few compelling incentives to cooperate on an equal footing with weaker states in the region. Whereas American hegemony in Europe is largely based on consent and is widely viewed as necessary and legitimate, the opposite sentiment appears to be prevalent among the peoples and states of the region. As street demonstrations in Haiti against foreign occupation suggest,[18] American leadership is far more suspect in Central America, the Caribbean, and Latin America than in Europe, the Middle East, or Northeast Asia. The legitimacy of American hegemony, like any other power resource, varies across regions, depending on the historical evolution and particular security problems confronting the area at any point in time.[19]

South Asia

A few final words about South Asia and Africa complete this scan of regional problems to illustrate the diversity of the security arrangements characterizing each region. India is perhaps the only self-contained regional subsystem. Both of the superpowers exercised considerable restraint in extending their competition to the region. In turn the principal regional powers, Pakistan and India, viewed the superpowers primarily as sources of arms and diplomatic support rather than as allies in the cold war struggle. Their regional security interests have invariably superseded cold war concerns. The superpowers, sensing these constraints even as they attempted to enlist these communal antagonists in their global struggle, generally pursued parallel policies toward the region, converging on ways to reduce Pakistani-Indian tensions as much as to gain the support of Islamabad and Delhi. The superpower sale of arms to the warring parties did not essentially negate a diplomatic effort to contain the regional conflict. The United States implicitly accepted Soviet mediating efforts in the 1960s and helped by restricting its arms flows to Pakistan. The United States signaled its displeasure with India's military intervention in the Pakistani civil war by sending naval vessels into the South Pacific, hinting that it might intervene in the South Asian conflict, but it quickly pulled back. Its clumsy moves served to irritate the Indian government more than to preclude Pakistan's partition.

Barring a catastrophic nuclear arms race and the breakdown of the fragile nuclear deterrent system that currently prevails, India will continue to maintain its military dominance of the region. Stanching nuclear proliferation is Washington's principal security objective in the region. It has succeeded, arguably, in slowing the rate of nuclear proliferation, but not in reversing the process, as it did in South Africa. Outside powers will not likely coerce or badger India or Pakistan to relinquish its nuclear weapons or to give up its efforts to acquire long-range delivery systems. The limited ability of outside powers to influence matters of crucial regional security importance to India and Pakistan is clearly evidenced in the failure of the United States and its Western allies to persuade India to sign the comprehensive test ban treaty, which India had championed for over thirty years.

Delhi and Islamabad view nuclear weapons as a deterrent against each other, no matter that these systems hardly approach the reach and explosive magnitude of those in the United States and Russia. These weapons are also a hedge for India against China. Reports of Chinese material and technical assistance to Pakistan's long-range missile delivery program do little to encourage Delhi to take an active role in restricting nuclear proliferation.[20] Nuclear weapons also seem to reflect a widely shared determination among Indian elites to seek a big-power position for India, consistent with its history, ancient culture, and hegemonic position on the subcontinent. Modernization of nuclear systems in India and Pakistan will likely go forward but whether at the current relatively slow pace is anyone's guess. The scare over India's "Operation Brasstacks," which threatened an unintended war with Pakistan, offers grounds for optimists and pessimists. Both Islamabad and Delhi pulled back to avert a collision, yet both are still bent on acquiring nuclear weapons and advanced delivery systems.

The problems of South Asia are still primarily internal, however much they are obscured by interstate rivalry—a rivalry that also deflects attention from serious domestic divisions. Pakistan continues to undergo severe domestic strain. Rival ethnic and communal groups battle for control of the cities. Civil disorder is particularly rampant in Karachi. India has its own communal problems. These show no signs of being resolved anytime soon. Kashmir remains a lightening rod for domestic upheaval in Pakistan and India and the principal threat to interstate peace. A definitive solution appears no closer on the horizon than at the time of partition, a half-century ago. Pakistani governments lack the military means and are too preoccupied with homegrown violence and ethnic strife to address the problem from a position of strength. India as the dominant power in the region cannot be budged on Kashmir. Stalemate and managed conflict appear to be the only solutions in the immediate future.

Sri Lanka's civil war appears insoluble, short of autonomy for the Tamil Tigers or their forceful suppression. India, which intervened militarily in the Sri Lankan fray, paid a heavy price for its decision; it had no appreciable effect on the vicious conflict and lost a prime minister for its pains. Delhi will very likely concentrate on containing the damaging effects of the civil war on the subcontinent rather than reassume an active military role in seeking to reconcile the warring ethnic factions. The Colombo government lacks the internal coherence to negotiate effectively with the minority Tamil community. The central government also lacks the military means to impose a solution. The result is a "hurting stalemate" that promises no decisive end to the struggle for a long time to come.

In the interests of space and given the vast complexity of the region, I will not try to unravel the African tangle. As in most underdeveloped regions of the world, the problems in Africa stem primarily from poorly developed political institutions, predatory governments—witness Zaire—widespread and lethal tribal and social conflict, increasing populations, deplorable health and sanitation, periodic famines and plagues, and a rate of economic development outpaced by rising human needs. These problems are well documented in scholarly works and U.N. reports and need not detain us here.[21] The problems appear so intractable that the advanced industrial states have been reluctant to increase their aid to the region in proportion to its many problems, pending a demonstration that increased resources will actually have positive payoffs. From the perspective of security, the diversity of the African system defies generalization and merits separate treatment to dissect the region's many daunting problems.

Conclusion

Developing mature regional security regimes will not be easy in the post–cold war era. The end of history and its legacy of hostilities is hardly at hand, as this overview of regional rivalries suggests. In greatly reducing the threat of global nuclear annihilation, the end of the cold war has, ironically, weakened incentives among the major states, principally the members of the Western coalition that emerged ascendant from the cold war struggle, to help manage or resolve local conflicts. The trend line points to a slow but discernible disengagement by the major states from many regions of the world, where their resources and leadership might well have had a positive effect (the United States in Somalia) and where feckless or temporizing interventions (Britain and France in Yugoslavia) might well have prolonged conflict, with appreciable losses in life and property. NATO expansion bucks this trend, but how much remains an open question.

This cursory review highlights the principal theme of this essay: the gradual regionalization of formerly globalized security systems. Regional self-help is the order of the day, notwithstanding regional rivals' continued need for outside resources and intervention, most notably a domestically distracted United States, which remains the world's largest arms supplier. History has left a complex legacy of security systems, each adapted to local circumstances, whatever their defects. If these systems are to be moved up the Deutschian security ladder, sketched in figure 1, they will have to address the diverse needs of each region and its principal actors. All this will take time, measured in generations, not years. It will have to be done in ways that create incentives to resolve endemic differences through negotiation, bargaining, and consensus over coercion. Movement up and down the ladder is likely to be uneven across regions and, where upward, always hard won and precariously maintained, as evident in the Middle East peace process. The European experience both cautions and advises that the climb is possible but slippery, never sure, and the danger of falling is always present, yet obstacles can be surmounted, and institutions and processes can be erected that move the peoples and states of the region from coercion to consensual cooperation.

The sheer complexity of the European system also demonstrates a hidden and unanticipated element that potentially has positive implications for the development of more mature security systems in other regions. Until now, the entwined sets of finely spun security arrangements, interdependent economic relations, and multiple cultural exchanges have tended to dampen incentives to resort to force and violence. One ironic conclusion of this entanglement is that calls for coherence and greater clarity in building Europe's security architecture may have the unwitting effect of forcing decisions that could inflame divisions instead of quieting them and diverting them toward peaceful pursuits. There may also be something to be said for muddling through the process of transforming the cold war system at the regional level to something that more closely fits Europe's present circumstances and future needs. These same considerations might well be applied to other regions of the globe.

If the security dilemmas confronting regions today have never been more difficult to surmount, partly because of a heightened appreciation of their many and often intractable features, it does not follow that the aim of international security is somehow equally difficult to grasp. From the perspective of international security outlined in this essay, the question to ask in evaluating a security complex or a proposal for change is whether it encourages (or discourages) ever lesser levels of violence and ever fewer appeals to coercive threats in settling differences between peoples and states. If the indicator points toward encouraging consensual over coercive cooperation, the proposal under review provisionally meets a positive security test, provided that the consenting parties move up together on the security ladder and lift themselves by the force of their conjoined wills. If you know where you are going, almost any road, arguably, will get you there.

Notes

1. U.S. Arms Control and Disarmament Agency, *World Military Expenditures and Arms Transfers* (Washington, D.C.: Government Printing Office, 1963 to the present), passim.

2. Superpower cooperation in the developing world is developed at length in a set of regionally focused essays in Edward A. Kolodziej and Roger E. Kanet, eds., *The Cold War as Cooperation: Superpower Cooperation in Regional Conflict Management* (Baltimore: Johns Hopkins University Press, 1991). Needless to say, the superpowers did not always get their way with determined clients, as the United States and the Soviet Union learned, respectively, in their relations with Israel and with Romania and Cuba. See Roger E. Kanet and Edward A. Kolodziej, eds., *The Limits of Soviet Power in the Development World: Thermidor in the Revolutionary Struggle* (Baltimore: Johns Hopkins University Press, 1989), passim.

3. *Economist*, April 12, 1997, 35–36.

4. Max Singer and Aaron Wildavsky, *The Real World Order* (Chatham, Mass.: Chatham House, 1993).

5. Samuel P. Huntington Jr., *The Clash of Civilizations* (New York: Simon and Schuster, 1996). This overview of security complexes parallels the work of other scholars and reflects the growing attention being devoted to regional security problems and theorizing. Notable are David A. Lake and Patrick M. Morgan, eds., *Regional Orders: Building Security in a New World* (University Park, Pa.: Penn State University Press, 1997); Efraim Inbar, ed., *Regional Security Regimes: Israel and Its Neighbors* (Albany: State University of New York Press, 1995); and Andrew Mack and John Ravenhill, eds., *Pacific Cooperation: Building Economic and Security Regimes in the Asia-Pacific Region* (Boulder, Colo.: Westview Press, 1995).

6. Karl Deutsch, *Political Community and the North Atlantic Area* (Princeton, N.J.: Princeton University Press, 1957).

7. Richard K. Betts, "Systems of Peace or Causes of War," *International Security* 17, no. 1 (1992): 5–43.

8. Charles A. Kupchan and Clifford A. Kupchan, "Concerts, Collective Security, and the Future of Europe," *International Security* 16, no. 1 (1991): 114–61; Charles A. Kupchan and Clifford A. Kupchan, "The Promise of Collective Security," *International Security* 19, no. 1 (1994): 52–61.

9. For a review of this debate, see Sean M. Lynn-Jones, "Preface: Debating the Democratic Peace," in *Debating the Democratic Peace*, ed. Michael Brown et al. (Cambridge, Mass.: MIT Press, 1996), ix–xxxiii.

10. John Mueller, "The Essential Irrelevance of Nuclear Weapons," *International Security* 13, no. 2 (1988): 55–79; John Mueller, *Retreat from Doomsday* (New York: Basic Books, 1989).

11. John J. Mearsheimer, "Back to the Future: Instability in Europe after the Cold War," *International Security* 15, no. 1 (1990): 5–57; Kenneth N. Waltz. "The Emerging Structure of International Politics," *International Security* 18, no. 2 (1993): 44–79.

12. Paul W. Schroeder, "The Nineteenth Century System: Balance of Power or Political Equilibrium?" *Review of International Studies* 15, no. 2 (1989): 135–53; Paul W. Schroeder, *The Transformation of European Politics, 1763–1848* (Oxford: Clarendon, 1994).

13. Janice Gross Stein, "Communications, Signaling, and Intelligence," in *Coping with Conflict after the Cold War*, ed. Edward A. Kolodziej and Roger E. Kanet (Baltimore: Johns Hopkins University Press, 1996), 247–70.

14. I. William Zartman, "Bargaining and Conflict Reduction," in *Coping with Conflict after the Cold War*, ed. Kolodziej and Kanet, 271–90.

15. Edward Luttwak, *The Endangered American Dream* (New York: Simon and Schuster, 1993).

16. Yoichi Funabashi, "The Asianization of Asia," *Foreign Affairs* 72, no. 5 (1991): 80.

17. For relevant literature on this point, see Gerardo L. Munck, *Authoritarianism and Democratization: Soldiers and Workers in Argentina, 1776–83, in Comparative Perspective* (University Station, Pa.: Penn State University Press, 1996), notes to each chapter.

18. *Economist*, September 30, 1995, 32.

19. John G. Ikenberry and Charles A. Kupchan, "Socialization and Hegemonic Power," *International Organization* 44, no. 3 (1990): 283–315.

20. *New York Times*, August 27, 1996.

21. See, for example, Paul Kennedy, *Preparing for the Twenty-First Century* (New York: Random House, 1993).

Part Two

Regional Conflict and
the Prospects for Peace

2

Understanding the Irish Conflict and the Hopes for Peace

William F. Kelleher

> And projects are of course often projected rather than realized: be-
> cause of their confrontations with indigenous interests, alternate civ-
> ilizing missions and their internal inconsistencies, colonial intentions
> are frequently deflected, or enacted farcically and incompletely. While
> the administrator might have wished that governing could be effect-
> ed as forcefully and simply as a flag could be raised, in practice the
> business of sustaining colonial control is often more like repairing an
> old car: the cost and energy absorbed into surgery is never reflected
> in results, parts are replaced, but connections fail, there are inexpli-
> cable rattles, and sooner or later the whole effort has to be aban-
> doned—not least (and here it is the analogy that breaks down) be-
> cause government and its conceptual categories are resisted.
>
> Nicholas Thomas, *Colonialism's Culture*

As we approach our "fin de millennium," the people of the island of Ireland, particularly the citizens of Northern Ireland, are grappling yet again
with their constitutional future. As they did at the end of the eighteenth
century, when rebellion led to the Irish Act of Union with Great Britain
in 1800, and at the end of the nineteenth century, when guerrilla warfare led to the home rule crisis and the eventual partition of the island
into unionist Northern Ireland and the quasi-independent Irish Free State
in 1921, the people of Northern Ireland today endeavor to make constitutional politics, not the politics of the gun, the means of struggling over
the future.

Northern Ireland faces a dramatic transformation. Yet the pathos is
hardly recognizable after nearly thirty years of planned political assassi-
nations, random murders, bombings of population centers by both nationalist and loyalist paramilitaries, and an assassination campaign by the
British army and police that led to the violent deaths of not only Irish
Republican Army (IRA) members but also children and other innocents

who happened to be in the wrong place at the wrong time.[1] Now the Irish people, both north and south of the border, are galvanized by the hoped-for return of a cease-fire, which, put into place in August of 1994, was put asunder by an IRA bomb in London seventeen months later. That act of terror was followed by IRA bombings of British army barracks in Germany and Northern Ireland, bombings of civilian centers in England, and a murder of a member of the Royal Ulster Constabulary (RUC) in April of 1997. The loyalist paramilitaries have kept their pledge to stop military operations, although they murdered a Roman Catholic taxi driver in Portadown, Northern Ireland, in the summer of 1996. Representatives of the loyalist paramilitary groups, the Ulster Volunteer Force (UVF) and the Ulster Defense Association (UDA), have been able to participate fully in the peace talks that were arranged after the 1994 cease-fire agreement.

These negotiations, chaired by George Mitchell, a former U.S. senator, have excluded representatives from Sinn Féin, the political wing of the IRA. Northern Ireland's unionist parties have threatened to abandon the talks if Sinn Féin participates, while the moderate Irish national party, the Social Democratic and Labour party, has agreed to loyalist paramilitary participation even though neither the IRA nor the loyalist paramilitary has disarmed. Senator Mitchell adjourned the peace talks in March of 1997, scheduling them to resume on June 3, 1997, after the Westminster elections. Sinn Féin participation would be a key issue in the peace talks.

At the time of this writing, the IRA was making its political wing's inclusion difficult. Before the May 1997 parliamentary elections the IRA disrupted the routines of daily life in England. They issued bomb threats on motorways into London, and they bombed commuter rail lines. After the British Labour party announced a possible schedule to meet with Sinn Féin if the Labour party won the general election, the IRA threatened to bomb the National Derby, a cherished British event. The Labour party withdrew its announcement of negotiations, but the IRA's attempts to disrupt daily life did not cease. These IRA tactics were rationalized as protests against Sinn Féin's exclusion from the peace talks, but the terror the IRA perpetrated makes its inclusion all the more difficult.

Compounding the difficulty of IRA terror is the civilian violence carried out by small groups of militant Protestants against their Roman Catholic fellow citizens. In the summer of 1996, when IRA violations of the cease-fire were relatively few and before any had occurred in Northern Ireland, the British government rerouted several of the summertime marches annually carried out by the Orange Order, the largest Protestant organization in Northern Ireland. It changed neither the destination nor the staring point of these parades, but it did create alternative routes to avoid contact with Catholic neighborhoods whose residents found the marches insulting and triumphalist. This government directive led to violent protest. Orange Order members, sometimes supported by loyalist paramilitaries, blocked roads, burned cars, and threatened the police who had to oversee the rerouted marches. Under threat, the government abandoned the restrictions it had placed on selected parade routes. The turnaround led to nationalist rioting and police violence against Roman Catholics that has made cooperation among the three sides—the British government, the Northern Irish nationalist, and the unionist—increasingly difficult. In the aftermath of these events more Protestant civilian violence occurred. Roman Catholic worshipers in Harryville, County Antrim, were subjected to weekly harassment, physical violence, and blocked roads as they tried to make their way to mass. A Roman Catholic church was burned to the ground.

These events signal the enormous difficulty of negotiating peace in Northern Ireland. Yet all groups hoped for a second cease-fire after the May 1, 1997, Westminster elections. The protests and violence of the past year demonstrate the variety and complexity of the issues to be addressed in the peace process. For a second cease-fire to come about Sinn Féin must be brought into the peace talks at some level, and the social and cultural divisions that so disturb much of everyday life in Northern Ireland must be addressed in localities as well as government centers. Sorting through the cultural practices and institutional exclusions that divide the people of Northern Ireland is a necessary step toward peace, though it will be an emotionally charged undertaking.

This essay explores what is at stake in the Northern Ireland peace process and the anxiety entailed in it by using concepts developed in recent studies of social transformation. It addresses concerns at the intersection of anthropology, sociology, and political science and pays special attention to the ethnographic aspects of Northern Ireland's divisions. In particular the essay explores the contributions that an ethnographic understanding of the practices of everyday life may make to interdisciplinary discussions of this and other conflicts. To make the contributions of an ethnographic approach understandable, it is necessary to begin with a historical delineation of the Northern Ireland state.

The Northern Ireland State

Northern Ireland, a region of the United Kingdom of Great Britain and Northern Ireland, opened its parliament in 1921. As the title of the state to which it belongs attests, the status of Northern Ireland differs from that of England, Scotland, and Wales. It is a twentieth-century creation and was formed after a long anticolonial struggle carried out by Irish nationalists and unionist resistance not only to that sometimes violent campaign but also to a series of home rule bills that came before the British Parliament from 1885 to 1914.[2] Northern Ireland was granted a devolved government at its formation, even though the unionists would have preferred a continuation of the Union established in 1800, that is a union of the entire island of Ireland with Great Britain.[3]

The 1920 Government of Ireland Act partitioned the island and created two parliaments in Ireland with local government powers.[4] One parliament was to be placed in Belfast to function as the seat of government for the island's northeastern six counties. The other, located in Dublin, would be the political center for the southern twenty-six counties. Although the 1920 act adhered to the principles of Irish home rule for which Irish parliamentary nationalists had struggled for more than four decades, by 1920, after the bitterly fought Anglo-Irish war, such a devolved government was out of the question in the southern twenty-six counties. Sinn Féin, which had won 124 of the 128 parliamentary seats, boycotted the Parliament in Dublin on its scheduled opening, June 28, 1921.[5] This abstention enabled Irish nationalists to negotiate the Anglo-Irish Treaty of December 1921, the pact that laid the foundation for the establishment of the Irish Free State in 1922 and provided the backdrop for the Irish Constitution of 1937, the document through which the southern counties eliminated the symbols of the imperial link with Britain.[6] The Northern Ireland Parliament convened on June 22, 1921.

Ironically, then, the Northern Ireland Parliament (Stormont)—an institution always controlled by Ulster unionists who campaigned against any independence for Ireland with the declaration "Home Rule Is Rome Rule"—was in practice Ireland's only home rule government. Since 1921 Northern Ireland has had political parties distinct from those in the rest of the United Kingdom. Citizens living in the region do not get a chance to vote for any of the parties that might control Westminster, but they do send representatives to that parliamentary body.[7]

From 1921 until 1972 Stormont legislated domestic social policy with considerable autonomy, controlling social welfare and domestic spending. Westminster controlled defense, foreign policy, and finance while retaining the right to intervene at will in Irish affairs. Stormont was ruled by one party, the Ulster Unionist party, throughout the fifty-one years of its existence, and that party was supported almost exclusively by Protestants. The state excluded members of the main opposition party, the Nationalists, from any public office above that of chair of an urban district council.[8] It did not conform to the norms of parliamentary democracy, especially in the areas of electoral representation and security. It gerrymandered voting districts, created an armed special constabulary staffed exclusively by Protestants, and passed security legislation, the Special Powers Act (1922) and the Public Order Act (1951), which drastically curtailed the rights of the accused and dissenters.[9]

In 1972 Stormont fell because of the upheaval created by the civil rights protests of Northern Ireland's Roman Catholic citizens and some Protestant supporters. The failure of the state not only to meet the demands of the protesters but also to quell the violent disturbances that followed led to its downfall. Northern Ireland has been ruled directly from the British Parliament at Westminster since, a legislative arrangement referred to as direct rule.[10]

The Northern Ireland state has been contested since its inception in 1921.[11] Those contesting the state are Irish nationalists, predominantly Roman Catholic. Those supporting the state are unionists who identify themselves as British citizens first and Northern Irish second. "Loyalist" best describes the politics of those unionists who feel they owe primary allegiance to Northern Ireland and only secondary loyalty to Westminster.[12]

Recent Political Developments

Sinn Féin accepted the terms of the British and Irish Peace Declaration of December 1993 in August 1994. Six weeks later the Ulster Defense Association, the umbrella organization of the various loyalist paramilitary groups, accepted the terms of that declaration as well. Both agreed to a total cease-fire, but neither turned over its arms to the authorities as both the British and Irish governments wished. Representatives of loyalist paramilitary groups participated in the peace talks and in discussions on the political future of Northern Ireland, but the British government did not grant Sinn Féin full participation because it did not decommission its arms stockpile. The IRA broke the cease-fire after seventeen months with the Canary Wharf bombing in London. Since then violence has been sporadic. Most of these violent acts have been carried out by the IRA, but violence has not reached the levels it did before the cease-fire.

As expected, difficulties pervade the search for a negotiating framework through which to debate the prospects for the region's constitutional future. Discussions between the Northern Ireland parties and the two governments have been stalemated since the Anglo-Irish Agreement introduced the possibility of talks in 1985. Northern Ireland's unionists, those who wholeheartedly support Northern Ireland's union with Great Britain and base their cultural and political identities on that association, believe that the document compromises their future by offering a consulting role to the government of the Republic of Ireland. Northern Ireland's nationalists offer differing interpretations of the 1985 accord. The Social Democratic and Labour party, led by John Hume, supports it and believes it offers fruitful ground on which to debate political possibilities. Sinn Féin, led by Gerry Adams, has opposed the agreement because it states that no constitutional change will take place in Northern Ireland without the expressed consent of the majority of its citizens. Sinn Féin believes this point provides veto powers to Northern Ireland's unionists; it wants voters in the whole of the island of Ireland to have a say in the political future of the six northeast counties.

Despite these opposing positions, the debates emanating from the Anglo-Irish Agreement, an accord whose inspiration came from the nationalist New Ireland Forum of 1983, led to the Joint Declaration of 1993, the cease-fire that followed, and the Frameworks for the Future of February 1995 (which came to be called the Framework Document), in which the British and Irish governments laid out proposals for talks between unionists and nationalists. That document put forth the following:

—The Republic of Ireland will amend its constitutional claim to Northern Ireland and will recognize, as they have done in signing the Anglo-Irish Agreement, the right of a majority within Northern Ireland to choose its political future.

—The United Kingdom will change its laws to allow the people of Northern Ireland to decide whether or not to join the Republic of Ireland.

—Northern Ireland will have an assembly with enhanced powers, and both the British and Irish governments promise support for this body without interference.

—A Cross-Border Council will be selected from the proposed Northern Ireland Assembly and the Irish Parliament to coordinate policies across the Irish border.[13]

These efforts to foster peace, at first rejected by unionists because of the cross-border dimension, were accepted by all nationalist parties and approved by British prime minister John Major's cabinet, which considered itself unionist. After much negotiation on agenda-setting issues the unionist parties in Northern Ireland accepted the framework and engaged in "all-party talks," a forum that excluded Sinn Féin. These meetings were intended to set the groundwork for debating Northern Ireland's future.

They have been led by George Mitchell, who was appointed to that role by President Bill Clinton, whose visit to Northern Ireland spurred these "all-party talks."

Ironically, a major reason for the existence of these talks is that the Ulster Defense Association (UDA), the loyalist group that has advocated violence for the last twenty-five years, accepted the Framework Document. In 1974 its supporters staged the Ulster Workers' Strike, the most widespread, virulent, and threatening protest of the last three decades of political upheaval.[14] The UDA's acceptance of the Framework Document signified an important change of position for this most militant of loyalist groups. Largely urban and working class, UDA supporters have experienced the greatest declines in quality of life and employment security of any Northern Ireland group since World War II. Yet their economic and social situations are still far ahead of working-class Catholics, with whom they share a variety of cultural practices and fragments of working-class ideology. Roman Catholics are still two-and-a-half times as likely to be unemployed as Protestants, even though the educational achievement of the two groups is about equal.[15]

Despite the economic and social advantages of its constituency, the UDA, by agreeing to the discussions outlined in the Framework Document, made public the fissures in the unionist bloc that usually go unacknowledged. Although noted by scholars, the divisions among Northern Ireland's Protestants have been little recognized in institutionalized political discourse.[16] By agreeing to the parameters of the 1995 proposals, the UDA leadership signaled not only that differing political positions exist within unionism but also that it is willing to contest and reassess the hegemonic view of unionist identity. This is a very propitious development because such reevaluations are important not only to the ongoing discussions about Northern Ireland's constitutional future but also to the practices of daily life that provide the context for such negotiations to bear fruit. For the differences between Northern Ireland's unionists and nationalists of whatever class to be recognized and tolerated through democratic means, changes will have to occur in how all groups understand themselves, their histories, and each other in this deeply divided society.

History, Colonialism, and Identity in Northern Ireland

But the term "British history" has been used here to express the need for something that shall include both the attempt to incorporate Ireland within English or British political structures, and the reactions against that attempt and its consequences. The history of Irish nationality is as much a part of "British history" in this sense as is the history of Union and Empire, and "British history" thus denotes the historiography of no single nation but of a problematic and uncompleted experiment in the creation and interaction of several nations. At this point "British history" becomes independent of Anglo-Irish union and will continue as long as there are a number of nations inhabiting the "Atlantic archipelago." But "British history" does not stop there; it extends itself into oceanic, American and global dimensions. . . . Our "British history" . . . includes the history of English-speaking America down to the point—however we determine it—when the United States is seen to have created a distinctive political culture and embarked upon a constitutional and global history that demands to be treated in its own terms. The pattern resembles that of Irish history in the sense that Anglicization and the revolt against Anglicization unite in determining it: "Ireland," however, is not able to depart from that archipelago history of which "America" ceased to be an extension.

John G. A. Pocock, "The Limits and Divisions of British History"

Virtually all commentators on Northern Ireland note the problem of national identity as a significant factor in the conflict.[17] Protestants want to preserve their British identity and fear minority status in an all-Ireland state. Roman Catholics aspire to membership in an Irish state and feel that the worth of their cultural tradition is not recognized in a British political entity. The identity question, however, is more complicated and nuanced than that coded by the aspirations for a particular nation-state.

Northern Ireland's unionists occupy a more ambiguous location than that of being stretched between two national entities. Having occupied a colonial frontier since the late sixteenth century, these people have responded to political exigencies that are different from those of their compatriots on the mainland, yet they must examine themselves through the cultural lenses developed there. Their loyalism indicates this. Ulster loyalists are militant unionists who pledge loyalty to the queen while refusing to submit to her government.[18] In other words, they put limits on their obedience to the crown in Parliament. The Stormont government's reluctance to implement British social welfare reform for its Roman Catholic citizens in the 1950s and 1960s, grass-roots opposition to the Sunningdale Agreement of 1974, and unionist intransigence toward the Anglo-Irish Agreement of 1985 all manifest this sentiment.[19]

Such loyalism is best understood in the context of the "British history" to which John G. A. Pocock alludes in the epigraph. As Pocock implies, British and Irish senses of national identity have been constructed in relation to each other. Both are products of an imperial history, and the conflict in Ireland is constructed in that history. Such historical understandings do not, however, often enter the social science debates on the Northern Ireland conflict. At present the internal conflict model predominates, and this representation of Northern Ireland's political problems enters the political arena as well. The former Irish taioseach (prime minister) Garrett Fitzgerald, for example, interprets the New Ireland Forum, over which he presided, as an important departure from Irish nationalism because it recognized two identities on the island. Fitzgerald writes that "the core of the Northern Ireland problem is seen by the Forum as lying in the clash of two identities and not the British presence."[20] This conception of the conflict is correct in that the British military presence is not the sole problem, as Sinn Féin holds. If British troops were to withdraw, the conflict over national identities would remain, but it is important to remember there is a British cultural presence that must be understood and sorted out. As Pocock insinuates in the epigraph, it is not only troops that constitute a British presence in Northern Ireland but also the symbols and history of British colonialism that have contributed so greatly to the development of Irish nationalism, Ulster unionism, and the struggles of identity Northern Ireland people are living through now. This more complicated picture must be addressed if the conflict is to be adequately assessed, and to do so the complex relationship of culture and colonialism deserves attention.

Colonialism and Ireland's Cultures

Particularly if our interest is in colonial culture, it is important to recognize that a variety of colonial representations and encounters both precede and succeed periods of actual possession and rule, and pertain in generalized forms about whole regions or continents at a level detached from particular imperial adventures. Colonial culture thus includes not only official reports and texts related directly to the process of governing colonies and extracting wealth, but also a variety of travelers' accounts, representations produced by other colonial actors such as missionaries and collectors of ethnographic specimens, and fictional, artistic, photographic, cinematic and decorative appropriations. To acknowledge that such a range of cultural products is in some sense inflected by colonial relationships is not to propose some new, highly inclusive definition of colonialism, as if that were a solution. The interest is rather in establishing how productive it is to pose a series of questions about, for example, how differences between colonizers and colonized are postulated in particular texts, and how the temporal development of those relations is imagined through narratives that may project conquest, assimilation, segregated development or some other transformation.

Nicholas Thomas, *Colonialism's Culture*

Recent works in historical anthropology and the history of colonialism, along with the interdisciplinary work of diaspora and postcolonial studies, have investigated the relationship between colonialism and culture in productive ways. In the epigraph the anthropological historian Nicholas Thomas suggests that colonial representations outlive colonial administrations. The past lives in the present through the cultural construction of colonial projects, the narratives that live on after colonial governments depart. This is certainly the case for all parts of Ireland, and the conflict over identity fuels the fires of these historical memories.

It is not so much that Irish people envelop the present with unreflexive stories of the past but that narratives of the past are used to interpret social, economic, and political problems that continue to accumulate. Geographically part of Western Europe, Ireland is marginal to it because historically it is part of the decolonizing world. People in both Northern Ireland and the Republic of Ireland live in what David Lloyd perceptively calls "anomalous states," cultural modes and political institutions that produce anxiety.[21] With a weak economy and the continuing loss of thirty thousand people or more to emigration annually, the Irish people, like many people from formerly colonized territories, live in multiple locations and forge their identity from very different geographic and political spaces. As Lloyd writes, "Doubtless only a culture similarly deracinated could pose the question of identity with such insistence as it has been posed historically in Ireland."[22] Ireland's difficulties with identity cannot be separated from either its colonial past or its weak economic position.

That Irish identity is shaped at many locations is not, however, a negative factor for political development, particularly at the present. Its effect on developments in Ireland is evident in the negotiations that enabled the IRA cease-fire and the laying down of arms by the loyalist paramilitaries six weeks later. William J. Flynn, chairman of the board of Mutual of America Life Insurance Company and the first Irish American chairman of the National Committee on American Foreign Policy; Niall O'Dowd, publisher of the Irish American newspaper *Irish Voice;* Charles Feeney, a wealthy Irish American entrepreneur; and Bruce Morrison, former congressman from Connecticut, headed a delegation to Northern Ireland that met with not only political representatives from the constitutional parties but also members of Sinn Féin and the IRA.

These Irish Americans tried to persuade those they met to give up arms. They outlined for Northern Ireland nationalists the support they could offer by lobbying the Clinton administration and organizing economic investment should a cease-fire take place. These meetings did much to precipitate the IRA cease-fire, and it is through the work of these men that Gerry Adams was granted a visa to come to the United States and address a meeting of the National Committee on American Foreign Policy, an event that had much to do with Sinn Féin's acceptance of the terms of the British and Irish governments' Joint Declaration. After the IRA committed itself to the cease-fire, these men returned to Northern Ireland to present their case to the various loyalist paramilitary groups whom they influenced to come to the United States to talk with groups of interested Irish Americans. Again, their work was important in leading the Ulster Defense Association, the umbrella organization of the loyalist paramilitaries, to accept the Joint Declaration.

This sequence of events gives credence to the notion that Irish identity is shaped through mediations at a number of locations. Such developments are related to Ireland's colonial past in that as Irish people mold their political culture, they look outward to both their diaspora populations and Britain. Colonialism is a complex process that introduces a variety of what Nicholas Dirks and Bernard Cohn call "cultural technologies of rule"—educational systems, political institutions, and historical narratives that produce in the colonized, as Lloyd puts it, "a perception of self-estrangement, of being perceived and perceiving through alien media."[23] In Northern Ireland this self-estrangement is extremely complicated. On the one hand, Irish Catholics, who were represented as unprepared for civilization during the conquest of Ulster in the sixteenth and seventeenth centuries, have had to live through variations on that trope since then. In twentieth-century Northern Ireland its most salient redeployment represents Roman Catholic citizens as traditional, not modern, and therefore not ready for the industrial job markets of modern society. Northern Ireland's Protestants, on the other hand, have been cast as colonial modernizers, as people who brought a sense of property and industrial values through a form of progressive, collectivist pioneering that was developed in Ulster and brought to America in the eighteenth century. Still, Ulster Protestants are modernizers with a difference. Tainted by that frontier position, they are judged as not quite capable of instituting full political modernization. British institutional culture considers them provincial.

This judgment arises from the metaphysical dimension of British nationalism, one common to all colonial and imperial nationalisms—the ambition to realize its essence in specific political forms and to perceive that essence, in the words of Irish writer Seamus Deane, as "the ideal model to which all others should conform."[24] Any departure from British forms is considered to be an act of the marginal. In the case of Northern Ireland, Ulster loyalism is marked as provincial, while Irish Republicanism is an abomination. Ulster unionists see themselves through those mainland lenses, a perception they have tried to make up for with their sacrifices in the service of the empire, especially in World War I and World War II. They must show their discipline, their loyalty, and their steadfast-

ness to enhance their Britishness. They must constantly prove they belong.[25]

The people in Ballybogoin, where I carried out ethnographic fieldwork
from 1985 to 1987 and in 1992, tell stories illustrating this cultural dynamic.[26] Their narrations describe the town's geography and function as
a cultural mapping of the town. How Ballybogoin people figure space—
Catholic space as disordered and appropriated and Protestant space as
ordered and modern—reveals much about their particular constructions
of the colonial past and the use of that past to discern the present.

The town square is an orderly public space with a police barracks and
an Orange hall overlooking it. Protestants take pride in the fact that no
Roman Catholic or nationalist group has ever assembled in the square.
To them, it signifies their ability to maintain order. Roman Catholic nationalists, however, cringe at the fact that groups of women marching for
welfare rights were spat on as they tried to enter the square in the local
Campaign for Social Justice, which preceded the more famous Northern
Ireland Civil Rights Association marches of the mid- to late 1960s. By
following the route Roman Catholics take to the town square and by lis-
tening to the stories they told me about this journey, we can understand
how they perceive their town.

Most Catholics from Ballybogoin and its surrounding rural district approach the town's square from Ann Street, which connects the Catholic-
nationalist, residential side of the town, its west side, to Irish Street, the
Catholic commercial street leading into the square, the place that inscribes
order. The residential units on both sides of Ann Street were razed in 1984
to make way for a proposed commercial development project whose plans
were never made public; they did not receive security clearance. The
muddy, unpaved lots that remain function as parking lots for the Catholics, who leave their cars there in crisscrossed patterns and make the easy
walk from this disorder to Irish Street or on to the square.

On these journeys from Catholic-nationalist residences to the square
space and time coalesce, and from the threshold of Ann Street the practices through which people bring them together become evident. To the
west, Ann Street's pedestrian path ends at the gateway to an old manse,
"the big house" Ballybogoin people call it, and at this juncture a road veers
off to the northwest and leads to the Catholic-nationalist housing estates
and on toward the hill country, whose social spaces many contemporary
Catholic townspeople identify as their ancestral homes. Their place-names,
anglicized by the British state in the middle third of the nineteenth century in the course of the attempt to map this territory, memorialize the
loss of a living language and provide an index to what Catholics see as

the social and political realities of both the past and the present: the realities of exclusion. These social spaces—Cornamucklagh, round hill of the
piggeries; Culnagor, hill back of the cranes or herons; Knocknaclogha, the
stony hill; Munderrydoe, the bog of the black oak wood; Aughagranna,
the ugly or bushy field—populated mostly if not wholly by Catholics, sig-
nify to the nationalists not only the poor terrain they and their ancestors
have inhabited but also the events, the sixteenth-century Elizabethan
Conquest of Ireland and the seventeenth-century colonial settlement,
which led to Protestant settlement there. In making these colonially created places into spaces, making the names on the map theirs through
cultural memory, Catholics say of their lowland, more richly situated
Protestant neighbors, "They got the land, we got the view," adding, "We
were pushed here over three hundred years ago."

In similar ways spatial stories make Ballybogoin, the first provincial
town created by the seventeenth-century colonial state, into a people's
space.[27] Ann Street, the thoroughfare between "the square" and the
town's western hinterland, stops at "the big house." It was owned by the
Stewart family, which accumulated its wealth in the area's nineteenth-
century linen industry. Catholics remember that family, its discriminato-
ry employment practices, and the exclusively Protestant ownership of that
industry through stories of Edna, the last Stewart heir to people the
place.[28] Edna, so the story goes, used to make her daily trip up to the
square by walking down the middle of Ann and Irish streets. Sturdy and
staunch, she stared straight ahead, people say, and did not look either left
or right. If a vehicle of any sort trailed her, it would have to wait. She
would not step into the "shuck," the gutter that flowed with the refuse
from the sidewalk sweepings of these entirely Catholic throughways, nor
would she walk on the "pavements," the sidewalks these people's homes
and shops abutted. She certainly would not talk. In this story, Edna's territorial practices represent the whole—the state, the Protestant people,
and its institutions. She bears a metonymic relation to that whole, but the
story also indicates that these streets have been made into "the natives'"
social spaces, appropriated culturally if not physically, as does a second
story almost always attached to memories of Edna.

Edna followed a determined path, and she did not look to or occupy
the margins, actions her family's inheritance practices attempted to reproduce. Her family's will stipulated that "the big house" be sold only to
a Protestant, and when Edna died, her heirs intended to carry out that
desire. They did this but, the Protestant man they sold the place to did
not intend to keep it. A Catholic, "part businessman, part gangster, a man
who will stick the arm into ye," Catholics say, put this Protestant busi-

ness associate from south of the border up to the purchase and had him turn around and sell it to him. When the heirs had their estate sale and this Catholic man, well known in the area, walked in and announced that he was the new owner and would take everything in the place, the heirs were reportedly stunned.

Irish Street is an uphill climb, and when Edna reached the top, she was at the square. Running perpendicular to its center and due west is Scotch Street, duly named to house the Scots dissenters who came to populate the seventeenth-century state's planned settler colony. This street divides the square in two. Both Catholics and Protestants shop and drink there. Only Catholics shop and, besides the rare exception, drink on Irish Street, designated as the place for the descendants of the natives, who started drifting back into the town in the late seventeenth century.

Thomas Street exits to the north. At the corner of Thomas Street and the square stands a now deserted but previously Catholic-owned hotel, the only edifice on the square owned by that "side of the house" until the late 1960s, when one other building was purchased by Catholics. Carved onto the outside window of that hotel, McAleer's, are the initials *TB*. Catholics say Tom Barry, a famous Irish Republican Army fighter of the 1920s who went on the run for a number of years, stayed there while the police and army were after him. He left his mark, and his exploits are sometimes sung in the pubs on Irish Street.

At the east end of the square stands a memorial to local men who died in the two great wars and the struggles to keep Ulster British. It is the ritual center of the local state and the Protestant community. Behind this, further up the hill, stands the old police barracks, more than a hundred years old but still used to house members of the security forces. A light brown, oddly designed building, it looks out of place among the dark gray sandstone buildings of Ballybogoin. Catholics say it is a mistake. It was intended for Bengal, but the plans got mixed up in the colonial office, and Bengal got Ballybogoin's building while Ballybogoin got Bengal's.

Behind the old police barracks is the modern British army lookout post, cameras clearly visible, and next to it is the Loyal Oranges Lodge, the home of the exclusively Protestant fraternal organization that organizes the bulk of the unionist political commemorations in Ballybogoin. Underneath these two edifices are the remains of the fort of Hugh O'Neill, the last Gaelic chieftain to rule the area. Catholic people remember him when they dream of the future. Talk has it that when Ireland is free, the Catholics will erect a historical park at the top of the hill, excavate the old fort and the old druid fort, which is under that one, and tell their history.

People say that under those forts are the tunnels their Gaelic forebears used to escape the British forces. Outfirepowered, they would incinerate the barricades; a few fighters would stay back as decoys; and once the British troops charged, they would escape through the underground tunnels dug for these maneuvers and join their comrades, who would attack the British army from the rear. No one knows, however, if these tunnels really exist. It is said they exit underneath the headquarters of the local Ulster Defense Regiment, the almost entirely Protestant, locally recruited unit of the British army, which is situated about half a mile from the top of the square. Someday, Catholics believe, their real story will be known. Now, they believe, their true story is hidden from them by the institutions of officialdom.

Settling Accounts

These stories and their vivid inscription of the colonial past on the contemporary landscape indicate that a narrative of Irish history that separates a colonial past from a liberal, postcolonial present will not hold. Culturally, Northern Ireland is still in a period of decolonization. Northern Ireland's rapidly changing situation, along with the even more remarkable social transformations taking place in other parts of Europe, particularly the formerly socialist states, is reminiscent of the fin de siècle predicament Emile Durkheim addressed a century ago when he attempted to theorize about such all-encompassing social change. On fracturing traditional structures, Durkheim wrote, "One after another, these [traditional structures] have disappeared either through the slow usury of time or through great disturbances, but without being replaced."[29] Northern Ireland faces a similar restructuring. Institutions from the family to regional industry to the devolved state are undergoing dramatic change and have not been replaced. But now, unlike Durkheim's day, social sciences are not seen as the sciences of morality that will serve to order the increasing disorder in our fin de siècle global system. Today, with the collapse of communism and the gradual dismantling of the welfare state, publics commonly believe that economics provides the best guide. It is cast as the beacon that will lead the states of Eastern Europe from socialism to capitalism, the postcolonial states to prosperity and democracy, and the industrialized states from big government to community and individual self-regulation. In the everyday talk of both nationalist and unionist Ballybogoin people, especially the middle classes, this evaluation of both past and future predicaments is heard.

Since mainstream economic discourse lacks a theory of change, however, it has had to borrow from sociology to address the problematic of transitions, whether those from war to peace or socialism to capitalism.[30] The current theories of transition and their application, as evidenced in the policies being instituted in east central Europe and the former Soviet Union, are wanting because, as the sociologist David Stark writes, they assume "an underlying teleology in which concepts are driven by hypothesized end-states. As in all versions of modernization theory, transitology begins with a future that is not only desired but already known. The destination has been designated."[31] To avoid this teleology, Stark advocates a more grounded approach, where the object of study is transformation, a process established through an empirical examination of events and institutions that shows how "new elements emerge through adaptations, rearrangements, permutations, and reconfigurations of existing organizational forms."[32] From this perspective it makes little sense to impose grand schemes of social engineering that have worked elsewhere. This approach holds that actors in transforming societies are accustomed to negotiating the ambiguity of contradictory social forms like those in capitalizing central Europe or decolonizing Northern Ireland and emphasizes the importance of studying the cultural scripts underlying people's understandings of society. It stresses the importance of routines and the embeddedness of choice in a network of multivalent social relations, not the rational choices of individuals guided by economic calculus. It also rejects the division of labor that the sociologist Talcott Parsons created, where the economists study value and the sociologists study values. Focusing on the question of social worth, Stark comes up with a concept that bridges this Parsonian division: accounting. The notion of accounts closes this gap between economic value and Durkheimian values by holding that economic assets and social standing can be mobilized only through a network of social relations but cannot be reduced to them. Social, economic, and cultural assets "must be bound in a network of measuring instruments, tests, and proofs of worth."[33] People give accounts, and they keep accounts:

> Both dimensions entail evaluative judgments, and each implies the other. Accountants prepare story lines according to established formulae, and in the accountings of a good story teller we know what counts. The literary critic, the moral philosopher, and the accountant are all engaged in a systematic search for value. These specialized professions, however, are just a starting point. More important for the sociology of worth is the basic social condition that we can all be called to account for our actions. When we make such an accounting, we draw on and reproduce social orders. We can competently produce justifi-

cations only in terms of established and recognized ordering principles, standards and measures of evaluation. Because we do not simply give reasons but also have reasons for doing things, accounts are not simply retrospective; the imperative of justification structures what we do and not simply how we explain. We can never merely "calculate" because we must do so with units and instruments of measurement that are deeply structured by accounts of what can be of value. We reproduce these units of measurement and we recalibrate the measuring instruments when we assert our worthiness, when we defer to the "more worthy," or when we denounce their status according to some other standard of evaluation. When we give an account, we affirm or challenge the ordering criteria according to which our actions (and/or those of others) will be evaluated at some point in the future.[34]

These concepts, developed through the empirical investigation of the organizational uncertainty of Eastern Europe, are applicable to the change taking place in Northern Ireland. Like the former state socialist societies, Northern Ireland is transforming. Since World War II it has experienced drastic economic decline, increasing rates of divorce, extensive out-migration, and political violence. Although violence in Northern Ireland has been curtailed for the moment, the structural and cultural problems that created the organizational ecology conducive to ethnic violence persist. As many commentators have noted, the conflict there is particularly difficult to resolve because Northern Ireland's cultural identities are based on that very conflict. Consequently, one of the major mitigating conditions—elite compromise usually facilitated by the existence of a common enemy or threat shared by the communities in conflict—is absent.[35]

Division is deep in Northern Ireland, and disorder occurs in all areas of social life. A notion of social order as the intersection of ties and accounts, of networks and social forms, enables an analysis of this problem. Northern Ireland, like all modern societies, is made up of several social orders, but the most salient are those labeled Protestant-unionist and Catholic-nationalist. The stories that Ballybogoin's Catholics tell to map their town point to these two orders. The Catholic, western hinterland is poor, and their side of the town is disordered, unpaved, and unbuilt. Their Protestant neighbors, personified by Edna, exclude them. The state does not fulfill its commitment to them and, worse, has them under surveillance. Their cultural mappings of the town convey their belief that law in Northern Ireland is a matter of control, not justice.

People perform identities in narrating these accounts, which evaluate their public spaces and mobilize ties to each other. Resistance figures prominently in these stories, and Roman Catholics in the town, although they differ markedly on the morality of political violence, share these narratives and question the legitimacy of the state. These accounts, then, contribute to making important cultural-political groups, but they work to exclude as well. The desire of Ballybogoin's Irish nationalists to find who they really are from those artifacts under Hugh O'Neill's fort replicates the essentialism of British nationalism. Through them, nationalists believe, they will realize their intrinsic essence. With them they return to the accounting problems that have led to the war in Northern Ireland: Catholics demand the right to define identity because their ancestors were there first, while Protestants demand authority because their ancestors were the first to institute civil society.

Such stories contribute to the conflict. In the interests of peace there should be another accounting, one that challenges the ordering criteria of British and Irish nationalisms. This is a difficult undertaking because in the interests of social justice the differences between the categories Protestant and Catholic need to be scrutinized. As mentioned earlier, Ballybogoin's Roman Catholics are almost three times more likely than Protestants to be unemployed. The town council has a history of gerrymandering voting districts to favor Protestants. These facts need to be known and addressed not only in Ballybogoin but also throughout the region, where discrimination against Roman Catholics prevails despite some positive remediations.[36] An accounting is needed in the bookkeeping sense.

At the same time, in the interests of peace there is an urgency to abolish Catholic and Protestant as political categories. The cultural accounts, the narratives that evaluate the events of everyday life, need deconstruction. The institutions proposed in the Framework Document of 1995— the Northern Ireland Assembly, the Cross-Border Council, and the "all-party talks"—will be particularly pressed to deal with these identity issues, along with the necessary constitutional ones. New organizational forms are new interweavings of social orders, and this particular historical moment is a propitious one for reworking Northern Ireland's problematic institutions and cultural accountings. The Paris Charter has realigned the security debate in Europe and rendered Britain's strategic considerations of Ireland obsolescent. The European Community, especially the single market, has made whatever economic considerations Britain has historically had regarding Ireland dramatically different. The international conflicts in Europe that historically have made Ireland a nodal point for British security concerns are over, and many Irish leaders are aware of this. John Hume of Northern Ireland's Social Democratic and Labour party notes this when he addresses the possibilities for Ireland:

Britain is pooling sovereignty not just with France and Spain but with Ireland and eight other European countries as well. Sovereignty and independence, the issues at the heart of wars in Europe and the issues at the heart of the British-Irish quarrel, have changed their meaning. The basic needs of all countries have led to shared sovereignty and interdependence as we move inevitably toward the United States of Europe and as we in Ireland rid ourselves of the obsession with Britain and rebuild our links with the rest of Europe.[37]

Hume stresses the importance of shared sovereignty and interdependence for all nation-states in dealing with the economic and technological changes occurring in Europe. By emphasizing this, he is reorienting Irish nationalist ideology, and this should help institution building on the regional and local levels. The emphasis on the Britishness or the Irishness of political institutions on both sides of the border has done much to alienate Catholics and Protestants in Northern Ireland. Eamon DeValera's 1949 constitution, which values a Gaelic and rural Ireland, pushed unionist identity toward a more solidly British identification and away from the British-Irish one emphasized earlier.[38] Northern Ireland's legal and political practices, under both unionist hegemony and direct rule, have not valued the distinctive traditions of Irish nationalists. The issue of multiculturalism—whether the institutions of liberal democratic government make room or should make room for recognizing the worth of distinctive cultural traditions—should receive attention in both the proposed Northern Ireland Assembly and the Cross-Border Conference.[39]

When these issues are publicly debated, it is hoped that changes on the local level will occur. As the stories from Ballybogoin demonstrate, Northern Irish identities have a strong local component. Narratives of towns, villages, and even the smaller townlands articulate to regional and international narratives that describe loss and violent recovery on both the nationalist and unionist sides. Yet one can envision the local Ballybogoin Council organizing a joint British and Irish march into the square. It would be the first time a Catholic organization ever freely assembled there. Such rituals would be difficult to stage, but the Ballybogoin people with whom I have communicated since the cease-fire see such public commemorations on the horizon, albeit several years from now. The peace process is a healing process. The dividend of terror is hard-to-heal wounds, but with considered institutional innovations a lasting peace is possible in Northern Ireland, providing attention is paid to the two senses of accounting outlined here: the bookkeeping sense, which tracks the employment and political discrimination still marring Northern Ireland, and the cultural accountings people use to make sense of their social world. Anthropologists are beginning to join political scientists and sociologists in bringing the fruits of their work to public policy questions in Northern Ireland, and it is hoped cultural questions will be inserted into future policy debates.[40]

There are luminous examples of such considerations contributing to peace. Not the least among them are the medical and physical scientists who counted the costs of weapons of mass destruction and in the course of that reevaluated the relations of science and society, giving a different accounting of the cold war. Such efforts have contributed immensely to worldwide efforts to make peace.

Notes

The field research cited in this essay was conducted from 1985 to 1987. It was supported by a dissertation grant from the Social Science Research Council's Fellowship Program. Funds for the program were provided by the Ford Foundation, the William and Flora Hewlett Foundation, and the National Endowment for the Humanities.

1. Jo Thomas, "'Shoot to Kill' Policy in Ulster: The Debate Rages," *New York Times*, April 12, 1985; Jo Thomas, "'Shoot to Kill' Rumors Will Not Die," *New York Times*, March 17, 1986; John Stalker, *The Stalker Affair* (New York: Viking, 1988); International Lawyers' Inquiry, *Shoot to Kill?: International Lawyers' Inquiry into the Lethal Use of Firearms by the Security Forces in Northern Ireland* (Dublin: Mercier, 1985); Anthony Jennings, "Shoot to Kill: The Final Courts of Justice," in *Justice under Fire: The Abuse of Civil Liberties in Northern Ireland*, ed. Anthony Jennings (London: Pluto, 1988), 104–30.

2. Patrick O'Farrell, *England and Ireland since 1800* (Oxford: Oxford University Press, 1975), 85–109; Oliver MacDonagh, *States of Mind: Anglo-Irish Conflict, 1780–1980* (London: George Allen and Unwin, 1983), 1–70; Oliver MacDonash, *Ireland: The Union and Its Aftermath* (London: George Allen and Unwin, 1977), 53–71; Robert Kee, *The Laurel and the Ivy: The Story of Charles Stewart Parnell and Irish Nationalism* (London: Hamish Hamilton, 1993), 476–532, 610–14.

3. Paul Arthur, *Government and Politics of Northern Ireland* (Essex: Longman, 1980), 14.

4. Joseph Lee, *Ireland, 1912–1985: Politics and Society* (Cambridge: Cambridge University Press, 1989), 43–44.

5. Alan J. Ward, "A Constitutional Background to the Northern Ireland Crisis," in *Northern Ireland and the Politics of Reconciliation*, ed. Dermot Keogh and Michael H. Haltzel (Cambridge: Cambridge University Press, 1994), 42–46.

6. Lee, *Ireland, 1912–1985*, 94–150.

7. Arthur, *Government and Politics of Northern Ireland*, 17–33.

8. Paul Bew, Peter Gibbon, and Henry Patterson, *Northern Ireland, 1921–1994: Political Forces and Social Classes* (London: Serif, 1995), 9.

9. Michael Farrell, *Northern Ireland: The Orange State* (London: Pluto, 1976); Michael Farrell, *Arming the Protestants: The Formation of the Ulster Special Constabulary and the Royal Ulster Constabulary, 1920–27* (London: Pluto, 1983); Arthur, *Government and Politics of Northern Ireland*, 28–29; Ward, "A Constitutional Background to the Northern Ireland Crisis."

10. Brendan O'Leary and John McGarry, *The Politics of Antagonism: Understanding Northern Ireland* (London: Athlone, 1993), 153–219.

11. Bob Rowthorn and Naomi Wayne, *Northern Ireland: The Political Economy of Conflict* (Cambridge: Polity, 1988), 28–50, 70–104; J. Bowyer Bell, *The Irish Troubles: A Generation of Violence, 1967–1992* (New York: St. Martin's, 1993).

12. Steve Bruce, *The Edge of the Union: The Ulster Loyalist Political Vision* (Oxford: Oxford University Press, 1994), 1–2.

13. The Governments of the Republic of Ireland and Great Britain and Northern Ireland, *Frameworks for the Future* (Belfast: HMSO, 1995).

14. Robert Fisk, *The Point of No Return: The Strike Which Broke the British in Ulster* (London: Andre Deutsch, 1975).

15. Rowthorn and Wayne, *Northern Ireland;* Vincent McCormack and Joe O'Hara, *Enduring Inequality: Religious Discrimination in Employment in Northern Ireland* (London: National Council for Civil Liberties, 1990).

16. Bew, Gibbon, and Patterson, *Northern Ireland, 1921–1994*, 55–80.

17. John Whyte, "Interpretations of the Northern Ireland Problem," in *Consensus in Ireland: Approaches and Recessions*, ed. Charles Townshend (Oxford: Oxford University Press, 1988), 24–46; John Whyte, *Interpreting Northern Ireland* (Oxford: Clarendon, 1990).

18. David W. Miller, *Queen's Rebels: Ulster Loyalism in Historical Perspective* (Dublin: Gill and Macmillan, 1978).

19. Fisk, *The Point of No Return;* Lee, *Ireland, 1912–1985*, 456; Paul Arthur, "The Anglo-Irish Agreement: A Device for Territorial Management," in *Northern Ireland and the Politics of Reconciliation*, ed. Keogh and Haltzel, 228–33.

20. Garrett Fitzgerald, Foreword to *Interpreting Northern Ireland*, by Whyte, vi.

21. David Lloyd, *Anomalous States: Irish Writing and the Post-Colonial Moment* (Durham, N.C.: Duke University Press, 1993), 3.

22. Ibid.

23. Bernard S. Cohn and Nicholas B. Dirks, "Beyond the Fringe: The Nation State, Colonialism, and the Technologies of Power," *Journal of Historical Sociology*, 1, no. 2 (1988): 225; Lloyd, *Anomalous States*, 1.

24. Seamus Deane, Introduction to *Nationalism, Colonialism and Literature*, ed. Seamus Deane (Minneapolis: University of Minnesota Press, 1990), 8.

25. Seamus Deane, *Civilians and Barbarians* (Derry, Northern Ireland: Field Day Theatre Company, 1983); Frank McGuinness, *Observe the Sons of Ulster Marching towards the Somme* (London: Faber and Faber, 1985); Terence Brown, "British Ire-

land," in *Culture in Ireland: Division or Diversity,* ed. Edna Longley (Belfast: Institute of Irish Studies, 1991), 72–83.

26. The town in which I did fieldwork is given a fictional name, in keeping with anthropological practice.

27. Michel de Certeau, *The Practices of Everyday Life* (Berkeley: University of California Press, 1984).

28. In keeping with standard anthropological practice, I use fictional names for individuals in ethnographic descriptions.

29. Emile Durkheim, 1897, quoted in Loic J. D. Wacquant, "Solidarity, Morality and Sociology: Durkheim and the Crisis of European Society," *Journal of the Society for Social Research* 1, no. 1 (1993): 4.

30. David Stark, *Recombinant Property in East European Capitalism* (Ithaca, N.Y.: Mario Einaudi Center for International Studies, 1994), 1.

31. Ibid., 2.

32. Ibid., 4.

33. Ibid., 30.

34. Ibid., 30–36.

35. Brendan O'Duffy, "Containment or Regulation: The British Approach to Ethnic Conflict in Northern Ireland," in *The Politics of Ethnic Conflict Regulation,* ed. John McGarry and Brendan O'Leary (New York: Routledge, 1993), 129.

36. Relative unemployment varies from region to region within Northern Ireland. Ballybogoin has a higher percentage of Catholic unemployment than do most regions. McCormack and O'Hara, *Enduring Inequality,* 5–9.

37. John Hume, "A New Ireland in a New Europe," in *Northern Ireland and the Politics of Reconciliation,* ed. Keogh and Haltzel, 226–33.

38. Brown, "British Ireland," 74–78.

39. Charles Taylor, *Multiculturalism* (Princeton, N.J.: Princeton University Press, 1994).

40. Hastings Donnan and Graham McFarlane, *Social Anthropology and Public Policy in Northern Ireland* (Aldershot: Gower, 1989).

3

The Case for Impartiality in Ireland

Robert J. McKim

The five million or so people of the island of Ireland can be categorized in various ways. There are Protestants and Catholics, and there are unionists and nationalists. There are conservatives and liberals, and there are various issues, including moral and religious issues, with respect to which people are either conservative or liberal. Most of the Protestants, who make up 18.4 percent of the population of the island as a whole and 50.2 percent of the population of Northern Ireland, are unionists. But many are not. For instance, the vast majority of Protestants in the Irish Republic are not unionists. Most of the Catholics, who make up 77.0 percent of the population of the island as a whole and 38.4 percent of the population of Northern Ireland, are nationalists, but many are not.[1] A good many people are neither Protestant nor Catholic, and a much larger number are neither unionist nor nationalist. There are secular nationalists just as there are secular unionists. Both Protestants and Catholics come in conservative and liberal varieties, and again there are numerous issues with respect to which they are liberal or conservative. The Protestants are mostly the descendants of settlers from England and Scotland, who from the sixteenth and seventeenth centuries on came to Ireland. Many of the Catholics are the descendants of natives who lived in Ireland before the settlements of the sixteenth and seventeenth centuries. In both communities, however, there are numerous exceptions to these generalizations about ancestry. While there is room for a distinction between natives and newcomers, many of the natives are descendants of those who arrived in earlier waves of immigration, including Celts, Vikings, and Normans. In these and many other respects the situation in the island of Ireland is a complicated one. In this essay, in which I focus on the two dominant competing political ideologies—unionism and nationalism—that have implications for the future of the island, I ignore most of these complications.

A central ingredient in the unionist ideology is the aspiration to continued union between Northern Ireland and the rest of the United Kingdom. A central ingredient in the nationalist ideology is the wish for Northern Ireland to be included in an expanded Irish state and for the island to be unified politically. In this essay I comment on the reasonableness, value, and worthiness of support of these ideologies, in whose name much blood has been spilled. I also comment briefly on the form that loyalty to either of them should now take. In the process I advocate a general perspective on disputes of the Irish sort. What follows, then, involves an interweaving of rather general theoretical points with more specific recommendations about the Irish case. The general theoretical points concern the notion of a right to self-determination, the form that loyalty to an ideology should take when certain conditions are met, and the correct attitude to take toward other groups when these conditions are met.

Two Reasonable Ideologies

I contend that the nationalist wish to have a single unified and independent state in the island of Ireland and the unionist desire to remain British are equally reasonable and equally deserving of attention and respect and that neither the nationalist nor the unionist ideology rests on false or unreasonable assumptions—or at least the advocates of each can present a version that is free of false and unreasonable assumptions. We should view with equal respect and take equally seriously the aspirations, hopes, and fears of these two main political communities. Let us first try to understand these ideologies.

The basic aim of Irish nationalists has been to unify the island of Ireland, to have a single state for all the people. Nationalists may well describe their aim as that of unifying the country, but that way of putting it seems to presuppose a certain conception of what "the country" consists of, a conception that probably is profoundly unsatisfactory to unionists. (Here and elsewhere I try to avoid controversial terminology and controversial ways of presenting issues.) Nationalists think that the natural political arrangement for the island is a single state. Irish nationalism traditionally has conceived of unionists as not really belonging on the island. Often they have been perceived as a relic of colonial occupation.

Most of these aims are reasonable. Indeed, the only indefensible part of what I have just imputed to nationalism is the idea that unionists do not belong on the island and are not entitled to own what they own.² All other things being equal, it is a perfectly splendid idea that people should live together rather than apart.

A central aspect of what matters to unionists is the preservation of what they conceive of as their distinctive way of life. They fear that in a one-state island their culture, identity, and religion—in effect what makes them who they are—will be submerged. They think that in the event of unity with the rest of Ireland they would be a beleaguered minority. At least as important to them is the aspiration signified by the very term *unionism:* they wish for the six counties that now constitute Northern Ireland to continue to be united with the rest of the United Kingdom. Unionists feel British, think of themselves as British, and want to remain British. Why, they ask, should they be forced into unity with the Irish Republic, which they regard as a foreign state, and with the people of the Irish Republic, with whom they feel they have a lot less in common than they feel they have with the people of Great Britain?

It is clear from this sketchiest of accounts that each side pursues a goal that, on the face of it, is not outlandish or unworthy of some allegiance.³ It is hard for the advocates of either ideology to concede this. For one thing, in practice an endorsement of either position is frequently inter-twined with mistrust and suspicion of the other community and some-times with bigotry and hostility toward it. Clearly the reasonableness of these ideologies is not compromised by this fact, just as it is not compro-mised by the folly, brutality, or past injustices of some of their adherents. I next provide more substantial evidence for the claim that both ideolo-gies are reasonable by considering the concept of a right to self-determi-nation. My contention is that if one examines what this concept amounts to, it actually supports an evenhanded approach to the two communities.

The Right to Self-Determination

According to international law, as encoded in the Helsinki Final Act, "[A]ll peoples always have the right, in full freedom, to determine, when and as they wish, their internal and external political status, without exter-nal interference, and to pursue as they wish their political, economic, social and cultural development."⁴ How is this right to be understood? And who has it?

Rights

Obviously no one can have a right to self-determination if there are no such things as rights. Whether there are rights is itself a controversial issue in moral theory, but one that will not be broached here. Suffice it to say that if there are no such things as rights, then there must be something else that takes their place in a rightless moral scheme of things. For instance, if people do not have a right to life, then we need some other way to express the fact that people's lives are worthy of protection and ought not to be taken except under exceptional circumstances, such as when soldiers are voluntarily fighting in support of an unjust cause. The same can be said for other apparent rights. Rather than enter into the complicated debate about whether there are rights—a morass from which we might never emerge—it will simply be assumed that there are such things as rights. Part of the justification for doing so is that if there are no rights, everything said in what follows about self-determination can be formulated in a way that would make no mention of rights. Another part of the justification for this approach is that talk of rights has the convenience that arises from being an established part of our moral vocabulary.

Self-Determination

I use some themes from an essay on self-determination by Avishai Margalit and Joseph Raz as a starting point.[5] Margalit and Raz observe that self-determination generally has been fairly narrowly construed and is understood to consist of the achievement of independence or autonomy.[6] They contend there is a right that is more fundamental than the right to self-determination, so understood—namely, the right to self-government. A group has achieved self-government when its members determine "the character of their social and economic environment, their fortunes, the course of their development, and the fortunes of their members by their own actions . . . in as much as these are matters which are properly within the realm of political actions," when "the general political power over a group and its members [is entrusted to] the group," and when "whatever is a proper matter for political decision [is] . . . subject to the political decision of the group in all matters concerning the group and its members."[7] Self-determination, in the usual and narrow sense, matters because it generally is the most effective way to achieve self-government.

This distinction between self-determination and self-government is reasonable and sensible. But the notion of self-government, which Margalit and Raz correctly think of as a more general and more fundamental notion, has various dimensions that need not go together and are actually best separated. I distinguish these and assign each of them a name for ease of discussion. The choice of names here is somewhat arbitrary; what matters is that we have a convenient way to refer to the different ideas.

First, there is the idea that "the general political power over a group and its members [is entrusted to] the group." Let's say that a group that has achieved this condition is sovereign. A group is therefore sovereign if it has political independence and control over its own affairs.[8]

Second, there is the idea that a group's wishes and choices about its destiny, including choices about what its political, social, and economic arrangements should be, are reflected in its situation in a significant way. Let's say that a group that has achieved this condition is fulfilled.

Third, there is the idea that a group is fulfilled, in the sense just explained, and that this has come about as a result of the group's actions. That is, "the character of their social and economic environment, their fortunes, the course of their development, and the fortunes of their members" are as they wish them to be, and they themselves are responsible for achieving this state of affairs. What this third idea adds to the second idea is that the group's actions have played a major part in bringing about its happy circumstances. Let's say that a group that satisfies this third condition is self-regulating.

Clearly a group can be fulfilled even though it is not self-regulating. It can also be fulfilled even though it is not sovereign. It may not aspire to being sovereign, yet it may have well-defined aspirations about its fate. It may wish, for instance, to align itself with some other group, either by forming some sort of association with it or even by coming under its control. In such a case, it can be fulfilled only if it is *not* sovereign. The notions of being sovereign and being self-regulating are also distinct. Since a group may not aspire to being sovereign with respect to its social and economic conditions and the like, it may achieve the condition it wishes and do so through its own efforts without achieving sovereignty. It is clear from what has been said thus far that there are a number of equally sensible ways to use the term *self-determination;* what matters is that we be clear about what we mean.

The really important idea here is the idea of being fulfilled. It seems most important that groups have the arrangements they want. What matters most, surely, is not that groups be independent or sovereign or self-regulating. It may not be important to them to be independent or sovereign; it may also be unimportant to them to be self-regulating. (It may not matter to them that their own actions have created the arrangements in which they find themselves—which is what is involved in being self-regulating.) Or at least if this is important, it seems to be less important than whether their circumstances are in accordance with their wishes, which seems to be what really matters here. Because of its importance, I refer to this idea of being fulfilled as self-determination. Self-determination, understood in this sense, is the focus of much of the discussion that follows.

Thinking of self-determination in this way circumvents the charge that to endorse the ideal of self-determination is to endorse the view that the ideal for international affairs would be every nation's having its own state. Partly because we have become more aware of the virtues of the liberal multicultural state and partly because the idea of every nation's having its own state seems to be a recipe for anarchy, many people feel that this idea that every nation should have its own state is a very dubious notion. This criticism does not, however, apply to the notion of self-determination under discussion.

Achieving self-determination (in the proposed sense, although this also applies in the case of the other related notions) is a matter of degree rather than an all-or-nothing affair. The greater the extent to which a group's wishes and choices about its political, social, and economic arrangements are fulfilled, the greater is the extent to which it has achieved self-determination. Further, there is a continuum here—from being in circumstances altogether at odds with the wishes and choices of one's group to being in circumstances altogether in accordance with those wishes and choices—and it would be arbitrary to specify some particular level of influence as the cutoff point for having achieved self-determination. (Must it be that, in the light of your wishes and desires, your situation is the best possible one? Or is it enough for it merely to be pleasing? Or satisfactory? Or tolerable?) However, if the cutoff point for when self-determination has been achieved is difficult to specify, it is easy to think of states of affairs in which a group is self-determining and other states of affairs in which it is not. (Again, corresponding points could be made about the other notions here, such as autonomy and sovereignty.) Since there are degrees of self-determination, it will take less for the lesser degrees to be justified.

Finally, I restrict discussion to cases in which a group's wish to be self-determining (henceforth used in my sense unless indicated otherwise) involves a territorial aspiration. This component can be included in two ways. One is to define self-determination as involving a territorial dimension, and the other is to think of this as a dimension that may or may not be present in a group aspiring to self-determination and then to limit discussion to cases in which it is present. Either way of including the territorial dimension would suffice for my purposes, but I take the second approach. Discussion thus is restricted to cases in which a group has aspirations to a distinct piece of territory; part of what the group wants is that a certain political arrangement will exist in this territory. Typically either the territory is occupied by the group in question or the group has some other special connection with it.

Who Has a Right to Self-Determination?

If this is what self-determination is, who has a right to it? One pleasing feature of Margalit and Raz's account is that it shifts the debate away from the notions of a nation and a people. There is therefore no need to seek a set of conditions that are either necessary or sufficient for a group to constitute a nation or a people. Margalit and Raz introduce the term *encompassing group* in the course of giving their answer to the question of who has a right to self-determination. (They understand this question in a slightly different way since their notion of self-determination is a little different from mine, but the same reasoning applies, and I ignore the resultant differences in the remainder of this discussion.) Encompassing groups have six characteristics that "in combination are relevant to a case for self-determination."[9]

First, "the group has a common character and a common culture that encompass many . . . varied and important aspects of life."[10] Associated with each culture are various "forms of life, types of activity, occupations, pursuits and relationships,"[11] and we expect distinctive cuisines, architectural styles, literary and artistic traditions, music, customs, dress, ceremonies, holidays, and so forth.[12] Second, "people growing up among members of the group will acquire the group culture, will be marked by its character. Their tastes and their options will be affected by that culture to a significant degree."[13] Third, membership "in the group is, in part, a matter of mutual recognition. Typically, one belongs to such groups if, among other conditions, one is recognized by other members of the group as belonging to it."[14] Fourth, membership is important for one's self-identification; membership "is one of the primary facts by which people are identified, and which form expectations as to what they are like."[15] Fifth, membership "is a matter of belonging, not of achievement. One does not have to prove oneself, or to excel in anything, in order to belong and to be accepted as a full member."[16] Sixth, "the groups concerned are not small face-to-face groups, members of which are generally known to all other members. They are anonymous groups where mutual recognition is secured by the possession of general characteristics."[17]

A seventh consideration, which Margalit and Raz do not mention, is that the group in question must value self-determination and their need to achieve it, if they have not achieved it. How people think of themselves in this respect is crucial. They must aspire to having political, economic, social, and cultural arrangements that reflect their traditions, or they must value the fact that they have achieved these if this has been their good fortune. This aspiration must be a subject of public discussion, and it must be publicly recognized. As mentioned, I am restricting attention to cases where people also aspire to having certain arrangements established in the territory that is their special concern. This seventh consideration and the first of Margalit and Raz's considerations seem to be the really important ones.

It is beyond my present purposes to give an account of why groups satisfying these conditions have a right of the sort under discussion, or of the many factors that bear on the possession of this right, and I will not discuss these topics beyond this and the next few paragraphs. Margalit and Raz sensibly link their account of the relevant characteristics of encompassing groups to their case for the value of self-government. They say that people find in such encompassing groups "a culture which shapes to a large degree their tastes and opportunities, and which provides an anchor for their self-identification and the safety of effortless secure belonging."[18] In their view the fact that encompassing groups are so important to their members explains why self-government and in turn self-determination (by which they mean independence and autonomy) matter. It is often true that an encompassing group can prosper only if it is self-governing: encompassing groups "that do not enjoy self-government are not infrequently persecuted, despised, or neglected."[19] Independence is often the best, and sometimes the only, way to achieve self-government:

> [The] great importance that membership in and identification with encompassing groups has in the life of individuals, and the importance of the prosperity and self-respect of such groups to the well-being of their members . . . makes it reasonable to let the encompassing group that forms a substantial majority in a territory have the right to determine whether that territory shall form an independent state in order to protect the culture and self-respect of the group, provided that the new state is likely to respect the fundamental interests of its inhabitants, and provided that measures are adopted to prevent its creation from gravely damaging the just interests of other countries.[20]

Margalit and Raz say that it may be no more than a brute fact that encompassing groups matter as much as they do to people, but it is a very important fact. Membership in such a group is important for well-being, and the fate of the group impinges on the fate of the individuals who constitute it. A case for the importance of self-determination in my sense, where this amounts to being fulfilled, is at least as easy to make on the basis of their reasoning.

A full account of the normative grounding of the right to self-determination would probably also proceed by extrapolation from the notion of an individual right to self-determination. Self-determination for individuals consists of something like living a life that reflects one's aspirations and choices and particularly not being prevented from doing so by others. It is the idea that what matters to individuals, how they see themselves, what they think is important to them, and so forth should be expressed in how they live. If a satisfactory version of the individual right to self-determination can be developed, then we might think of the group case as a matter of summing up the rights of individuals.

A full discussion of the basis of the right to self-determination would be complex and multifaceted and would also include such points as the following. All other things being equal, a group has a stronger case for self-determination to the extent that it has a unified culture and a well-defined conception of itself and to the extent that it differs from the other groups around it. Grievances of various sorts can also enhance a case for self-determination. Insofar as some other group will be disadvantaged if a group achieves self-determination, its case for self-determination is accordingly weakened. In addition, if the group is aspiring to become a new political unit, the new unit ought to be economically viable. As the costs and burdens of achieving self-determination increase, the justification must be that much stronger. A full discussion would have to take into account such considerations. It would also have to pay attention to the details of the arrangements to which a group aspires. To the extent that the purpose is to dominate another group, the case for its having a right to self-determination is weakened. Whether a group has a right to self-determination is also partly a function of its guarantees to protect minorities in a new arrangement. If guarantees cannot be provided, the right is diminished, and a demand for self-determination is correspondingly less worthy of support.

There are some points that bear specifically on the sort of cases to which I am restricting discussion, namely cases in which the group in question has a territorial aspiration. Normally a group that aspires to a certain political future for a territory and its population must be a significant presence in that territory.[21] If independence is at issue, the territory must not contain all or more than a fair share (and what that is obviously requires discussion) of the assets of the larger unit of which it has been a part. The economic viability of the larger unit that is being dismantled should not be undermined. There is also a prima facie case for compensating the larger unit for the assets that it will lose. Obviously the nature of the historical connection with the territory in question is also crucial. If, for example, it began with violent conquest, then we should be less favorably disposed to the claim of the conquerors that they now have a right to self-determination. And so on. Many of these considerations are offered just by way of example. In what follows I simply assume that a compelling case for self-determination can be made. It seems intuitively clear that the greater the extent to which groups are self-determining, the better off they are, all other things being equal.

Other issues are worth exploring here. Whether a group has achieved self-determination is a matter of its relations with other groups rather than its internal arrangements, such as whether its political system is a democratic one. But, as indicated earlier, a group has a right to self-determination only if its members aspire to achieve self-determination. Hence, if a group is not a democratic one, there must be another way to discern the will of the people. If we are concerned with self-determination because we believe that groups of people should have the sort of political, economic, and social arrangements they want, we have reason to prefer democratic arrangements within countries. There therefore is a loose connection between these ideas.

Two further points about the right to self-determination should be mentioned. First, every group that satisfies the seven conditions spelled out earlier has a right to self-determination. We need not, however, commit ourselves to the view that only groups that do so have this right. For example, political entities consisting of more than one encompassing group or groups composed of individuals who lack a common culture but share a particular territorial ambition may sometimes have this right. Second, since the right to self-determination is prima facie and defeasible, one group's right to self-determination will sometimes take priority over that of another.

Self-Determination and the Irish Case

What are the implications of this sort of analysis for the case of Ireland? It seems clear that both unionists and nationalists have a right of the sort discussed. This is very controversial. Irish nationalists have generally argued that the group that should make decisions about the future of Northern Ireland is the population of the island of Ireland as a whole, in which case the unionists would be outvoted many times over. Here, for instance, is a typical statement of this view from the Irish artist Robert Ballagh:

> [The plain answer to the] question as to whether the decision about the future of . . . "Northern Ireland" ought to be left to the people there . . . is "no."

"Northern Ireland" was and is a glorified gerrymander whereby six Irish counties were partitioned from the rest because they were the largest area that the unionists could dominate. The truly democratic demand is for majority rule in Ireland, albeit on the basis of devolution and non-discrimination and [for] Britain to accept that and to start a process of disengagement to help realize it.[22]

Francis Boyle, a professor of international law at the University of Illinois at Urbana-Champaign, takes more or less the same line.[23] He says that the sort of group that has a right to self-determination is a people and that international law requires "one state for the Irish people." By "Irish people" he means all of the inhabitants of the island.[24] He takes it as obvious that the occupants of the island of Ireland together constitute a people, that the people who inhabit Great Britain are another people, and that the people of each island should be regarded as having a right to self-determination. The relevant documents in international law, however, are vague about what is meant by a people, even though they say that a people has a right to self-determination. We might try to rectify this situation in either of two ways: one is to try to get a clearer understanding of what exactly a people is, and the other is to leave that murky notion aside and give an account of the conditions of the possession of the right that does not refer to this notion. The latter route, which is the one taken here, is the better one; Margalit and Raz show us how to make progress on it. If encompassing groups, or groups that satisfy the seven conditions identified above, have a right to self-determination, it follows that both the unionists and the nationalists have a right to self-determination for they both satisfy all seven conditions, including the crucial first and seventh ones. It seems that if the one group has the right, so does the other. Although some of his proposals are worthwhile and his attitude to the communities in Northern Ireland is in many respects evenhanded, Boyle, along with many other commentators on Northern Ireland, fails to recognize that the unionists and nationalists ought to be seen in this light.

Boyle believes his approach is supported by the Downing Street Declaration, also known as the Joint Declaration, which John Major, who was then the British prime minister, and Albert Reynolds, who was then the Irish taoiseach, concluded in December 1993. Boyle quotes this passage from section 4 of the declaration:

> The British Government [agrees] that it is for the people of the island of Ireland alone, by agreement between the two parts respectively, to exercise their right of self-determination on the basis of consent, freely and concurrently given, north and south, to bring about a united Ireland, if that is their wish. They reaffirm as a binding obligation that they will, for their part, introduce the nec-

essary legislation to give effect to this, or equally to any measure of agreement on future relationships in Ireland which the people living in Ireland may themselves freely so determine without external impediment.[25]

Of course even if the British government (or the Irish government) were to declare that the people of the island are to be treated as one people and that the Irish people as one unit ought to decide the political future of Northern Ireland, that would hardly settle the question of what ought to be the case, which is my concern here. The quoted passage does not seem to have the import that Boyle takes it to have, however. The main point in this passage is that the British government will not stand in the way if the people who live on the island of Ireland choose en masse to be part of a united and independent Ireland. But this is of course compatible with recognizing that there are two groups on the island, each of whom must separately agree to a united and independent Ireland before it will have the backing of the British government. These remarks seem to suggest that there are in fact two groups that must separately agree. It is, I suppose, a clever formulation, designed to offer something to everyone. On the one hand there is the pronouncement that the Irish people have a right to self-determination and a right to achieve a united Ireland through the exercise of this right. This is designed to please the nationalists. On the other hand the right that is recognized presupposes agreement that has been freely entered into between two different groups; and if there is no agreement, there is no recognition of the right to achieve a united Ireland. This part is designed to please the unionists.

But what exactly are the two groups that must freely agree to a united Ireland for there to be recognition of the right to self-determination? In pondering this question, we should consider the so-called Framework Document, which was issued jointly by the Irish and British governments on February 22, 1995.[26] The relevant part of the Framework Document is section 16, which I quote in full:

In their approach to Northern Ireland [the Irish and British Governments] . . . will apply the principle of self-determination by the people of Ireland on the basis set out in the Joint Declaration: the British government recognise that it is for the people of Ireland alone, by agreement among the two parts respectively and without external impediment, to exercise their right of self-determination on the basis of consent, freely and concurrently given, North and South, to bring about a United Ireland, if that is their wish; the Irish Government accept that the democratic right of self-determination by the people of Ireland as a whole must be achieved and exercised with and subject to the agreement and consent of a majority of the people in Northern Ireland.

This passage has a number of striking features. Both governments re-affirm the principle of self-determination for the people of Ireland.[27] Both agree that the right may be exercised only if there is agreement. But agree-ment between which groups? The position imputed to the Irish govern-ment is clear in this respect: the populations of each of the two political parts of the island, namely, Northern Ireland and the Irish Republic, must agree to a united Ireland. The position imputed to the British government, however, retains an ambiguity from the Downing Street Declaration, an ambiguity that appears to have been retained with sufficient care that one assumes it was done intentionally. The same ambiguous locution is re-peated verbatim: "it is for the people of Ireland alone, by agreement be-tween the two parts respectively" to exercise their right to self-determi-nation. But what are the parts in question parts of? Is it Ireland that has the relevant parts, or is it the people of Ireland that have the parts in question? If it is Ireland, then what is required for recognition of the right to self-determination by the British government is just what the Irish government requires: agreement on the part of the population of the Republic of Ireland and the population of Northern Ireland. But if it is the people that have the parts in question, the situation may be otherwise. Someone might think of the people of Ireland as having as its parts the populations of the Irish Republic and of Northern Ireland, but the two parts may be the nationalist and the unionist communities. At the very least a formulation is used that is open to this interpretation. Moreover, reading it so that both communities must agree is very much in the spirit of much of the remainder of the Framework Document, which repeat-edly mentions the need for structures that will "reflect the reality of di-verse aspirations," that will "reconcile as fully as possible the rights of both traditions" (section 18), and that will "respect the full and equal legiti-macy and worth of the identity, sense of allegiance, aspiration and ethos of both the unionist and nationalist communities [in Northern Ireland]" (section 19).[28] Such remarks come close to recognizing a right to self-determination on the part of both encompassing groups, namely, nation-alists and unionists. My contention, in any case, is that whatever rights the populations of Northern Ireland and the Republic of Ireland may have, and indeed whatever may be the import of these documents, encompass-ing groups such as Irish nationalists and Northern Irish unionists have a right to self-determination.

Although Irish nationalists typically have stressed a right to self-deter-mination, Irish unionists have not done so. Sometimes the unionists have construed the notion of self-determination as amounting to sovereignty;

and since they want to preserve the union with Britain, sovereignty is a second-best option. Patrick J. Roche, an economist at the University of Ulster, says that "the entire mode of nationalist argument lacks authority for unionists. Unionists are not part of an Irish nation, but neither do they perceive themselves to be a distinct nation. Unionists have a localized territorial identity ('Ulstermen') but their political perception is of belonging to a British nation constituted by a shared allegiance to the state."[29] This emphasis on nationhood as crucial to self-determination is a mistake, however. Nationhood—unless that amounts to satisfying the seven conditions specified above, in which case both the nationalists and the unionists count as nations—is not necessary for having the right to self-determination.[30]

There is a further consideration that may help explain why unionists have been wary of endorsing the idea of self-determination, although I am not sure about the extent to which it has actually played a role in their thinking. Insofar as they think of themselves as British and think that the right in question would be possessed by the British people as a whole, unionists obviously are aware that the British people as a whole might well decide that the union should not be maintained, especially at the cost of a few billion pounds a year. This consideration ought not to be given much weight, however. Unionists are sufficiently distinct to constitute their own encompassing group. They have this status by virtue of their history, their attitudes to this history, their culture, their religious orientation, their style of life, and their general outlook. Unionists may also have been reluctant even to define themselves as a group that is distinct from the people of Great Britain, which is a prerequisite for thinking that they have a right to self-determination, because they have thought that to do so is, in effect, to concede that they are not British. This line of thought ought also to be given little weight. For one thing, their being a distinct group that has a right to self-determination is consistent with their exercising that right by choosing to continue to belong to the United Kingdom.

Traditionally the appeal to self-determination has been part of the basis on which Irish nationalists have made a case for Irish independence from Britain, but the appeal to self-determination can equally well serve as the basis of unionists' right to the political, social, and economic arrangements of their choice. Anyone who thinks favorably of the independence achieved early in this century by the twenty-six counties that now constitute the Republic of Ireland has good reason also to look favorably on the unionist aspiration to achieve their goal, provided of course that no minority community is disadvantaged in the process. If unionists have this right, however, this hardly settles the question of what political, economic, and social arrangements should obtain in Northern Ireland. All that is settled is that this right is one of the many considerations that have to be taken into account.

What is really important to recognize is that a case for either group's right to self-determination can reasonably be made only by appealing to the general principle that a group that satisfies the specified conditions has such a right. But then the other group probably has such a right too. If we look for a basis in principle, the framework we lay out will reveal that the right is possessed by both sides. My main suggestion is that, roughly speaking, we have an equally good case for self-determination (of the sort that counts) in each case. This short discussion does not suffice to show that both communities are on an equal footing in this respect, much less that each ideology is equally worthy of support. But what I have said provides some support for both of these claims.

The Case for Diminished Loyalty

There is another dimension to the case for impartiality in the Irish case. I want to define in general terms certain cases in which different groups are loyal to ideologies that are in conflict with one another. To subscribe to an ideology is to hold certain beliefs to be true as well as to have certain hopes and commitments, and to subscribe to ideologies that are in disagreement with one another is to have disagreements or differences in all, or at any rate most, of these areas. I have in mind particular cases in which the groups that disagree satisfy all of the following conditions. Each group has enjoyed a long history and has its own unique traditions and practices. It also has among its members people who are intelligent, reflective, and wise. In general, let's say that people on each side have integrity. This integrity has two dimensions, an intellectual dimension and a moral dimension. Intelligence and reflectiveness, for example, are intellectual virtues, whereas being fair-minded and just in the assessment of relevant interests, for instance, are moral virtues.

Disagreement among people who lack integrity has much less significance. One reason is that in that case the beliefs that partly make up ideologies may not have been adequately reflected upon and therefore may not have the same claim on our attention. The process of reflection, particularly if it is engaged in by people with integrity, increases the probability that the beliefs in question are true. People with integrity are also less likely to be careless in acquiring and maintaining their beliefs as well as in forming their commitments. That people of integrity support an ideology suggests it is worthy of support. I want also to restrict discussion to cases where an outsider can see the point of each side's aspiration. Needless to say, the hard-liners in cases of conflict will be loath to admit there is anything to their opponents' aspirations. They will dismiss those aspirations, calling into question the character, motives, intentions, or perhaps even the parentage of their adherents, and it will seldom be possible to show they are wrong.

In situations where loyalties are divided but people on each side of the divide have integrity, loyalty to one's own ideology should be diminished. This idea has various dimensions corresponding to the various aspects of what it is to accept an ideology. This reduction in loyalty involves certain changes in the belief part of one's ideology. It also involves taking seriously the other point of view, seeing what is to be said for it, and considering the flaws in one's own relevant beliefs. The claim is that once ideologies satisfy certain standards, they make claims on the proponents of competing ideologies. This is a condition that governs the worthiness of ideologies to receive our support. Loyalty to the goals or ideology of either side has to be mediated through an awareness of the value of the other side's goals.

The application of this line of thought in the Irish case is just that those who endorse either the nationalist or the unionist ideology need to incorporate an awareness of the legitimacy of the other side's ideology. Either group's allegiance to its ideology needs to be tempered by an awareness of the appeal of the competing ideology in the ways I have sketched.[31]

Tolerance and Respect

I have offered two independent lines of thought that provide some support for an evenhanded approach to the claims of the two communities in Ireland. I also want to comment on the sort of attitude toward the practices, interests, style of life, beliefs, institutions, pastimes, and symbols of the other community as well as toward them as individuals and as a group that ought to accompany this evenhanded approach. The crucial distinction is between tolerance and respect.

What is it for the As to tolerate the Bs? In the view of the As, at least, there must be something wrong with the Bs, ranging from being truly offensive and morally repugnant to being merely distasteful or unpleasant. If there is indifference to the B's behavior to the Bs themselves, there is nothing to tolerate. In that case one of the necessary conditions for tolerance is not met. Tolerance involves living with something, accepting it, enduring it, or putting up with it. It involves refraining from reacting negatively to something even though there is something wrong with it or it is not as one would wish it to be. Thus if the *A*s tolerate the *B*s' behavior, the *A*s restrain themselves from doing something to stop the *B*s' behavior. Tolerance of a group involves a willingness to live with it in the sense that one lets them be as they are.

Respect involves a more positive attitude. Tolerating or putting up with something always involves reluctance. Presumably it would be better in your view if you did not have to put up with it. Respect, however, involves an appreciation of the other position, tradition, group, or nation, to some extent for its own sake; it sees it as worthy of preservation and perhaps exploration. Respect is likely to be accompanied by a willingness to protect and preserve its object, whereas tolerance is likely to be accompanied by a mere willingness not to attack it. Respect also involves an element of humility. It involves a recognition that our group may need to learn from our competitors and that their culture has its own virtues. Respect is therefore more demanding than tolerance. It may require that we study our own culture and our own institutions and practices to see if they can be improved in the light of the alternative. It thus has a self-critical dimension. The thought is that if the others have a valued way of life, valued institutions, and so forth, perhaps we had better pay attention to what they may have to offer, just as in turn they ought to have a similar attitude toward us. To have respect is also, in effect, to acknowledge that we can see how reasonable people might belong to the other group. The fact that a group consists of (or an ideology is supported by) reasonable people recommends it to us. There is a sense that being one of them is not outrageous or ridiculous or foolish, never mind distasteful or repugnant.

Respect permits new possibilities to emerge. In the Irish case it might unleash a new shared sense of identity. The two sides might come to focus more on their shared history. This is perhaps farfetched, but even the struggles and conflicts that the two communities have engaged in might come to be looked upon as matters of shared experience through which both communities have come together. New loyalties and affections could emerge. For example, a new perspective might emerge that would involve focusing on the sense of being an island people at the edge of Europe. Other possible, though less plausible, dimensions of a new shared sense of identity might include the development of a sense of being different from a more secular British mainland[32] or even European mainland. It has also been suggested that a shared sense of Gaelic tradition and culture might provide a common bond, though I doubt that this is realistic.[33]

One reason for advocating respect is provided by the pragmatic thought that although tolerance will help us get along with one another to some extent, it will probably always make for unstable relations, for it is likely to become clear that we are merely tolerating others. The most important consideration, however, appeals to principle rather than to pragmatism. It is relevant in contexts where impartiality is the right attitude. In such contexts it is not enough for one group to put up with, or endure, the others and their beliefs and practices; this attitude is too begrudging and insufficiently generous. In such a context each group needs to go a lot further than that. The important point is that something has to be really wrong with others for it to be appropriate to settle for mere tolerance of them.

There is another argument for respect. If we were to identify ourselves with, say, the cause of Northern Irish unionists in such a way that we failed to respect the ideals and aspirations of Irish nationalists, we would not be able to understand properly what makes the nationalists tick; we could not feel what they feel, and we would be blind to their ideals. The same of course would hold if we were to identify with the cause of Irish nationalists in a way that involves a failure to respect the ideals and aspirations of the unionists. When impartiality is the correct attitude toward groups, and many of the aspirations of each of them are reasonable, something like respect is needed. Otherwise, a whole set of worthwhile concerns will not be appreciated; a whole set of symbols will lose their power, and to some extent a way of life will be alien.

Conclusion

The connections between the considerations I have introduced are various. In part the discussion of respect is a discussion of what will be the appropriate, and perhaps also the natural, response if you are persuaded by the case for impartiality. But the attractiveness of respecting the other group is itself part of the case for impartiality: we contribute to the case for impartiality by revealing its pleasing implications for practice. A case for respecting another group can also contribute to a case for reduced identification: if respect is the appropriate attitude to have toward others and what they stand for, that should make a difference to how we think about our own political ideology and to our relation to it. The different considerations are therefore mutually reinforcing.

In reflecting on the polarized political situation in Northern Ireland, it is interesting to trace some of the contours of a perspective that treats the two main ideologies with equanimity. It is also interesting to discover that some of the considerations that it is natural to appeal to in support of one side support the other side as well. No doubt the advocates of realpolitik will find the perspective taken here to be unduly idealistic. My response is that no position can be more realistic and practical than one that takes seriously the convictions, aspirations, and hopes of the two main communities.

Obviously it is not possible here to probe the policy implications of the sort of neutral stance I have advocated. To do so, we would need to address such questions as these: what arrangements would reflect an even-handed, respectful, and generous attitude toward each community and toward its ideology, culture, and traditions? What arrangements would permit both communities to feel at home, not to feel like strangers in their own land, and to feel that they are achieving a good part of the social, economic, and political arrangements to which they aspire?

Notes

I thank Eamon Boyle, Frank Gourley, Norma Mahmood, and Paddy Roche for valuable discussion of the themes in this essay.

1. The figures for the Northern Irish population are taken from the 1991 census in which 38.4 percent of the respondents declared themselves Catholic and 50.2 percent declared themselves Protestant. However 7.3 percent of the respondents in that census did not register their religion, and 4 percent said they had no religion. There is some debate about how many of the people in these last two groups have a background in one or the other cultural group and hence about how many of them should be counted as cultural Catholics or cultural Protestants. See, for example, John McGarry and Brendan O'Leary, *Explaining Northern Ireland* (Oxford: Blackwells, 1995), 502–3n24; and Paul Compton, "No Certainty of a Catholic North," *Parliamentary Brief* (Northern Ireland Supplement), 3, no. 1 (1994): 23–24.

2. I discuss this issue in Robert McKim, "Some Remarks on a Historical Theory of Justice and Its Application to Ireland," *Philosophical Studies* 32 (1988–90): 224–44.

3. For useful sources on Northern Ireland, some partisan and some neutral, see Padraig O'Malley, *The Uncivil War: Ireland Today* (Boston: Houghton Mifflin, 1983); John Darby, ed., *Northern Ireland: The Background to the Conflict* (Syracuse, N.Y.: Syracuse University Press, 1983); Geoffrey Bell, *The Protestants of Ulster* (London: Pluto, 1987); Eamonn Hughes, ed., *Culture and Politics in Northern Ireland* (Philadelphia: Open University, 1991); Michael Ignatieff, *Blood and Belonging: Journeys into the New Nationalism* (New York: Farrar, Straus and Giroux, 1994); Kevin Boyle and Tom Hadden, *Northern Ireland: The Choice* (London: Penguin Books, 1994); Jürgen Elvert, ed., *Nordirland in Geschichte und Gegenwart/Northern Ireland—Past and Present* (Stuttgart: Franz Steiner, 1994); and Patrick J. Roche, "Northern Ireland and Irish Nationalism—A Unionist Perspective," *Irish Review* (Institute of Irish

Studies, Queen's University of Belfast), no. 15 (1994): 70–78. The best and most up-to-date book is McGarry and O'Leary, *Explaining Northern Ireland*.

4. "Final Act of the Conference on Security and Cooperation in Europe, Adopted by the Conference on Security and Cooperation in Europe at Helsinki, August 1, 1975," in *Basic Documents in International Law and World Order*, 2d ed., ed. Burns H. Weston, Richard A. Falk, and Anthony D'Amato (St. Paul, Minn.: West Publishing, 1980), 117. It is clear from many other U.N. documents that the central aspect of the notion of self-determination is that a group has a right to decide its political status. See, for example, "Declaration on the Granting of Independence to Colonial Countries and Peoples, Adopted by the U.N. General Assembly, December 14, 1960," in *Basic Documents*, ed. Weston, Falk, and D'Amato, 343; "International Covenant on Economic, Social and Cultural Rights (1966)," in *Basic Documents*, ed. Weston, Falk, and D'Amato, 371; "International Covenant on Civil and Political Rights (1966)," in *Basic Documents*, ed. Weston, Falk, and D'Amato, 376; and "African Charter on Human and People's Rights (1981)," in *Basic Documents*, ed. Weston, Falk, and D'Amato, 448.

5. Avishai Margalit and Joseph Raz, "National Self-Determination," *Journal of Philosophy*, 87, no. 9 (1990): 439–61. Initially my discussion takes the form of a set of reactions to some of the claims in this essay, which is the best piece of writing I have come across on this topic.

6. Stanley French and Andres Gutman, for example, take self-determination to mean "[constituting] an independent state and [determining] its own government." French and Gutman, "The Principle of National Self-determination," in *Philosophy, Morality, and Public Affairs: Essays Edited for the Society for Philosophy and Public Affairs*, ed. Virginia Held, Sidney Morgenbesser, and Thomas Nagel (New York: Oxford University Press, 1974), 138. Allen Buchanan takes the ideal of national self-determination to be that each nation achieves complete political independence or sovereignty. Buchanan, *Secession: The Morality of Political Divorce from Fort Sumter to Lithuania and Quebec* (Boulder, Colo.: Westview, 1991), 48.

7. Margalit and Raz, "National Self-Determination," 440.

8. This notion of sovereignty greatly resembles self-determination in the sense of autonomy and independence. This suggests that self-government is the more comprehensive as well as the more fundamental notion, including in it the idea of self-determination. But I am going to ignore this point because my main concern is with the second and third ingredients.

9. Margalit and Raz, "National Self-Determination," 443.

10. Ibid.

11. Ibid.

12. Ibid.

13. Ibid., 444.

14. Ibid., 445.

15. Ibid., 446.

16. Ibid.

17. Ibid., 447.

18. Ibid., 448.

19. Ibid., 457.

20. Ibid.

21. According to Margalit and Raz, the "encompassing group that forms a substantial majority in a territory" (ibid.) has the right in question. But being in the majority seems less important once we focus on the idea of being fulfilled. For example, this allows us to say that in cases in which two or more sizable encompassing groups share the same territory but neither is in the majority, each of them has a prima facie right to be fulfilled.

22. Robert Ballagh, Letters Page, *Irish Times,* August 7, 1992.

23. Examples of others who take this position are not hard to come by. Clare O'Halloran, *Partition and the Limits of Irish Nationalism: An Ideology under Stress* (Atlantic Highlands, N.J.: Humanities Press International, 1987), mentions many such examples. This is also more or less the position of Sinn Féin: "The island of Ireland, throughout history, has been universally regarded as one unit. . . . The Irish people have never relinquished their claim to the right of self-determination. In the words of [Séan] MacBride, winner of the Nobel and Lenin Peace Prizes: '. . . Ireland's right to sovereignty, independence and unity are inalienable and indefeasible. It is for the Irish people as a whole to determine the future status of Ireland.'" Sinn Féin, "A Scenario for Peace," quoted in Bob Rowthorn and Naomi Wayne, *Northern Ireland: The Political Economy of Conflict* (Cambridge: Polity, 1988), 189–90.

24. Francis A. Boyle, "The Decolonization of Northern Ireland," *Asian Yearbook of International Law* 4 (1995): 37.

25. Ibid., 45.

26. The Governments of the Republic of Ireland and Great Britain and Northern Ireland, *A New Framework for Agreement* (Dublin and London: Government Printing Offices, 1995).

27. The Framework Document does not say what is meant by self-determination, but I take it as obvious that central to it is the notion of being fulfilled or having the wishes and choices of one's group about its destiny—including choices about what its political, social, and economic arrangements should be—significantly reflected in its situation.

28. For similar sentiments, see sections 10, 20, and 38 of the Framework Document.

29. Patrick J. Roche, "Nationalism and British Policy in Northern Ireland" (Unpublished paper), 3. On this, see also D. George Boyce, *Nationalism in Ireland,* 2d ed. (London: Routledge, 1991), 364.

30. In "Unionism and Self-determination," in *The Northern Ireland Question: Myth and Reality,* ed. Patrick J. Roche and Brian Barton (London: Avebury, 1991), Arthur Aughey, a unionist political theorist, makes some suggestions about how to decode unionist statements that appear to support the idea of independence for Northern Ireland (9). He also says, in remarks that betray something less than complete admiration for his neighbors to the south, that insofar as there has been

support among unionists for self-determination, it has been self-determination of a negative sort: "namely, that British citizens ought not to be compelled against their will to become part of an economically backward, politically authoritarian and religiously exclusive Irish state" (9).

31. I develop and clarify the suggestions sketched in this and the next section in Robert McKim, "National Identity and Respect among Nations" in *The Morality of Nationalism*, ed. Robert McKim and Jeff McMahan (Oxford: Oxford University Press, 1997).

32. O'Halloran, *Partition and the Limits of Irish Nationalism*, 204.

33. Ibid., 172.

4

Pakistan's Search for Security and Prosperity

Marvin G. Weinbaum

More than ever before, the thrust of Pakistan's foreign policy has shifted to its west, more precisely to its near west. The challenges as well as opportunities for Pakistan are found most in its relations with the region's non-Arab and Arab countries and, more recently, in Central Asia. While India remains the principal military concern and Kashmir continues to dominate the political discourse, Pakistan is locked in an adversarial relationship that has become stagnated and stalemated. Recent attempts at reconciliation between India and Pakistan have gone slowly. Both have embarked on nuclear development policies that, in effect, reduce the possibility of conventional war—even if the outcome of any conflict promises to be far more lethal. The Kashmir dispute shows no signs of abating and is unlikely to move toward compromise while governments in Islamabad and New Delhi are constrained by domestic pressures. Economically, very little can be expected of the South Asian Association for Regional Cooperation (SAARC). Without greater convergence on a political agenda, the regional organization is bound to remain moribund. Any progress with India is thus likely to be limited to modest confidence-building measures, which, while not unimportant, testify to the lack of options in reaching serious agreements on basic issues dividing the two states.

Pakistan continues to look toward its Islamic neighbors to its near west for political and conceivably military leverage against India. It is a more realistic vision than one held during the prime ministership of Zulfikar Ali Bhutto, when it was hoped Arab money would boost Pakistan to regional parity with India, or during the Zia ul-Haq regime, when geostrategic depth often seemed to be some magical solution to deter or overcome Indian aggression. The advantages of having friends to its near west are now seen in more unassuming terms militarily and are likely to be defined by their potential political and economic returns. What small hope

exists for concessions from India on Kashmir is thought to rest on diplomatic pressures that Pakistan can elicit from outside the region. Similarly, salvation from most economic woes is found abroad in visions of new
trade partners and profits. Pakistan seems to require, most of all, political cooperation and stability across its near west.

Contemporary relations with states to its near west are not without
strain. Policies that once converged in opposition to a Soviet and communist presence in Afghanistan—as in the case of Pakistan's ties to the
United States and to once favored Afghan resistance factions—have in the
1990s often taken divergent paths. Domestic pressures in several states
now loom larger in their policy determinations. Ideological, economic, and
strategic differences among countries that had been put aside in the face
of a common threat have, not surprisingly, reemerged. New regional players have appeared with their own particular problems. National interests
and concerns create some degree of competition and incompatibility, even
while the possibilities for cooperation remain strong. A community of
interest among those to Pakistan's near west has thus become subject to
regular readjustment and renegotiation.

In forging a foreign policy with those countries to the near west, decision makers in Islamabad have tried to orient their actions to several specific challenges. The first has been one of balancing policies where possible and sidestepping incompatibilities among allies. Second, it has been
necessary to weigh these policies for their possible impact on Pakistan's
continued confrontation with India, in particular to consider the policy
implications of resolving the Kashmir question satisfactorily. Third is reconciling policies in the near west with domestic politics, particularly the
overriding concern among government leaders to retain positions of power. The fourth challenge involves balancing the demands posed by the
broader international community—those organizations and national powers on which Pakistan remains dependent for financial assistance and
military equipment—with regional and domestic priorities. An examination of bilateral relations with several adjacent and more distant countries in Pakistan's near west illustrates these challenges.

Restoring Afghanistan

Plainly things have not gone as planned or desired in Afghanistan. The
expectation that a postwar Afghanistan might become, in effect, a satel-
lite of Pakistan—an unrealistic view given the Afghans' historic struggle
to defend their independence—was quickly dashed. Even those who were
prepared to settle for a friendly government in Kabul that would strong-

ly orient its trade and foreign policies toward Pakistan are disappointed, at least for the foreseeable future. For Pakistan, any positive outcome in Kabul requires, at a minimum, a reasonably stable and effective government. Order and security, for so long absent across most of the country, are needed to permit the unimpeded movement of goods and people. A strong central authority is not necessary, only one able to attract and absorb international aid for reconstruction and to provide a legitimate framework for the country's various powerful leaders to manage their differences.

Pakistan's Afghan policies have gone through a series of readjustments since the fall of the communist regime in Kabul in 1992. Until fairly recently Islamabad's strategies had failed badly. The Pakistan government not only was at deep odds with a sitting (until September 1996), if beleaguered, mujahidin-led government in Kabul but also had created tensions with all the neighboring powers over its choices among the Afghan factions. Clearly Islamabad did not have the kind of control that it had when the resistance parties were headquartered in Peshawar during the 1980s. The Pakistan government's public stand was noninterference in the factional politics and conflict. It claimed to have cordial relations with all Afghan groups and insisted it was trying to arrange a political solution through mediating a peace conference among factions. It also welcomed the diplomatic efforts of other Islamic countries.

In reality Pakistan repeatedly shifted its preferences among factions, not so much on ideological grounds, as is often asserted, but for highly pragmatic reasons. Islamabad regularly reassessed the forces likely to prevail and lent its political and covert military support to those leaders in Afghanistan likely to be able to consolidate power and, above all, protect the free flow of commerce to and from Pakistan. Islamabad thus withdrew postvictory commitments to a Kabul government led by Burhanuddin Rabbani and protected by the former mujahidin commander Ahmad Shah Masoud. Policymakers hedged their bets as they came to view an earlier favorite, Jamiat-i-Islami's Gulbudin Hekmatyar and his short-lived ally General Abdur Rashid Dostum, as possibly having a better chance of consolidating power. The Islamabad government subsequently gave substantial material support to the Taliban, initially an Islamic student movement, in its armed challenge to Hekmatyar and then to the forces of Masoud and Dostum.

The history of Afghan relations has witnessed decision makers in Pakistan often working at cross purposes. Differences among elements in the military, especially given the de facto autonomy of the Inter-Service Intelligence (ISI) in several areas of policy, as well as frequently contradictory approaches by the Foreign Office, have often left Pakistan's Afghan policy confused and ineffective.[1] The lack of a coherent policy was manifest, for example, in differences of opinion between the bureaucrats of the Ministry of Interior, supported by Interior Minister Nasirullah Khan Babar, and the Foreign Office over the decision, once the fratricidal conflict among the victorious mujahidin groups had begun, to seal the border with Afghanistan to prevent a fresh entry of refugees.[2] Later the misgivings about the Ministry of Interior's patronage of the Taliban felt in the bureaucracy and among opposition politicians also became well known.

The policy giving massive logistical aid to the Taliban was a particularly contentious one. Noted for its rigid Islamic doctrines and made up almost entirely of Pashtuns, the Taliban, for all its promise as a fighting force free of the corruption and personal feuds associated with the other warring Afghan factions, was nonetheless a risky choice for Pakistan. Its brand of Islam sat well with one of the more influential religious parties in Pakistan that pressed for covert assistance to the students and other elements joining in their armed campaign. Ideologically, however, it was difficult to understand why Benazir Bhutto's pro-Western, moderate Islamic government would welcome the new force, given its contrary worldviews. The Taliban posed an even more obvious problem for Pakistan if its battlefield success fell short of full territorial dominance and if Afghanistan became ethnically fragmented.

For more than a decade Pakistan's traditional concerns about Afghan irredentism had been dismissed. When communists were the enemy, the distractions of the fight, not to mention the sense of gratitude to and dependence on Pakistan, seemed to put aside, if not finally to rest, the explosive Pashtunistan issue. Yet the very real possibility of ethnic and geographic division of Afghanistan could revive nationalistic Pashtun claims for a state that would encompass Pakistan's North-West Frontier Province and parts of Baluchistan. An Afghanistan divided into ethnic enclaves also poses related security problems for Pakistan as other groups, namely Tajiks, Uzbeks, and Hazaras, seek allies and material support in India, Iran, and especially the bordering Central Asia republics backed by Russia.

International pressure on Pakistan to take a more constructive part in bringing about an Afghan peace increased when the fighting seemed stalemated. Islamabad had begun to reassess it policies. It took sharp criticism from other states in the region for its continued backing of this increasingly brutal and uncompromising force in possession of the southern and much of the western parts of Afghanistan. Pakistan was also encouraged to take a second look by the revived interest of the United Nations and the United States, both arguing for an arms embargo and new dialogue.

Everything seemed to hinge on a willingness among the Afghans themselves; no one expected a peace to be imposed on the country, certainly not by outside military forces. Nothing so unites the Afghans as the belief that foreign domination threatens. Deep suspicions about Pakistan's supposed designs for Afghanistan have never entirely vanished among nationalist-minded Afghans, including factions that were not too long ago principal recipients of arms through Pakistan's military. Indeed, much of the goodwill built up during the course of the war has dissipated.

By early 1996 there were signs that the level of exhaustion setting in among the fighting groups could, along with a growing shortage of arms, drive the leaders to a compromise in the form of a broadly representative government. Peace in Afghanistan appeared to turn on a willingness among the several countries in the region, Pakistan above all, to push their clients toward a settlement by threatening to deny them political and material support. Then, as had happened twice before, when a diplomatic solution appeared close, events overtook the negotiators. The Taliban captured Kabul and did so, as it had in early victories across the country, through intimidation and bribery of its adversaries rather than in a fight.

It remains to be seen in the spring of 1997 whether the Taliban will complete its conquest of the north. What is clear is that most Afghans, after nearly two decades of warfare, welcome any force that can bring a lasting peace. Although the Taliban is without coherent foreign or domestic policies (aside from its Islamic prescriptions), it is viewed by most people as authentically Afghan, a legitimate ruler of a restored and united Afghan state. To succeed, however, it must be able to fashion a way of accommodating non-Pashtuns, probably through a system of local autonomy that adheres to the Taliban's core principles. Whatever the outcome, Pakistan, the dominant neighbor, will be part of any solution. Postwar rehabilitation and reconstruction are hardly conceivably without Pakistan's cooperation. At the same time, the possibly diminished influence of Pakistan's military after a sweeping parliamentary victory in February 1997 by Nawaz Sharif could lead to less interventionary policies toward Afghanistan.

Accommodating Iran

Iran occupies a pivotal place in Pakistan's near western policy, primarily because of its location and potential political leverage in the region. Yet Iran and Pakistan have enough differences in their foreign policy agendas that really close collaboration is not always possible. Ideologically there is much that separates them. Their political systems are at considerable variance, and their alliances have often been in opposition. Despite this, areas of common purpose easily outweigh the differences. For Pakistan, normal and, if possible, warm ties with Iran have to be maintained at almost all costs. Fortunately for Pakistan, Iran also sees friendship with its eastern neighbor as highly desirable. Although previous notions of strategic depth were overdrawn, stronger linkages to Iran based on culture and religion are meant to suggest that Pakistan has bought some additional security by its attachments to other Islamic states. Ties with Iran are meanwhile convenient for extracting statements from Tehran that are supportive of Pakistan's criticism of Indian policy in Kashmir. Iran regularly obliges by speaking out on Indian atrocities.

Because policymakers in Islamabad have no desire to see tensions along Pakistan's border with Iran compete for attention and resources with its Indian problems, Pakistan has long minimized its differences with Iran, despite evidence of Iran's involvement in Pakistan's domestic troubles. Money and mullahs are alleged to have been put at the service of Pakistan's Shiites, and Iran has been implicated, if only indirectly, in serious incidents that have occurred between Sunnis and Shiites in the country's northern areas and in Karachi and Lahore in recent years. Pakistan has nonetheless publicly downplayed its suspicions or knowledge of Iran's involvement. Islamabad's determination to avoid confrontation with Iran over the sectarian issue has, in effect, allowed the Tehran government to have a relatively free hand in Pakistan. Concern that Iran might embark on more disruptive meddling in local affairs also gives Tehran some leverage over Pakistan's foreign policy.

Iran's relations with India are worrisome to Pakistan. The idea of a Tehran-Delhi axis—basically economic in content but containing political implications for the region as well—that developed in the mid-1970s has reemerged. The countries have explored several areas of economic cooperation. By mid-1996, with the completion of a rail link with Turkmenistan, Iran could provide India with a commercial route to Central Asia, bypassing Pakistan and Afghanistan. India looks on the former Soviet republics, where consumers are familiar with Indian goods, as a promising market. Returning a visit by the Indian prime minister, in 1995 President Hashemi Rafsanjani became the first Iranian head of state since the 1979 Islamic revolution to visit India. In his wide-ranging talks he left the impression not only that a mutually beneficial economic partnership was in the offing but also that Iran recognized India's political preeminence in the region.

The Iranian regime's continued support of Pakistan on Kashmir is seen in Delhi as Tehran's dues to the Islamic cause and is not likely to sour relations. Public pronouncement aside, Iran has sought to play a more evenhanded role between India and Pakistan. On several occasions Rafsanjani has offered to mediate the conflict. Iranian envoys have already sought, although without success, Indian approval for an OIC fact-finding mission to Kashmir; they did succeed, however, in gaining permission for an OIC representative in India.[3] Highly revealing is Tehran's handling of Pakistan's attempts to bring the Kashmir issue before the Geneva-based U.N. Commission on Human Rights in March 1994. Fearing criticism of its own domestic rights policies, Iran convinced Pakistan's representatives to withdraw the resolution—which had no chance of passage anyway. Nevertheless, the long history in Iran and the Arab states of sacrificing their presumed Islamic obligations for Third World solidarity and economic advantage with India leaves Pakistani policymakers understandably sorely disappointed.

Similarly, Pakistan finds both common cause and reasons for apprehension over Afghanistan. Each has been anxious to have an end to the hostilities, although not necessarily with the same outcome in mind. Over the course of the war, the two countries accorded different priorities to ending the conflict, and each had its own favorites among the ethnic-based resistance parties and commanders in the field. The Iranian government gave aid and comfort to the Afghan Hezb-Wahdad, a Shiite party of ethnic Hazaras, and adjusted its policies to fit the goals and shifting alliances of its clients. Through most of the decade of its war with Iraq, a politically isolated Iran, while absorbing some two million Afghan refugees, also coveted Moscow's aid and maintained fairly cordial relations. Since the Soviet's 1989 departure from Afghanistan, the policies of Iran and Pakistan have often been both parallel and convergent. They consulted regularly in the early 1990s in trying to mediate among the warring factions. The two countries see eye-to-eye on the need to contain the conflict in Tajikistan and allay Russian fears in the region. However, Iran and Pakistan have viewed quite differently the successes of the Taliban, especially after the death of the leading Shiite commander at the hands of this Islamic (Sunni) group. The Tehran government's active diplomatic efforts during 1996 to find a formula for reconciling the Afghan factions created suspicions in Pakistan. Least appreciated was a conference convened in Tehran, which Indian representatives attended, along with those from Russian, China, and the Central Asian republics. Pakistan and Saudi Arabia were conspicuously absent.

Pakistan and Iran have had a limited economic interdependence. At present there is only a $300 million annual trade volume, which is mainly an exchange of Iranian oil for Pakistani rice. Economic gains are, however, very much part of both countries' plans. Significantly, Benazir Bhutto's first official travel abroad after returning to power as prime minister in 1993 was to Iran (and Turkey), where she made every effort to portray the visit as being substantive, not merely symbolic. She reached an agreement with President Rafsanjani on building an oil refinery in Pakistan and a pipeline to carry Iranian natural gas to Pakistan.[4] The proposed 1,100-mile pipeline, intended to deliver 1.6 billion cubic feet of gas each year, could be connected to a projected pipeline from Qatar, but its $7 billion price tag means it will require heavy outside financing. If it materializes, the loans are most likely to come from Qatar and Oman, the Asian Development Bank, and the World Bank.[5] More immediately possible is a joint Pakistan-Iran oil refinery venture in Karachi, the cost of $1.36 billion to be shared equally between the two countries.[6] A sugar refinery to be located in Iran is also under serious consideration. In turn Pakistan could be critical to discussions between the Tehran and New Delhi governments on building a submerged gas pipeline from Iran to feed Indian industries. But this pipeline would probably be routed across Pakistani territory, and pressures in both Iran and Pakistan would make it difficult to proceed without a resolution of the Kashmir issue.

Iran's progress in building a defense industry is also mentioned by some as being of interest to Pakistan. Pakistan is unlikely to require the kind of military hardware the Iranians produce. All the same, Pakistan is willing to join Iran in conventional military exercises. Joint maneuvers by the two countries' navies over ten days ending in early March 1994 included four warships, reconnaissance planes, and antisubmarine helicopters.[7] The limits of cooperation with Iran are most apparent in the field of nuclear development. Pakistan has repeatedly assured Washington and the West that it has no intention of transferring nuclear technology to other countries. Despite the view that the United States is prejudicially targeting nuclear developments in Islamic countries, great care is taken in Islamabad not to be seen as the potential source for an Islamic bomb. Pakistan's policy is very unlikely to change in the case of Iran, if only because the Islamabad government has no desire to be faced with nuclear armed powers on two borders—Islamic and economic ties notwithstanding.

Pakistan is aware that its usually cordial relations with Iran rankle the United States. Many in Pakistan think the United States opposes the strengthening of Pakistan's ties with Iran because it wants to prevent strong cooperation between the two countries that would exclude Washington from economically dominating the area. Although these voices badly overestimate and mistakenly identify Washington's stakes in the region, it is true that the United States is concerned about losing what little political influence it still has with Pakistan over the nuclear development and drug issues. In pursuing its policy of containing Iran, Washington is uneasy about any Pakistani agreements that might strengthen Iran's hand in the region. Recognizing this, Pakistan's leadership lets it be known that it will be pushed closer to dependence on Iran as well as China if left politically isolated and cut off from military assistance.[8] At another time perhaps, when Washington and Tehran are ready for a rapprochement, Pakistan may be best positioned to assume the intermediary role it once played between Washington and Beijing.

Playing the Islamic Card

A leading foreign policy challenge for Pakistan has been how to capitalize on its friendship with the Arab states and at the same time avoid offending both Iran and the United States. The task is highlighted by the balancing act Islamabad must perform to avoid taking sides between Iran and Saudi Arabia in their continual and wide-ranging competition in the region. Pakistan's leaders have also managed to avoid getting caught up in the ideological and power politics among the Arab states. It is a diplomatic record of considerable, even remarkable success. What has made it possible is mutual advantage: Pakistan had something to gain from each of its Arab links, mainly from workers' remittances, development assistance, and political support, while the Arab states could draw on Pakistan's human resources, not the least of which is the reliability and skills of its military. Pakistan has also been valued as neutral ground for surrogates.

Arab sources have been generous with financial credits, government and private. In the immediate future Pakistan's development opportunities in its near west lie mainly with the affluent ministates of the Persian Gulf. The leaders of these states see ties with Pakistan through cooperative, Arab-financed projects as helping assert their independence of an often overbearing Saudi Arabia and an unpredictable, possibly threatening Iran. The Pakistan connection, carrying no hegemonic overtones, can serve to strike a balance among the region's largest states. Thus private Kuwaiti sources early in 1994 approved $50 million to finance petroleum product imports by Pakistan State Oil. Qatar announced intentions to build a natural gas pipeline laid under the Strait of Hormuz to Pakistan. Oman, which has also proposed a gas pipeline, holds out the possibility of still another pipeline to carry water imported from Pakistan. Officials from Pakistan have met to discuss economic cooperation and plans to boost trade with a joint United Arab Emirate committee in Abu Dhabi. Unwill-

ing to overlook a traditionally important benefactor, Benazir Bhutto, while
prime minister, made a pilgrimage to Saudi Arabia in February 1994,
ostensibly for reasons of piety but no less so to nurture that political relationship. Although Pakistan some years earlier withdrew the troops that
once guarded the Saudi royal family, officers of their armed forces continue to meet on a regular basis.

Among countries of the Gulf, only with Iraq has Pakistan had at times
strained ties. Despite Zulfikar Ali Bhutto's aim to solidify Arab relations,
including those with regimes pursuing a more anti-Western course, links
between Baghdad and Islamabad were less than cordial. Bhutto, who had
sought to become a major figure in nonaligned Third World politics and
draw economic support for Pakistan,[9] could not ignore evidence—including the discovery of arms—of Iraq's involvement in Pakistan's Baluchistan
uprising during 1973–76. Relations with Iraq further deteriorated over the
period of General Zia's rule, largely because of Iraq's generally pro-Sovi-
et policies throughout the 1980s. Pakistan was also understandably more
sympathetic to Iran in its war with Iraq, and in turn Iraq generally endorsed the Indian position on Kashmir. Under the first Sharif government
(1990–93), Pakistan dispatched troops to the Desert Shield operation and
expelled an Iraqi diplomat. In 1993 Iraq captured and imprisoned two
Pakistani soldiers and a civilian involved in demining operations who were
found on the Iraqi side of the border with Kuwait.

Despite the disappointments and confrontations, diplomatic ties with
Iraq have never been severed. Moreover, the second Benazir Bhutto government (1993–96) made concerted efforts to establish more harmoni-
ous relations. By obtaining the release of nearly all Pakistanis in Iraqi jails
in March 1994, Prime Minister Bhutto helped herself domestically, but
the successful diplomacy also served a larger goal: it demonstrated Pakistan's potential role as an intermediary among Islamic countries, in this
case possibly in helping restore Iraq's ties with the international community—without offending Iran, Kuwait, and Saudi Arabia. Bhutto and her
foreign minister argued the humanitarian case for Iraq and called for
easing economic sanctions. But Pakistan had also been careful to insist
that any agreements with Iraq remain within the limits imposed by the
United Nations and that the principle of territorial integrity remain invi-
olate. The Bhutto government joined most of the international community in expressing concern over the October 1994 deployment of Iraqi
military forces close to the border with Kuwait.

Pakistan's conspicuous role in Somalia—having placed under U.N. command 5,300 troops in 1992 and 1993 and augmenting them by 1,500 in
March 1994—came at a time when other countries were reducing forces.

It served to ingratiate Pakistan with its Arab friends and also to underline the country's ability and determination to assume international responsibilities. Unlike the hesitation of Western leaders, especially in the United States, to put troops on the ground, Pakistan's leadership considers the projection of military force outside the country to be in most cases good politics at home, bringing pride in the country's military forces. Of course, Pakistan also hopes to cash in its chips by asking for support on Kashmir from the international community, most especially those Muslim states that remain reluctant to press the case.

On the issue of Bosnia, where no dissent is found among Arab and other Islamic governments, Pakistan sought to push to the forefront of a consensus. The Bhutto government had for some time indicated its willingness to send peacekeeping troops to Bosnia—at a time when U.N. forces there were badly undermanned and before NATO's intervention. In rejecting the offer, U.N. officials claimed that the world organization had neither the money to get them there nor the weapons to provide them. After a year of negotiations, however, Germany and Austria agreed in April 1994 to provide the arms, trucks, tanks, and so forth for a Pakistani contingent. The long delay naturally left the suspicion that Western leaders had no strong interest in having any Muslim troops on the ground in Bosnia, but if any were acceptable, they would be Pakistani. In any case, Pakistan's offer was not an empty gesture, and, unlike Iran and several Arab states, Pakistan continues to be envisioned in other future peacekeeping roles.

The need to placate its Arab friends has forced authorities in Islamabad periodically to move to evict from Pakistan's soil Arab expatriates from Egypt, Algeria, and Tunisia, among other countries. Arab volunteers began arriving in Pakistan in the early 1980s to fight in the Afghan jihad. Plainly, during most of the Afghan conflict these Arab mujahidin used their Pakistan base of operations to further their own long-term interests and, as such, played a minor role in the military effort against the communists. Whatever the initial view of their home countries—many had been anxious to get their young radicals out—these governments became alarmed, having witnessed the return of men highly indoctrinated in militant Islam and trained in the use of weapons. Most arrived home ready to join and inspire armed antigovernment groups.

Despite repeated threats to deport Arab volunteers in Pakistan, the Islamabad government was slow to evict them. Officials in Pakistan were not anxious to shed the image of Pakistan as defender of those struggling for Islamic causes. The absence of extradition treaties with most Arab states was often used to explain Islamabad's refusal in some cases to turn over some known opposition activists to their home countries.[10] Whether these countries in fact always wanted the volunteers deported is questionable. They more likely preferred their nationals to be watched, and Pakistani intelligence keeps a close eye on the remaining Arabs in the country. The number of young Arabs still located in Pakistan totals no more than three or four hundred—working mainly with nongovernmental organizations, most of which are legitimately engaged in welfare activities and the rehabilitation of refugees. Most volunteers either returned to Arab countries beginning in 1990 or followed their Afghan mujahidin sponsors into Afghanistan, where some became involved in the civil war.[11] The government in Islamabad bears responsibility, however, because many of those trained in camps in Afghanistan went there through Pakistan.

The government in Islamabad initially welcomed the agreements between Israel and the PLO. This was above all to please the United States and Egypt. Only later did Pakistan's leadership soften support, largely to satisfy domestic skeptics and mounting popular Arab criticism. In the past, as noted earlier, Pakistan has successfully handled contradictory alliances, but at least in this policy area the room for maneuvering has narrowed. The media and public opinion preclude any official policies that could be interpreted as suggesting support for Israel's rights to the Arab territory it now holds. The Pakistan government was thus embarrassed by reports of secret contacts with Israel. The alleged exploratory talks were said to be about future areas of cooperation and eventual diplomatic relations. Both the Bhutto government and the opposition, which was also accused of having talked to the Israelis, vehemently denied contacts and proceeded to use the issue against each other—blaming their political opponents for having initiated the talks. This controversy obscured the issue of whether such meetings, if they actually occurred, were in Pakistan's interest, especially since many Arab countries had begun talking formally to the Israelis and there were already formal agreements between the Palestinians and Jordanians.

In the light of warming diplomatic relations between India and Israel, the question naturally arises whether Pakistan might be ignoring an opportunity to alter or modify Israeli policy. Opening lines of communication are arguably a way to induce Israel to reassess its support for the Indian position on Kashmir and, more important, its apparent willingness to supply India with advanced military equipment and technology.[12] Some may contend that it is naive to believe that establishing contacts with Israel will neutralize or minimize Israel's growing ties with India. Even so, it could also be asserted that a normalization of relations with Israel by such Islamic states as Pakistan might serve as an incentive for the Jewish state to make concessions in its dealings with the Palestinians and the Arab states. In so doing, Pakistan would be assuming the kind of facilitating role that it has succeeded in performing so well in its near western foreign policy.

Reaching Out to Central Asia

A strong community of interest exists among leaders in the Central Asian Muslim republics as well as Russia to contain the fighting and ideology of the Afghan civil war. As already mentioned, Pakistan is interested in defusing the tensions in Tajikistan, which have badly retarded Pakistan's economic opportunities in Central Asia. Only a permanent cease-fire among the factions in Afghanistan can secure the land bridge to Central Asia that will be necessary for Pakistan to realize its commercial aspirations. Drawing on cultural affinities and economic promise, Pakistan is also anxious to enlist these republics in the campaign of international pressure on India over Kashmir.

The new states may serve to energize and expand the purposes of the Economic Cooperation Organization (ECO). There is much discussion of further strengthening communication links among the ECO countries. At least in its expressions of cooperation the ECO stands in sharp contrast to SAARC, although the ECO has yet to realize the kind of joint measures, including tariff reductions, that could be significant in drawing Pakistan into greater cooperation. For the time being the ECO is better at providing a forum for high-sounding pronouncements on international affairs and global and regional problems. As a result, Pakistan's serious overtures to the new states and the organization's original members have been more bilateral than multilateral.

It seems increasingly clear, moreover, that Pakistan's expectations from the more formalized contacts with the several Muslim republics will have to take Russia into account. Moscow has already indicated that it is none too pleased at the prospect of other Muslim states' developing close ties through the ECO. Plainly the Russian government is not anxious to see serious alternatives to a northern dependency emerge. Realistically speaking, Pakistan and its ECO partners cannot compete with Russia in furnishing industrial goods or large markets. In particular, Pakistan has no interest in poaching on the Russians' interests in Tajikistan and, by and large, has supported the political status quo. Islamabad has publicly promised the Russians that Pakistan's territory would not be used to mount interference in Central Asia. The Bhutto government and Nawaz Sharif before it put pressures on President Rabbani and his associates in Kabul to use their influence—limited as it was—to halt the direct involvement of Afghan mujahidin across the border. When a propagandist for the Tajik rebels, Mohammed Sharif Himmatzada, the chief of the Islamic Renaissance party, arrived in mid-1993 for a stay in Peshawar, Pakistan acted to mediate talks between him and the Russians. When the process became unrewarding, the Islamabad government expelled Himmatzada for his propagandistic efforts while in Pakistan.

That Pakistan may also have a constructive role to play in the region is suggested by its offering the venue for many of the diplomatic efforts to end the conflict in Tajikistan. Prime Minister Bhutto responded positively in April 1994 to Tajikistan president Ali Rakhmanov's request that talks seeking a cease-fire and political settlement between the warring sides be held in Islamabad. Pakistan joined Iran and Russia as observers in U.N.-sponsored negotiations held in Moscow and Tehran during the summer of 1994. Pakistan also hosted President Rakhmanov and a large delegation from Tajikistan to discuss trade and transit issues. Ignoring the civil war in Tajikistan, the Islamabad government offered $10 million in credits to bolster trade between the two countries. The money would be used to help Tajikistan import Pakistani commodities. A total of $110 million had already been promised to all the former Soviet republics during the first Nawaz Sharif administration.

Viewed in cultural and economic terms, however, Pakistan would not seem to be competitive with Turkey or Iran for influence in Central Asia. Turkey has strong linguistic ties to Uzbekistan, Turkmenistan, Kyrgyzstan, and Kazakhstan, as well as Azerbaijan, and early on took the initiative in providing for exchange programs as well as financial and technological aid. Iran's linguistic affinities are with Tajikistan, where in a low-keyed way it has tried to exploit cultural connections. The Tehran government has also sought trade links with the other republics and worked to allay their fears that Iran was bent on exporting revolutionary Islam. Even so, both Turkey and Iran are viewed with some apprehension in the new republics. The same ties that draw them to the new Muslim states also disqualify them as disinterested parties. Meanwhile, Pakistan has at least some of the same attractions for the republics, including an expanding market economy. Its port of Karachi provides the most convenient passage to trade with East Asia. While Pakistan offers Islam, it is of a less doctrinaire kind than in Iran. Pakistan lacks many of Turkey's resources, but, like Turkey, it has long been pro-Western and mostly democratic. More important, Pakistan cannot be accused of cultural imperialism; it is therefore in a better position to assume the role of an honest broker should one be sought. Moreover, because its interests in Central Asia generate fewer suspicions, Pakistan in any role is probably more acceptable to Moscow than are the other countries of West Asia.

If Pakistan looks increasingly to its near west, then what about the pull of China, its longtime ally? Is there also an attraction for Pakistan in the Koreas and countries of Southeast Asia that could substitute, as does its near west, for the dearth of opportunities in South Asia? Pakistan's leaders have regularly applauded their ties with China as exemplifying the kind of binational relations they value. In reality much of this has been symbolic. Although China has long been seen as a counterweight to India, China has failed to relieve military pressure on Pakistan when armed conflict has occurred in the subcontinent. Its cooperative programs in arms production are of course welcomed, and China is alleged to have played a role in Pakistan's nuclear development program. But the close relationship hinges essentially on China's and Pakistan's mutual concern with India. If in time the Beijing government finds reasons for normalization with Delhi, relations with Pakistan are bound to be affected. China cannot consider Pakistan a significant trading partner, and while the ghost of a warm alliance may be kept alive for sentimental reasons, the reality may make it increasingly empty.

The direction of China's South Asian policy was probably revealed by its stance at a meeting of the U.N. Commission on Human Rights in Geneva in March 1994. China joined in pressuring Pakistan to rescind its motion on Kashmir that was highly critical of India. Seemingly in return India supported China in its successful effort to have a motion pending against it withdrawn. More recently, resolutions on Kashmir have been left off the U.N. agenda. From every indication China appears determined to adapt a flexible, perhaps more balanced set of policies in South Asia. Much the same can be expected across the rest of East Asia. Japanese private investment, so freely flowing to India, has bypassed Pakistan, largely following the calculations of hard-nosed businesspeople that Pakistan remains too politically unstable. Notwithstanding the cultural links to Malaysia, that country's own regional economic ties and distance from Pakistan leave little on which to build a relationship. North Korea's warm overtures, including promises of cooperation in power generation and heavy industry, are transparently political in the Pyongyang government's search to lessen its international isolation. The communist regime in North Korea is likely to make similar advances to India once China has cleared the way. These circumscribed options leave Pakistan with fuller, more sustainable opportunities in its near west.

Conclusion

Pakistan is potentially a major actor in West Asia. It is the country with the greatest population and the largest army, and of course it is the only one with access to nuclear weapons. Yet it is not in Pakistan's interest, or capability for that matter, to try to impose its will on the region. Pakistan lacks the economic resources and human capital to play a hegemonic role, even if it were so inclined. Under the circumstances, then, Pakistan's national interests and its regional security depend on an equilibrium in the region. This implies a stability that is born of a balance of forces, where Pakistan can often assume the role of a "go-between." While some of the solutions may involve multilateral regional approaches, most will also continue to require well-conceived binational strategies.

As this essay has shown, governments in Islamabad have in a sense been playing this diplomatic game for some time. Over several decades Pakistan has managed its near western relations so that it has somehow maintained good ties with countries that are themselves antagonistic. Whether it was Iran and the United States, Iran and Saudi Arabia, or, earlier, the United States and China, strong diplomatic skills were needed to sustain friendships. Pakistan's role in the Afghan war—the prevention of a Soviet domination over Afghanistan—was also on two tracks, one military, the other diplomatic. The aim was to undo the threat that communist forces posed to the future of a sovereign Afghan state and ultimately to maintain a balance of forces on the subcontinent. Continuing efforts, albeit at times misdirected, to bring about a modus vivendi in Afghanistan are part of the same story.

Pakistan comes to its system role with few preconditions, and its involvement is likely to be nonthreatening. It has no territorial ambitions toward countries to its west. Aside from the Afghans, few are suspicious of its intentions. Although an Islamic country, it has no particular brand of the religion that it seeks to export. Despite the championing of an Islamic identity, Pakistan has shown itself to be a pragmatic practitioner. The country's experiences with its own religious parties suggest that it may be a useful role model for other officially designated Islamic states. More than any other, Pakistan has demonstrated that given an opportunity to compete freely, Islamic political parties and movements will choose to play by the system's rules. More important, Pakistan conceivably demonstrates that when given real choices, voters tend to avoid those offering the more radical solutions.

Much of Pakistan's possibilities for success with its near western neighbors will, as in the case of any regional player, rest largely on its reliability—the consistency of its policies. In this respect Pakistan's record is mixed. Its policies in supporting the Afghan resistance, building a nuclear deterrent, and endorsing Palestinian rights, as well as in its steadfast adherence to its alliances, have wavered very little. Nevertheless, Pakistan is handicapped by the absence of continuity in political succession. No elected government has finished its term since 1977. As a result, uncertainties about foreign policies are unavoidable. Although the military and the civil service have remained largely unchanged, different domestic alliances and policy priorities require that agreements may be subject to adjustment and possible reinterpretation. For example, a more coherent and consistent Afghan policy is one possible victim of Pakistan's domestic political turmoil in recent years. Hopes for greater political stability and policy continuity increased as the Sharif government, after gaining a large parliamentary majority in the February 1997 elections, succeeded in revising the constitutional provision that since 1985 had given Pakistan's president the discretionary power to dismiss popularly elected governments. No doubt the stabilization of Pakistani democracy would further the country in its regional role.

The search for counterweights to India, particularly in the confrontation over Kashmir, often seems to drive Pakistan's involvement in its near west. This same issue, however, could also forfeit for Pakistan many of its opportunities in West Asia. Of course, Kashmir succeeds as an issue in solidifying opinion in the country where few others do. The claims over injustices are real and for the most part sincere. Yet continuing preoccupation with Kashmir diminishes or can even deny Pakistan its larger geostrategic role. The price that Pakistan pays for its preoccupation with Kashmir is that the issue necessarily diverts attention from pursuing opportunities that exist in West Asia as well as South Asia. Even if Pakistan avoids armed confrontation over Kashmir, the country is captive to an issue that draws off scarce resources, uses up political capital, distorts domestic priorities, and puts critical alliances under some strain. Pakistan's will and capacity to provide a much-needed intermediary role for countries to its near west is sure to be affected.

As long as the Kashmir issue continues to dominate foreign policy, Pakistan will be unable to reassess its wider security interests, for in the end national security for Pakistan is not just military and political but increasingly involves economic strength, which is undermined by the country's inability to deliver adequately on welfare and enlightenment for its citizens. Some contend that the region is on the verge of an economic spurt that will mirror much of the boom in East Asia. This growth assumes a continuation of the economic reforms that have unshackled entrepreneurial energies. For Pakistan to attract foreign investment on a scale that has already begun in India, it will also have to make progress in building its technological and human resource base, as well as its physical infrastructure. Cooperation among South Asian states leading to increased trading and investment will enhance growth and improve chances for greater economic equity in Pakistan, but those opportunities for security and prosperity lying beyond the subcontinent promise most in the long run. The most attractive of these are in West Asia, where, as we have seen, significant political, cultural, and economic links have already been forged.

Notes

1. Marvin G. Weinbaum, *Pakistan and Afghanistan: Resistance and Reconstruction* (Boulder, Colo.: Westview, 1994), 94–95.

2. Zaffar Abbas, "The Battle for Kabul," *Herald*, February 1994, 44.

3. Pakistan News Service, March 12, 1994.

4. UPI, Islamabad, December 11, 1993.

5. William Scott Harrop, "Benazir Bhutto in Iran," *U.S.-Iran Review* 2, no. 1 (1994): 3.

6. Radio Pakistan, February 12, 1994.

7. Voice of the Islamic Republic, Tehran, March 3, 1994, in *FBIS-NES*, March 3, 1994.

8. See U.S. Congressman Lee Hamilton's comments in *New York Times*, February 25, 1994.

9. Marvin G. Weinbaum, with G. Sen, "Pakistan Enters the Middle East," *Orbis* 22, no. 3 (1978): 595–612.

10. See *Muslim* (Islamabad), January 5, 1994. In late March 1994 Pakistan signed an agreement with Egypt on international terrorism that provided for extradition of criminals between the two countries.

11. In February 1994 a group that included Egyptians, Sudanese, and Algerian nationals was reported killed in the Afghan capital when forces loyal to the then Afghan president Rabbani seized one of the positions of Gulbudin Hekmatyar. Middle East News Agency, Cairo, February 1, 1994.

12. *Pakistan Observer* (Islamabad), December 30, 1993.

5

Causes of Conflict and Conditions for Peace in South Asia

Stephen P. Cohen

What are the origins of war and the conditions for peace in South Asia? Surprisingly, only one study attempts to answer these questions, and even that one refers only to the wars between India and Pakistan.[1] This essay offers the preliminary conclusions of a larger study that explores the causes of conflict in South Asia and the conditions for peace.[2]

I make two assumptions about peace and war in South Asia. First, regional conflicts do have origins; conflict is not an inherent condition of either human society or the states constituting South Asia. This assumption is shared by virtually every regional strategist, scholar, soldier, and politician. There is, however, profound disagreement as to what those causes are.[3]

Second, the conditions for peace—or at least an absence of violent conflict—can be established. An accurate theory of regional conflict should help us develop policies and strategies that address the causes of conflict or, if they cannot be influenced with resources at hand, their worst manifestations. This is not an assumption that is widely shared. In and out of the region there is pessimism about the possibility of eliminating or even alleviating regional conflict. Many Westerners have vague ideas about the sources of regional strife but strong views on its consequences; they are easily persuaded that the region is doomed to war. Led by the CIA, U.S. officials have believed since at least 1992 that South Asia is the most likely site of a nuclear war in the world today and that the Kashmir conflict is the most likely cause of such a war. Many Indians and Pakistanis hold well-defined theories of regional conflict, but they do not think that the conditions that would end conflict can be reached soon or easily.

Before I set forth a theory of regional conflict, three theoretical puzzles, each with important policy implications, should be noted. The first is the discrepancy between events in South Asia, especially over the past ten years, and the trend toward regional peace elsewhere. The India-Pakistan conflict is now one of the few remaining wide-ranging and globally significant security complexes.[4] That is, it encompasses ideological differences, it has a potential for large-scale military conflict (and some of the systems themselves that could be developed, such as ballistic missiles and nuclear weapons, have a logic of their own), and it involves other substantive differences among the states over territory, water, trade, and the like. Why, when such disputes have subsided elsewhere, have they intensified in South Asia? Why have Sri Lanka, Nepal, and Bangladesh been drawn into disputes with New Delhi? When peace seemed to be breaking out in so many other regions, why was South Asia apparently countercyclical?

Second, both India and Pakistan are now democracies—indeed, every country in the region barring Bhutan is now a democracy.[5] Yet the relationship between the two seems to have worsened under conditions of democratic government. This also runs counter to the historical record, since few, if any, pairs of democracies have ever gone to war.

Third, both states are in the midst of a fundamental economic transformation, liberalizing their economies and allowing significant foreign investment. As India and Pakistan grow more prosperous, will they change the way in which they conduct foreign and security policy? Will their perceptions of neighbors alter, and will their newfound economic prosperity lead them to adjust their hierarchy of threat, which seems now to place the other at the top of its list?[6]

Conflict Models and the Model Conflict

There are abundant theories or explanations of the cause of war. It is possible to explain South Asia's conflicts in terms of balance of power theory, the role of personality, mutual or one-sided misperceptions, civilizational differences,[7] the existence of particular kinds of states (such as military dictatorships), the benign or malign influence of outside powers, racial theories, the prevalence of poverty in South Asia, the influence of the region's entrenched civilian and military bureaucracies, or simply the deeper and darker qualities of humankind.[8] My larger study provides an inventory of explanations and concludes that they have all been put forth at one time or another, although rarely in a systematic fashion (see table 1 for the major theories or explanations that strategists offer for conflict in several states and regions).

In perhaps the only extended attempt to answer the question "Why war?" in South Asia, Sumit Ganguly sets forth a model based on "irredentism."

Table 1. Origins of Conflict in South Asia: An Overview

	India	Pakistan	United States	Bangladesh, Nepal, Sri Lanka
Major source of conflict	Outsiders upsetting natural Indian dominance	Indian hegemonic ambitions	Regional poverty; unstable region threatens rest of world	Indian domination, arrogance
Secondary source of conflict	Unrepresentative states or leadership, e.g., Pakistan military dictatorship, Nepali monarchy, Sri Lankan/ Sinhala elites	Outside powers' failure to support Pakistan against India	(Formerly) external communist threat against region	Ethnic, environmental, and economic pressures
Self-image	Equivalent to "region" of South Asia	"Homeland," then frontier for Islam, then pure Islamic state and people	Benevolent, well-intentioned outsider	Benign and neutral
Image of India-Pakistan conflict	May last a long time, but India will prevail	Pakistan serves larger regional interests by countering Indian threat	Fundamentally wrong: highest priority should be development; now threatening wider spread of nuclear weapons, etc.	Bangladesh and Nepal: risks regional conflagration; Sri Lanka: may be useful to divert India from south
Role of outside powers	Their misguided meddling defers regional normalization	Draw them into regional struggle against India, since Delhi may threaten their interests	Establish barrier to spread of regional conflict; encourage regional cooperation	Primarily aid and assistance, though risk of angering India with an alliance is great
Approach to regional conflict resolution	Bilateral; covert pressure to force other side to dialogue or cessation of disruptive activity	Multilateral, extraregional powers helpful in ensuring the containment of India	Send delegations; threaten cutoff of aid; avoid direct involvement	Multilateral and regional

His argument is that disputes arising over minority rights or the claims of separatist groups are particularly difficult to solve.[9] The 1947 and 1965 wars between India and Pakistan were fought over Kashmir; the 1971 war was precipitated by the separatist movement that arose in East Pakistan and was assisted by India. This is an accurate but partial explanation.

Fearful Minority Psychologies

The most enduring and difficult cause of conflict in South Asia is each side's perception that one's own state, nation, or ethnic group or subnational entity is vulnerable and under attack from outsiders. Each side sees itself as a minority, or as a weaker state, facing a more powerful entity. In these "paired minority conflicts" it is extraordinarily difficult for one side to offer reassuring concessions or to agree to compromise on even the most trivial issues. To do so is seen as merely confirming others' perceptions of one's own weakness and to invite further demands. These conflicts are the societal equivalent of a machine that produces a surplus of energy—a sort of fusion-based power reactor. They seem to be able to draw on an inexhaustible supply of hatred toward the other side and distrust of advocates of dialogue or compromise. They are machinelike in their operation over time. When either side feels at a disadvantage, it invariably refuses to compromise because it fears being driven further down the road of concession. When in a position of advantage, however, this same leadership also refuses to compromise on the grounds that the stronger power can bend the weaker to its will. As if they were on a teeter-totter, the two sides take turns moving up and down, momentarily reaching a state of equality but always in a state of dynamic imbalance that inhibits the prospect of long-term negotiations.

These conflicts are further energized by their moral dimension. Aristotle has taught that people enter politics because they seek justice; in South Asia, goaded by a sense of injustice, conflict is legitimized because it seems to offer the only way to protect a threatened group. Further, the group sees itself as threatened because it is morally or materially superior. Past Indian or Pakistani defeats and current weaknesses are thus "explained" by Indian and Pakistani virtues: one's problems stem from the jealousy or envy of others.

Perhaps the best-studied case of a paired minority psychology is the Middle East. There Israelis point to the numerical superiority of the Arab (or Islamic) world and make a persuasive case that Israel stands isolated, surrounded, and threatened—David facing Goliath. Yet many Arabs see themselves as the threatened minority. While Arabs may outnumber Israelis, they see Israel as an extension of Europe, and the Arab (or Islamic) world remains in a position of political, military, and even numerical inferiority relative to this larger alliance. A similar and perhaps more pathological variant is found in the former Yugoslavia, where—in Bosnia—the complex struggle between and among Muslims, Serbs, and Croats is reminiscent of the three-cornered politics of Punjab on the eve of partition.

There are two acute cases of paired minority psychologies in South Asia. One is in the island state of Sri Lanka. Here the minority Tamil population feels under political, economic, military, cultural, and even societal threat from the dominant Sinhala community. Yet the Sinhalas, incited by intellectuals, politicians, and a militant Buddhist clergy that imagines itself to be defending the faith (against Hinduism, represented on the island by the predominately Hindu Tamils), believe themselves to be a threatened minority. Sinhalese Buddhists may be a majority on Sri Lanka, but some sixty million Hindu Tamils live just across the water in India. The Indian Tamils represent the sharp edge of this threatening and militant enemy. Both Sri Lankan Tamils and Sinhalese, like Arabs and Israelis, thus see themselves as threatened and vulnerable.

In these and similar cases, history plays a key role in perpetuating a dual minority psychology. Arabs, Sinhalese, Tamils, Serbs, Croats, and Bosnian Muslims all draw sustenance from the way in which they situate the present and future in the context of the past. Each refers back to an era of majority status, of great power, of an expanding civilization. Although now a threatened minority, they all believe that their culture and society were once especially notable. Their present minority status is thus incongruent with their past, and significant chauvinist elements thrive in each community. Israel is a somewhat different case. Although there are "great power" Israelis (represented by elements of the Likud), the Holocaust and, before that, centuries of oppression and discrimination teach the vulnerability of minority status and the real possibility of extinction.

The Core Conflict

South Asia's core regional paired minority conflict is between India and Pakistan—although it is complicated by the India-China pair, which is structurally somewhat different and does not demonstrate the same degree of pathology. While many Indian strategists regard Beijing as a fundamental (or, using Samuel Huntington's term, "civilizational") threat, the fear is not fully reciprocated, and Chinese disdain for India just accelerates the Indian sense of grievance and threat.

In India there is a widespread belief that the Indian state is under threat from one or another combination of Islamic, Western, Chinese, and small regional powers. Some Indians see India as surrounded by a sea of extremist Muslims, who already have infiltrated the Indian Muslim minority. Others see India as threatened by an alliance of extremist Muslims and Western powers—the U.S.-Pakistan alliance. Until quite recently China was also seen as a threat, in alliance with Islamic and Western foes. Indian perceptions of threat have rotated among these, singly or in groups.

Why is India threatened by some combination of Pakistan, Islam, China, and the West (led by the United States)? It is because outsiders are jealous of India, and they try to cut it down to size. This Indian sense of weakness, of vulnerability, is contrasted with India's "proper" status as a great power, stemming from its unique civilization and history.[10] However, the reality of an India divided between north and south, east and west, with rebellious and ungrateful minorities (tribals, Sikhs, Christians, Muslims, even Parsis) adds up to a fragmented, vulnerable state under siege from without and within—and their opponents are increasingly in alliance with one another.

In Pakistan the central explanation of peace and war is that from the first day of Pakistani independence all evidence points to a concerted Indian attempt to crush Pakistan, despite India's overwhelming size, military capabilities, and support from the outside world. Pakistanis see themselves as overwhelmed and overpowered by a militant India, increasingly Hindu and extremist, a state dominated by religious considerations and a sense of missionary zeal to extend Indian influence to the furthest reaches of South Asia and neighboring areas. Pakistanis have also turned inward against their own minorities or have created minorities by declaring certain Islamic sects to be non-Muslim.

Pakistan's self-image bears some resemblance to that of Israel. Both states were formed by a people who were persecuted when living as a minority, and now, even though they have their own state (which is, coincidentally, based on religion), they remain under threat from powerful enemies. Both contain zealots who see the ability of their state to hold off external enemies as compromised by "secular" or insufficiently religious Pakistanis or Israelis.

Origins: From Majority to Minority

How are psychological minorities created out of physical majorities or pluralities in South Asia, especially in India, which because of its population and size would seem to possess the attributes of a great power? Three processes seem to be at work: the influence of South Asia's own multilayered history, the lessons learned by politicians and others from the very societies in which they grow up, and generational differences among and within the Indian and Pakistani strategic communities.

Traditions, Old and New

Both Hindu and Islamic traditions contribute to the idea of a war-crowd, of inherently hostile rivals.[11] One major ancient Hindu tradition of statecraft defines antagonists in terms of proximity to oneself. Any king whose realm shares one's border "is an antagonist," because he is either a potential threat or a potential victim of one's own expansion. For Kautilya all statecraft revolved around the manipulation or balancing of a ring of antagonists. Some were more easily defeated than others, in some cases allies (the enemy's enemy) might be at hand, and in still other cases subversion and espionage were appropriate ("A single assassin can achieve, with weapons, fire or poison, more than a fully mobilized army"),[12] but the wise leader had to bear in mind that not only force and war but also diplomacy, deceit, and moral authority were instruments of statecraft, to be applied when and where appropriate.

As L. N. Rangarajan and other commentators have pointed out, this psychology of a ring of enemies (indeed, only states along this ring are enemies) flows from the existence of many competing small states. The Arthashastra offers no instruction on the maintenance of an empire, only on the conquest of others and their absorption into the state itself. For Kautilya "waging peace" was a strategy to be pursued only when the king "finds himself in relative decline compared to his enemy"; he could "remain quiet" when neither he nor his enemy could harm the other, wage war, prepare for war, build alliances with others, or wage peace in one direction and war in another. In all of this, the goal of the king is "progress," defined solely in terms of the security and welfare of one's own state.[13]

The Arthashastra's labyrinthine permutations of peace, war, alliance, deception, strong, weak, near, and far yield an astonishing variety of policies, very much in the Hindu tradition of exhaustive analysis of every position and possibility—it is the Kamasutra of statecraft. The underlying assumptions have not changed over time, and they remain influential among some regional strategic elites. These assumptions undergird a powerful image of a state surrounded by threats, not opportunities, of a dog-eat-dog world in which the welfare of one's own state (in the Arthashastra, embodied in the welfare of the king) comes first, always.

As for Islam, some of its teachings portray a world divided between believers and unbelievers and set forth the believers' obligation to convert the unbelievers. For South Asians this is not a theological or theoretical abstraction—the region was transformed by the great waves of Islamic invasion from both Central Asia and the Arabian peninsula that began in the eighth century. These invasions displaced or destroyed many dominant Hindu castes throughout north India, while others were forced to enter into alliance with Muslim rulers. From the perspective of most Pakistanis this invasion purged and reformed the unbelievers, which was a matter of pride and progress. For Pakistani extremists this process of purging a corrupt Hindu-dominated India has only begun, and they await the breakup of India with some relish.

More recent Indian history, read and written differently by Indians and Pakistanis, reinforces the notion of threat. The nineteenth-century Hindu revivalist and modernization movements stressed India's vulnerability vis-à-vis the West but asserted its spiritual superiority. India was seen as temporarily weaker but morally greater. India's riches and treasures attracted outside predators, who despite their temporary technical or military superiority lacked the deeper moral qualities of an old and established civilization.

The Indian view of regional conflict, especially its own relationship with Pakistan, is strongly dominated by a historical experience of conquest, domination, and absorption. For most elite Indians the very existence of Pakistan, as well as the period of British rule over India, is de facto evidence of Muslims' betrayal of India to other Muslims and then to the Western powers. In Islamic-Christian relations Hindus are the odd ones out.

Although India's past greatness has not been quite so evident in the twentieth century, India has, in the minds of most of its intellectuals and political leaders, the potential of "emerging" once again. The decadent states of the West particularly feared competition from India, with its greater moral and spiritual authority; hence, they kept India backward, even as they professed friendship. The liberal Indian intellectual Rajni Kothari blames India's social problems on the Ford and Rockefeller foundations (and their Indian collaborators) because they fostered the Green Revolution, which he sees as generating inequalities. The leading conservative Hindu party, the Bharatiya Janata party (BJP), blames the World Bank. Until recently everyone blamed the United States; Islam is also a convenient target. This view of the past is that someone is trying to cut India down or prevent it from again assuming a great role in regional and world affairs. That "someone" or "other" often enters into a conspiracy with local enemies, since Bangladesh, Nepal, Sri Lanka, and even Pakistan are not credible threats in their own right.

Internal Sources of External Perceptions

An Indian general once characterized the India-Pakistan wars as "communal riots with armor." I have frequently used the phrase to describe relations between the two states because it suggests a deeper truth about their conflict and the way in which it is conducted.[14] The communal riot is a set piece in South Asian political history. A conflict between two ethnic, religious, or linguistic groups erupts because of both proximate and long-term factors. In almost every case the leaders of both sides tell their followers that they are vulnerable and threatened and must strike first because waiting would put their side at a disadvantage. It is easy to do this in India because it is a country that does not contain a domestic majority. In South Asia communal riots do not always involve "ethnic cleansing" (an attempt to rid a city or region of a minority community). More often both sides see the riot as one of a series, each followed by a temporary truce but sooner or later breaking out again when the tactical situation requires it. In the typical communal riot both sides not only battle each other but also keep one eye on outside forces (the police, the civilian administration, politicians) that may or may not play favorites and may or may not speedily act to end the conflict.

In many ways the wars between India and Pakistan in 1947–48, 1965, and 1971 and the near wars in 1955, 1987, and 1990 follow a pattern resembling a communal riot; while both states have conflicting relations with other neighbors and other states, they appear to return again and again to each other. As in the riot, the causes of conflict between the two states run deep, and wars are assumed to be as predictable as riots stemming from religious, linguistic, or caste hatreds. It should be noted, however, that most communal riots in South Asia, like the wars between regional states, are not fought for total objectives—although with the advent of nuclear weapons, India and Pakistan now have the means to conduct a total war.

This element of inevitability is the most destabilizing element of the communal riot with armor model. In the end it leads one to ask not whether Indians or Pakistanis can be trusted to fulfill their obligations in a negotiated agreement that lacks incentives for compliance but whether, under the influence of a communal image of their destiny, they can be trusted in cases where it is in their self-interest to comply.

Generation and War

The strategic and political communities that now dominate India and Pakistan can be viewed in terms of "generation," groups or clusters of individuals who were differentially influenced by important regional events.[15] The foreign service officers, generals, politicians, academics, and journalists who constitute the core foreign policy elite number several thousand in Pakistan and perhaps five times that in India. They can be divided into at least three generations, two of which are discussed here and the third in a later section.

The first generation, the founding fathers—Mahatma Gandhi, Sardar Patel, Mohammed Ali Jinnah, and Jawaharlal Nehru—was an exceptionally talented group. Their lives were devoted to two goals: achieving independence and building new states and nations. With the exception of Gandhi, they did not believe that partition would lead to conflict between India and Pakistan. On the Indian side some expected Pakistan to collapse anyway, but they did not see the need to precipitate that collapse by war. On the Pakistani side Jinnah assumed that the two countries would have good relations; he expected a multireligious Pakistan would counterpoise a predominantly Hindu India, with both possessing significant minorities, whose presence would serve as a hostage to good relations. This was a generation that had been trained by the British and had, along the way, imbibed its share of British anti-American attitudes.

The second generation of Indian and Pakistani leaders was unprepared to solve the problems left by partition. Nothing in their experience had led these leaders to develop a strategy of regional reconciliation. They reached a number of agreements that cleaned up the debris of division, and there were trade and transit treaties, hotlines, and other confidence-building measures (CBMs) in place as early as the 1950s. At the rate they were moving, India and Pakistan were headed toward an uneasy truce. But the second generation, especially in Pakistan, was made of lesser mettle. These leaders turned to foreign policy as a means to shore up weak domestic positions, and everyone except Nehru was infected with the Manichaean bipolarity of the larger cold war.[16]

Both sides thought time was on their side, and little thought was given to the consequences of a major war in South Asia—after all, such a war would be trivial when compared with the universal nuclear holocaust between the United States and the Soviet Union about which everyone was talking. The view in both India and Pakistan was that if one waited long enough, the other side would falter, collapse, or yield. As for the United States, it was acknowledged to be a superpower, and both India and Pakistan accommodated themselves in different ways to that reality, often by moving closer to an alternative major power (China for Pakistan, the Soviet Union for India), but in neither case was the second generation any more interested than the first in U.S. conflicts.

What set the second generation apart from the first were the two great postpartition traumas. For India this was the defeat by China in 1962, and for Pakistan the vivisection of the country at Indian hands in 1971. Note the ten-year difference. Indians are further into a reconsideration of their great humiliation than are Pakistanis, although the rise of China as a major economic power has rekindled old anti-Chinese fears in New Delhi.

The two events have more similarities than differences, because they shaped the worldview of successor generations in both countries. First, in each case the seriousness of the event is denied by the other side. In 1962 Ayub Khan did not believe there was a real India-China conflict, and even today Pakistanis belittle Indian obsessions with Beijing. Indians blithely assume that Pakistanis have more or less forgotten the events of 1971 and cannot understand why Pakistani officials remain suspicious when New Delhi professes its good intentions.

Second, an external conflict had profound domestic political consequences, not a small matter in a democracy. No Indian politicians have been able to admit publicly that the Indian case is flawed or to suggest that territory be exchanged with China lest they be attacked for betraying the homeland. No Pakistanis can publicly talk about a settlement of Kashmir short of accession to Islamabad lest they be attacked for being pro-Indian and anti-Islamic.

Third, each trauma led directly to the consideration of nuclear weapons and the further militarization of the respective countries. In India's case the lesson of 1962 was that only military power counts and that Nehru's humanity and his faith in diplomacy when not backed up by firepower were disastrously naive. Like Pakistan, India has been spending too much on defense ever since. When the Chinese tested a nuclear weapon in 1964, members of the Indian strategic community began their thirty-year debate over the nuclear "option" (although Indians have also had the good sense to realize that nuclear weapons would provide little defense against either another conventional attack or a nuclear one). The linkage between the trauma of 1971 and the nuclear option is even tighter in Pakistan—and for Zulfikar Ali Bhutto a nuclear weapon had the added attraction of enabling him to reduce the power of the army. What a great irony that Pakistan has wound up with both a nuclear program and a powerful if bloated army.

Finally, each crisis helped shape, in a hostile fashion, attitudes toward the United States. Although the United States initially supported India against China and still, technically, endorses India's position on the McMahon line, it retreated from a major military assistance program and withdrew from the region entirely after 1965. For Indians of this generation, disappointment in America turned to fury when they learned of the U.S.-China rapprochement. This, more than anything else, drove New Delhi into the arms of the Soviets. For Pakistanis, of course, the support provided to them in 1971 was worthless, and from that moment the Pakistani leadership, whether civilian or military, developed a deep distrust of the United States. When Pakistan and the United States did cooperate on Afghanistan, Islamabad exacted a very high price.

Second-generation leaders, still in power, like to rehearse history, their own lives, and careers as a chronology of the unremitting hostility of the other side. They conclude that any regional failings are entirely the responsibility of someone else. They offer a litany of grievances against outsiders, especially the United States, for failing to see the region accurately. They also resent the perceived apathy and ignorance of the West, because it defines their own careers and lives as unimportant.

Indians thus acquired a persecuted minority psychology after Nehru's death. Along with Mahatma Gandhi and other members of his generation, Nehru had a vision of India as such a great country that others could not easily threaten it. They saw Indian history as so magnificent that they were confident India could stand up to any external threat without much outside help and without concern that it would fail. For them India could wait, could be patient. Gandhi's assassination was linked to his acceptance of Pakistan and sending it the agreed upon share of undivided India's economic and military assets. The second generation, which witnessed the traumatic 1962 loss to China, lacked such confidence. This insecurity led to alliance with the United States, an alliance with the Soviet Union, anti-American hysteria, an arms-buying spree, and the forcible division of Pakistan, but not to an honest appraisal of the past, including the 1962 defeat.

The ring of states around India provides a ready-made image of encirclement, of threat from all quarters. India has threats from the north, the east, the west, and even over the horizon. Indian naval propagandists eagerly point out the threat from the sea, from whence both the Arabs and the Europeans came, and—twenty-three years ago—the USS *Enterprise*.

Pakistan is similarly gripped by an image of encirclement. After the Soviet invasion of Afghanistan, mortal threats were visible just across both borders. This threat is magnified for Pakistan by the refusal (amounting to a betrayal) of Pakistan's Islamic allies and China, let alone the fickle United States, to provide effective assistance to Islamabad when it was under attack in 1971. The *Enterprise* incident, which Indians of the second generation recall as a threat, is seen by their Pakistani counterparts as the cynical gesture of a false friend.

Strategies for Threatened Minorities

When a group or a state defines itself as a threatened minority, a number of coping strategies suggest themselves. In the abstract, these include:
—Assimilation: joining the dominant power if allowed
—Alignment with the larger state against a third or outside threat, turning it into an ally
—Accommodation: living as a minority or weaker state by yielding, compromising, or negotiating with the dominant power
—Alliance against the threatening neighbor: seeking outside support to turn one's minority status into equal or majority status
—Reducing the power of the larger state by war or some other strategy
—Attempting to change the behavior of the dominant state
—If all else fails, fleeing the region or erecting impenetrable walls that protect against the dominant power

India's South Asian neighbors differ in the intensity of their fear of New Delhi. Some are less pathological than one would expect. Nepalis and Bhutanese understand their weak and vulnerable position but are not obsessed by it. They have the wisdom of the weak—the knowledge that weaker states can draw on a wide range of stratagems to protect their integrity from the worst excesses of neighbors. Like Sri Lanka, they cannot hope to redress the military balance with India and thus do not seriously consider an alliance with a larger or distant power, an alliance that would turn them from a minority to a majority power.[17]

This is not the case for Pakistanis and some in Bangladesh. Many of their leaders come from families that pursued a strategy of fleeing from India. (The Pakistan movement was to create a homeland for Indian Muslims, and millions made the trek from India to East and West Pakistan.) They believe they can avert minority status vis-à-vis India through several strategies: building up their own power and forming alliances with outsiders (who will come to share their view that India is a threat to world order) and with other regional states. An alliance that turns a weak state into a powerful state, thus balancing Indian power, is seen as desirable.

Others, especially in Pakistan, have gone further. Some hard-line Pakistanis believe that India is an artificial state and not only predict but also eagerly work to precipitate its breakup. This would turn Pakistan into the majority state implied by Pakistan's newly constructed history.

The Operational Code of Paired Minority Conflicts

Paired minority conflicts seem to be especially rich and complex in their dynamics. Their state-to-state interactions seem to exacerbate conflict or at least make it harder to resolve than conflict between confident powers or asymmetric relations between an acknowledged dominant and an acknowledged weaker state. Abstracting from the India-Pakistan case, the following seem to occur with some regularity:

1. History is used—and abused—to confirm current interpretations of the dispute, especially of the legitimacy of one's own side and the malign qualities of the other. India-Pakistan relations, particularly on the most contentious issue, Kashmir, are characterized by careful historiography on both sides that has proven the correctness of the Indian, or the Pakistani, position many times over. This is done by seizing on that moment in history when the evidence favors one's own case.

2. India-Pakistan relations have a "fractile" quality about them: in bilateral discussions it is common to find arguments deployed at one level being met by arguments drawn from another level. Meetings between Indians and Pakistanis rarely last long enough to discuss systematically the differences between the two sides and how those differences might be ameliorated or accommodated. Any discussion on the strategic and structural problem of a large India working out its differences with smaller neighbors is likely, sooner or later, to move upward to a discussion of civilizational differences (presumably incompatible ones), or downward to personality differences or the intractability of certain issues (nuclear proliferation, trade, water, and so forth), or laterally to the responsibility of outside powers for regional disputes.[18]

3. The same arguments, suitably disguised, are often adopted by both sides, although care is taken not to agree at the same time. A good example of this is the "joint defense" and "no-war" proposals. When Pakistan accepted the renewal of American aid in 1981, it proposed to India the same "no-war" agreement that had earlier been offered by New Delhi (and rejected by Islamabad). The no-war proposal could be made without much risk that India would actually accept it or that it would lead to serious discussions.

4. There is resistance to compromise because compromise would be seen at home at best as a sign of weakness or at worst as a sign of collaboration with the enemy. The bureaucracies responsible for negotiation with the other side soon decay, losing their capacity for solving problems with the opposing state, even though they perform brilliantly elsewhere. The

Indian and the Pakistani foreign services are among the finest in the world and are in demand by many international organizations, but they have yet to deal seriously with each other.

5. Much the same can be said of cooperation. Cooperation is urged on South Asian leaders by outsiders as a no-risk, high-gain process. However, in South Asia, especially in India and Pakistan, cooperation is seen as low-gain and high-risk. If cooperation fails, losses will be public and politically damaging; there might also be a multiplier effect in that the risk of conflict might increase if an active attempt at cooperation fails and if the costs of conflict are very high.

6. The regional arms acquisition process is, by definition, an arms race; both sides see any acquisition by the other side as threatening. Here the pressures exerted by the armed services and, in India, the arms production sector are additional factors. The motto of the respective armed services is "More Is Enough."[19]

7. Because each state contains large minorities with links to the other side, it is easy to raise the specter of a fifth column. In Pakistan this would include some Muhajirs (descendants of Indian Muslims who came to Pakistan after partition) and Sindhis (a large community that had strong Congress sympathies before partition). In India, according to extreme Hindu chauvinists, all Muslims are suspect until they prove their allegiance to Bharat.

8. Threatened minorities elsewhere are routinely praised as role models. To this day Indians and Pakistanis share their praise of the resistance of Britain against the Nazis during World War II, of Iraq against U.N. and U.S. pressure, of Cuba against the United States, of Palestine against Israel, and (in Pakistan, privately) of Israel against the Arabs. In each case a morally superior threatened minority holds off a larger force that may possess more weapons.

9. The rules of behavior are relaxed for threatened minorities. Since their very existence and identity are at stake, their struggle is a form of total war, not a limited conflict. Any means, fair or foul, may be used because the enemy has destruction in mind.

10. Finally, time is a critical element in the calculations of paired hostile minorities. Is the calendar working for you or against you? These disputes are especially difficult to solve if one or both parties are looking to a time when they can achieve some special advantage or when the other side will collapse. Do long-term demographic trends, real or imagined, appear to be threatening? Is your country or your group acquiring some special advantage in terms of technology, alliances, or economics that will change your relative position of power in the future? Such considerations are evident

even in the India-China dispute. Both know that severe domestic problems in the other might provide new opportunities—India in Tibet, China in India's northeast and even in Nepal, Bhutan, and Kashmir.

Kashmir

Kashmir is an especially important component of the India-Pakistan relationship because it is part of each country's self-image. It is economically, strategically, and militarily important to both sides and personally important to a number of South Asian leaders (the Nehru family originally came from Kashmir, and the contemporary Pakistani politician Nawaz Sharif is of Kashmiri origin), but Kashmir's entanglement with competing national identities sets it apart from these other issues.

Sisir Gupta, the eminent Indian strategist, wrote that the Kashmir problem was composed of "the images that India and Pakistan had created of themselves on the eve of Partition."[20] From the very beginning Kashmir has had this quality of being both a problem and a solution. It is hard for Indians or Pakistanis to talk objectively about Kashmir since it is now intimately connected to their national identities.

Kashmir is seen by both sides not only as lost territory but also as hostage territory—a piece of the political order that has been lost or is threatened. For many Indians Kashmir is seen as essential for maintaining secularism: if Kashmiri Muslims achieve separation from the rest of India, what would prevent the remainder of India's huge Muslim population from making special, even territorial, claims on the Indian enterprise? Directed by Pakistan, such a movement would result in the further break-up of India. For Pakistanis Kashmir is also a hostage, only in this case less of a threat to the existence of Pakistan as a state (after all, Pakistan has accommodated itself to the loss of East Pakistan) than to the identity of Pakistan, a state created to preserve and protect Muslim identity in South Asia. As long as Muslims are being forcibly denied their full freedoms or even the opportunity to vote on whether they want to join with Pakistan, Pakistan's original purpose remains unfulfilled.

Ironically, the emergence of a separatist Kashmiri movement with its assertion of a unique national identity (however imperfectly defined) comes as a challenge to both Delhi and Islamabad and may, paradoxically, make a resolution of the Kashmir problem possible. It has created a situation of nested minorities. Kashmiris are a minority in both India and Pakistan; Indians and Pakistanis are afraid that the wrong solution to the Kashmir problem will further exacerbate their own weaknesses; within Kashmir, Hindus and Buddhists live as minorities in a Muslim population;

the Valley Kashmiris, Hindus and Muslims, are a minority in the larger state of Jammu and Kashmir, as are other Kashmiri communities: Mirpuris, Jammu Hindus, Ismaili Muslims who live in the northern territories, and so forth.

Since all of the parties to the dispute view themselves as threatened or as a minority in one sense or another, a resolution of the dispute must rest on principles that reassure minorities, or putative minorities, or "nested" minorities. Two of these principles suggest themselves now that India and Pakistan are both democracies and most of the Kashmiri separatist or militant groups accept democracy. One principle is some variety of self-determination (if not a plebiscite, once but no longer agreed to by India, then some variation on it that would associate Kashmiris of various religions and ethnicities with the process). The second principle is the protection of minority rights that is embedded in India's constitution and, at least for Jinnah, was to be an important part of Pakistan's identity.

Will the Future Be Different?

A paired minority conflict does not imply that war is more likely or would be fought more savagely in South Asia. It does imply that achieving a dialogue leading to peace in the region may be difficult. Four strategies, or processes, seem to be of special importance in bringing about such a dialogue and, subsequently, a state of normal relations between democratic India and Pakistan.[21] Such a normal state of affairs would not eliminate important differences between these two countries, but it would create a mechanism by which they could be resolved—or if necessary deferred.

The Third Generation

I have noted the important, albeit intransigent, role played by the second generation of Indian and Pakistani decision makers scarred, respectively, by the traumas of 1962 and 1971. Particularly in India they came to view their country as weak and threatened and tried a number of coping strategies (alliance, an arms buildup, nuclear weapons) or lapsed into conspiracy theories or xenophobia.

Now a third generation is emerging.[22] At the very top, especially in Pakistan, decision makers have been exposed to a wider variety of international influences through television, films, and cheap air travel; they have cousins in New York and sisters in Chicago. They are more concerned than the second generation about environmental and economic issues, and the women of this generation have a special interest in gender issues.

Pakistan, perpetually disappointing in so many other ways, has one of the world's strongest women's movements.

Above all the third generation does not have a sense of responsibility for the gloomy history described earlier. Members of the third generation have all heard this history from their parents, their uncles, and their superiors, but it is not quite their history. They do not see the United States as one of the two (equally, if not more culpable) antagonists in the cold war,[23] they do not blame the cold war for their own country's misfortunes, and they do not hate the other side as do many in the first and second generation because they do not know the other side. At least as of 1993, no Indian was studying in Pakistan, and one lone Pakistani was studying in an Indian university.

In brief the coming of the third generation is about to happen. Their competence and their interest in the things that matter—above all, a fresh approach to economic issues, plus the collapse of many institutions dominated by a generation living in the past—will bring them to power sooner rather than later.[24] There is a distinct absence of hatred even among the younger officers of the Pakistan army; they distrust India, they fear India, but they are realistic about India. They understand what India did to their country, and they debate among themselves the merits of revenge. But most I have talked to would not sacrifice their own country to get even. In that respect they are moving to the position many Indians now hold on China. A "victory" that also destroys one's own country does not make military, political, or moral sense. At the other end of the spectrum is a new effort on the part of liberal Indians and Pakistanis to make contact and engage in serious dialogue.

Successive summer schools in security and arms control that I have chaired, which bring younger Indians and Pakistanis together, have had two components. The daytime sessions feature lectures and discussions of current strategic issues. The evening sessions, organized by the students themselves, explore the most profound and important aspects of India-Pakistan relations: What does it mean to be a Pakistani or an Indian? What was your image of Pakistan before you came here? Are we monsters, or are we people like you? Why is religion a part of your politics? Why isn't religion a part of yours? It is hoped this dialogue will continue, acquire a momentum of its own, and serve as one of many new bridges that are being built between India and Pakistan.[25] In comparative terms this group is about where the Israelis and Palestinians were fifteen years ago.

The third generation is not something that can be invented or halted; it is just happening. More than any other development in the region, this new group of regional leaders will make it possible for a dialogue to occur. Without other developments, however, that dialogue may not take place, or will take place later, or will take place under less than favorable circumstances.

A New Regional Economic Order

Westerners have always been puzzled by the existence of democratic governments in South Asia. How can such a poor region of the world (more than half of the world's poor live in India and Bangladesh alone) sustain democracy? Of course, South Asians have looked at European history and have asked how the world's most advanced industrialized states could sustain imperial policies for a century and produce two or three of the most horrific states ever seen on the face of the earth.

In truth, the relationship between democracy, peace, and economic development is weak and is still the subject of considerable academic debate. However, my observation is that the transformation of regional economies just now beginning will have important consequences for regional peace. Rapid and sustained economic growth is bound to create strains on all of the major regional economies and could generate radical or populist political movements made up of groups that feel they are not sharing in the growth. Further, if things go very wrong, rapid economic growth could provide the money for a vast increase in regional arsenals. Such growth could, however, provide both the incentive and the means for enhanced regional dialogue.

While India and Pakistan formally trade very little, about $2 billion of unpublicized trade goes on between the countries, which consists of items not readily identifiable by nationality (sugar, coal, salt, spices, cheap consumer goods, textiles). There is also a vast smuggling and third-country operation. Recent conversations with businesspeople in both countries indicate new, rising pressures for formal, open trade between India and Pakistan. Such trade would for the first time create a visible, legal stake in good relations between the two countries and further liberalization of at least economic ties.

Along with enhanced trade, we have already begun to see the influence of new forms of communication and movement made possible by extending various technologies to South Asia. All kinds of groups can now communicate (although with some difficulty) by e-mail and fax, and cheap regional airfares make it possible literally to fly over the new barriers to ground travel that have been established. Despite the existence of two suspicious (if not hostile) governments, private Indian and Pakistani citizens have been able to engage in serious discussions on a whole range of issues— security, environment, gender, and rural poverty, among others.

Reestablishing the Subcontinent's Strategic Unity

The one group most unforgiving of the partition of India and Pakistan was the senior officer corps of the Indian army. Virtually all British officers—and many Indian ones—opposed the creation of two new states with two armies on the grounds that partition would destroy the strategic unity of South Asia, exposing the region to threats from the Soviet Union. Even they, however, did not anticipate that the successor states would turn against each other, making the region vulnerable not only to Soviet pressure, which manifested itself in 1979 in Afghanistan, but also to Chinese pressure, exemplified by the 1962 war and subsequent support of separatist movements in India. Further, neither India nor Pakistan carried the influence of the raj in regions adjacent to South Asia—the Persian Gulf, East Africa, Central Asia, and Southeast Asia.

With the end of the cold war, however, both the Indian and Pakistani armies have discovered (or more appropriately, rediscovered) a role for which they were originally designed. In an era of splintering states and ethnic separatism, all of the subcontinental armies except Sri Lanka's have demonstrated phenomenal integrity and are among the best services available for international peacekeeping operations. In Somalia three subcontinental armies saw duty (India, Pakistan, Bangladesh), the Nepal army is everywhere, and Bangladesh is not far behind with seven separate peacekeeping missions. These operations have brought regional officers into professional contact. Further, both India and Pakistan now have military-to-military ties to the United States, which is planning regional peacekeeping exercises that could involve several South Asian armies.

Until very recently any contact with the Pakistan army was impossible for India, because Pakistan was ruled by the armed services and because military intervention might be contagious. But as long as Pakistan remains a democracy, such contact should be unobjectionable and, from an Indian perspective, even useful in influencing Pakistani strategic perceptions. These contacts would go a long way toward undercutting the paired minority psychology of both India and Pakistan. They would show both sides that a relationship based on professional principles is possible. They would also demonstrate how similar the two armies are, despite their five-decade separation. The process would be gradual, but inevitably strategists in both countries would begin to understand the gains open to the two countries if they were to engage in further cooperation.

A Helping Hand, Not a Foreign Hand

Finally, South Asia could use a peace process.[26] There is a difference between examining the policy choices open to individual regional and non-regional states and shaping a strategy that will deal with the larger problem of regional peace and war. There is also a difference between a policy designed to get the region (or an individual state) through a short-term crisis and one designed to address underlying causes of conflict. Single-state policies or short-term policies (or single-issue studies) are important, but they do not deal with the long term. The lesson of other regions or states with paired minority conflicts is that a systematic peace process can take place, but it may need an outside facilitator—a helping hand, although not a foreign hand.

One of the first things such outsiders can do is ensure that Indian and Pakistani strategists have a better understanding of the limited but critical role outsiders have played in the Middle East, South Africa, and elsewhere. In some of these cases—regarded as impossible, intractable, or not yet ripe for solution—a paired minority conflict was transformed into a cooperative bargaining game by a combination of subtle changes among the antagonists, changed social or economic circumstances, and private and governmental outsiders who first initiated dialogue and then kept it going over rough patches. Ironically, India once played such a role in the U.S.-Soviet dispute, and Pakistani officials have served as intermediaries for other contentious pairs, most notably the United States and China, and the United States and Iran. Neither the role nor the process should be unfamiliar to South Asian strategists.

The only state that can plausibly serve the role of intermediary or sponsor of a regional peace process is the United States. Hitherto, however, Washington's views on South Asia have been distorted by an emphasis on the region's poverty and backwardness. For Americans the overwhelming image of South Asia has been one of poverty; the notion that India and Pakistan might have legitimate or real security concerns that transcend poverty has been hard to accept. American involvement in South Asia, when not steered by extraneous cold war considerations, was thus economic and developmental in its emphasis. More recently the region has been seen through the prism of an overreaching nonproliferation policy, which has, if anything, pushed both India and Pakistan further toward overt nuclear deployment of nuclear weapons and ballistic missiles. For fifty years American policymakers have been reluctant to adopt a systematic approach to regional conflict resolution. The recent Asia

Society reports on America and South Asia and the Council on Foreign Relations report on U.S. policy toward Pakistan and India stopped short of recommending such a regional peace process, but the response to the council's report among officials, Congress, and the press indicates that American views may be shifting and old stereotypes fading.[27] If this is so, the United States would be the best-situated power to facilitate a regional peace process. It is the only major state with strategic, economic, and cultural ties to both India and Pakistan and with considerable expertise in initiating and managing such processes.

To the Future: Some Questions

The answer to the question, What are the causes of conflict in South Asia and the conditions for peace? is that the existence of a paired minority psychology in two important regional states both contributes to regional conflict and impedes the prospects for regional peace. Yet such paired minority conflicts have existed elsewhere and have been ameliorated, if not eliminated.

The accuracy of this conclusion, especially when compared with other plausible explanations of regional conflict, has yet to be measured. It is also uncertain that a regional peace process, once initiated, will achieve success. We will have to study carefully the region's own record of cooperation, the politics of establishing a regional peace process, and the consequences of doing nothing. A better understanding of the region will also have to be gained by those outsiders who have so much influence in it.

This conclusion suggests many clusters of questions or lines of inquiry that might guide future research. First, what are the likely costs and risks of continued conflict? What will the defense burden for India and Pakistan be in ten years, and what impact will it have on development? What are the costs of lost opportunities of trade, foreign investment, or multinational cooperation in managing the region's enormous water resources if there is no movement toward a settlement of the major regional disputes? The question could also be asked another way: What are the prospects for a strategic understanding between India and Pakistan that would allow each to reduce defense spending or at least reduce the risk of war between them? A "military balance" project to bring leading retired generals and strategists from both sides together to outline the contours of such an understanding would constitute the first serious attempt at a "net assessment" of the region's conventional and nuclear military balances. It would also have to factor in China's role.

Second, will Americans alter their attitudes toward India and Pakistan and the prospect for a regional dialogue? Most Western evaluations of the region are wrong in projecting onto South Asia the apocalyptic calculations that have dominated Eurocentric war since 1914.[28] Will the continuation of democratic government in all of the region's states and the prospect for rapid economic growth change Japanese, Western, and American attitudes toward a regional peace process?

Third, regional scholars and strategists need to look at other pairs of states that have deep antagonisms. The relevance of the Middle East and South African peace processes to South Asia have been mentioned, but other cases may be instructive. The United States and Japan, France and Germany, and the United States and Mexico are worth careful examination. All are democracies, and democracy provides both the framework and the reason to reach agreement. India and Pakistan are democracies. Will this eventually overcome their paired minority conflict, leading them to transform their relationship?

Finally, South Asia's past is rich in examples of both failed and successful cooperation.[29] Almost without exception, scholars working on the region and most from the region have ignored these data and the reasons for past regional cooperation. Under what conditions did India and Pakistan work together? What role did personality, the bureaucracies, or outsiders play in obtaining cease-fires, getting U.N. supervision, achieving the Indus waters treaty, and so forth. Why did the Simla Agreement appear to succeed, and why has it now failed? What led the region to the brink of war in 1987 and 1990, and what kept it out of war in both cases? Do the same mechanisms still operate, or were they just lucky?

Postscript, May 1997

Since this essay was completed two dramatic events have significantly enhanced the outlook for peace in South Asia. First, a new Indian government, headed by Deve Gowda, appointed Inder Kumar Gujral as minister of External Affairs in early 1996, and Gujral initiated a proactive regional diplomacy, popularly called the "Gujral Doctrine." This was characterized by generous diplomacy toward India's smaller and weakest neighbors: Sri Lanka, Bangladesh, and Nepal. It produced startling results, and by early 1997 India's relations with all three had dramatically improved. Gujral did not neglect Pakistan, and he unilaterally eased the visa problem for Pakistani journalists and others.

Then in February 1997 Pakistan held a dramatic, truly free election that gave Nawaz Sharif's Pakistan Muslim League a large majority. This was big enough to amend Pakistan's constitution, restoring full parliamentary democracy to that country. Within a few weeks of Sharif's democratic coup India was plunged into its own political crisis. On April 21, 1997, Gujral himself emerged as prime minister of India, pledging to continue the kind of proactive diplomacy toward Pakistan that had eased Delhi's relations with other regional states.

The stage is now set for a significant improvement of India-Pakistan relations, not excluding the resolution of the Kashmir problem. Gujral is a man of the first generation, originally from what is now Pakistan but not embittered by partition and still optimistic about the emergence of a South Asia at peace with itself. Sharif is a man of the third generation, a former businessman eager to restore normal trade and commercial relations with India. Ironically, both studied at the same college in Pakistan (Government College, Lahore), Gujral before petition, Sharif more recently. Both are Punjabis, and both have a special, personal connection with the very communities that were most embittered by the partition. This conjunction opens wide a window of opportunity.

The prospects that an India-Pakistan dialogue will achieve success are enhanced by a number of other developments:

—All major outside powers (the United States, China, Russia, Japan, and the European Community) have expressed their support for the peaceful resolution of the Kashmir dispute.

—Both India and Pakistan are in the midst of transforming their economies and cannot afford either a war or high levels of regional tension.

—The Indian and Pakistani undeclared nuclear programs have made conventional war unthinkable.

—"Track II" diplomacy (meetings of important but unofficial figures from both sides, which Gujral had strongly supported for many years) has brought many Indians and Pakistanis into close contact.

In brief, a peace process is now underway. It will have its fits and starts, but the underlying dynamic is likely to propel India and Pakistan toward a "normal" relationship. Although the Kashmir problem itself may take several years to resolve, both countries appear to be headed toward resolving other outstanding disputes.

Above all, the images held in both countries of the other are now beginning to change: Pakistanis hold out great hope that the Gujral Doctrine will lead to a more generous and less threatening India; Indians welcome the full restoration of democracy in Pakistan and hope that this will encourage Islamabad to seek political rather than military solutions to their disputes.

Notes

I wish to express my appreciation to Sumit Ganguly for comments on this essay.

1. Sumit Ganguly, *The Origin of War in South Asia,* rev. ed. (Boulder, Colo.: Westview, 1994). There is a vast literature that poses the question "Why war?" but the most interesting, and disappointing, is Albert Einstein and Sigmund Freud, *Why War?* (Paris: International Institute of Intellectual Cooperation, 1933).

2. This will be forthcoming in book form under the tentative title "Every Fifth Person: The Origins of War and the Conditions for Peace in South Asia." Some of the conclusions of this essay have been presented in seminars in India and Pakistan and at the University of Illinois. I am grateful especially to current and former students, Kanti P. Bajpai, Sue Burns, Shivaji Ganguly, Sumit Ganguly, Chetan Kumar, and Swarna Rajagopalan.

3. Indians and Pakistanis agree on one aspect of their special relationship and its origin. In both states one hears how the British practiced "divide and rule," and (sometimes) how the United States has continued such a practice, pitting the two South Asian states against each other or against third countries, such as China. The implication of this view is that the divided successor states could learn how to live with each other.

4. The term *security complex* was coined by Barry Buzan and refers to deep-rooted, long-lasting conflicts between states. Barry Buzan and Gowher Rizvi, eds., *South Asian Insecurity and the Great Powers* (New York: St. Martin's, 1986). The major thrust of this essay and much of my own work is that "deep rooted" is not quite an adequate description of the India-Pakistan relationship.

5. Afghanistan to the northwest and Burma to the east are only marginally "South Asian" states, and neither belongs to the main regional organization, the South Asian Association for Regional Cooperation (SAARC).

6. The answer of the recent Asia Society Study Group, cochaired by Ambassador Arthur Hartman and Carla Hills, to all of these questions is a qualified yes. See Asia Society, *South Asia and the United States after the Cold War: A Study Mission* (New York: Asia Society, 1994).

7. *Civilizational* is used in the sense it is used by Samuel Huntington, *Clash of Civilizations* (New York: Simon and Schuster, 1996): the highest level of cultural identification, which may transcend the individual nation-state.

8. Without doubt, the finest overview of theories of war remains Kenneth Waltz's first book, *Man, the State, and War* (New York: Columbia University Press, 1959). Waltz categorizes explanations of war according to whether they locate war at the level of human nature, at the level of the state, or the interaction of states in a particular system.

9. Ganguly, *The Origin of War.*

10. The Australian strategic writer Sandy Gordon has termed India a "weak-strong" state. Gordon, *India's Rise to Power in the Twentieth Century and Beyond* (New York: St. Martin's, 1995).

11. The most insightful thinker on how hostile groups or crowds are generat-

ed is Elias Canetti, whose book *Crowds and Power* (New York: Seabury, 1978) is a modern classic. For the perspective of a clinical psychologist who has studied the origins of ethnic conflict and war, see Vamik D. Volkan, *The Need to Have Enemies and Allies: From Clinical Practice to International Relationships* (New York: Jason Aronson, 1988).

12. Kautilya, *The Arthashastra,* trans. and ed. L. N. Rangarajan (New Delhi, India: Penguin Books, 1987), 555.

13. Ibid., 553.

14. Stephen P. Cohen, *The Indian Army: Its Contribution to the Development of a Nation,* rev. ed. (Delhi, India: Oxford University Press, 1990).

15. For an initial attempt to apply this concept to the officer corps of the Pakistan army, see Stephen P. Cohen, *The Pakistan Army* (Berkeley: University of California Press, 1985).

16. There are many exceptions to this characterization; perhaps the best known is Jagat S. Mehta, who worked closely with Nehru as a young foreign service officer and eventually rose to the position of foreign secretary under both the Janata and Indira Gandhi governments.

17. Sri Lankan strategists, however, see the India-Pakistan conflict as useful to Colombo because it tends to draw Indian attention away from the south toward the northwest.

18. One of the most striking components of India-Pakistan dialogues is how easily the two sides agree that the British, by practicing "divide and rule" politics in the subcontinent, laid the groundwork for the present conflict. Moderates on both sides (in other words, those who do not trace the differences between India and Pakistan to pre-British Islamic and Hindu differences) hold the British to be the original culprits, with the United States soon taking up the mantle.

19. This may be changing. Recently, when I have confronted senior officers of both armies with this characterization, they have readily agreed, and both believe that their country is spending too much on defense and not enough on development. Informed officers in India and Pakistan are aware their own strength rests on a strong civil society and economy, they favor the recent economic reforms in both states, and they are not averse to a trade-off between arms control and political dialogue on the one hand and arms reduction on the other.

20. Sisir Gupta, *Kashmir: A Study in India-Pakistan Relations* (Bombay: Asia Publishing House, 1967), 441.

21. The qualifier *democratic* is necessary; a different kind of strategy would be required should one or both states cease to be democracies. The prospect for a lasting peace between the two countries rests on their remaining democratic and learning how to apply to each other the principles that govern their internal order.

22. For an elaboration of this argument, see Stephen P. Cohen, "The Third Generation," *Seminar* (New Delhi), no. 422 (1994): 17–20.

23. The exception to this statement may be the subgeneration trained in some religious schools, especially in Pakistan, where the public educational system has broken down. Here anti-Americanism is a component of the core curriculum.

24. This conclusion is based on my own experience over the years as a lecturer in regional universities and military schools and since 1993 as chair of the South Asian Summer School in Security, Technology and Arms Control, directed by Chris Smith of Kings' College, London.

25. An overview of private contacts between India and Pakistan is provided in Sundeep Waslekar, "Track-Two Diplomacy in South Asia," 2d ed. (ACDIS Occasional Paper, Program in Arms Control, Disarmament, and International Security, University of Illinois, 1996).

26. For some 1993 and 1995 thoughts on the structure, assumptions, and organization of such a process applied to the region as a whole and to Kashmir in particular, see Stephen P. Cohen, "Is Peace Possible in South Asia?" *Journal of the United Services Institution of India* (New Delhi) 123, no. 513 (1993) 146–53; and Stephen P. Cohen, "Kashmir: The Roads Ahead," in *South Asia Approaches the Millennium,* ed. Marvin G. Weinbaum and Chetan Kumar (Boulder, Colo.: Westview, 1995), 127–44.

27. Asia Society, *South Asia and the United States after the Cold War;* Asia Society, *Preventing Nuclear Proliferation in South Asia,* Report of the Study Group (New York Asia Society, 1995); Council on Foreign Relations, *A New U.S. Policy towards India and Pakistan,* Report of an Independent Task Force (New York: Council on Foreign Relations, 1997).

28. Regional strategists—who claim that deterrence theory does not operate in South Asia and that South Asian wars are more civilized than other wars—have, however, neglected the possibility of total war brought about by nuclear proliferation and the overwhelming evidence that regional decision makers have been just as competent, or as incompetent, as their Western counterparts in their policies.

29. For a summary list, see Chetan Kumar, "A Chronology of India-Pakistan Cooperation: 1947–1994," in *Brasstacks and Beyond: Perception and Management of Crisis in South Asia,* edited by Kanti P. Bajpai, P. R. Chari, Pervaiz I. Cheema, Stephen P. Cohen, and Sumit Ganguly (New Delhi: Manohar, 1995).

Part Three

Intervention
and Peacekeeping

6

Grounds for Hope or Pessimism?

Paul W. Schroeder

This essay begins not, as is usual in American speeches, with one joke or anecdote but with two—both intended to introduce and illustrate the message. The first is a Jewish joke, but its point is universal. A passenger liner blew up and sank in the South Pacific. The sole survivor, a Jew, was washed up on an island entirely uninhabited but filled with trees and vegetation. This enabled the Jew, an energetic and ingenious man, not only to survive but in time to fashion tools and build himself shelter. Stranded for many years, he used the time for more building, eventually constructing a whole village. When a British warship finally appeared on the horizon, the Jew set off signal fires and was rescued. The captain of the British ship, however, was so impressed by what the Jew had done that he asked him to show him around the village. The Jew readily agreed, and began to give him the tour.

"Here is my house; this is the town hall; here is a synagogue; here is the police station; here is the general store; here is a synagogue—"

"Wait a minute," broke in the captain. "What do you do in this synagogue?"

"Why, that's where I pray three times a day, and celebrate the high holy days, and—"

"Yes, I understand," interrupted the captain. "But if you do all that here, what do you do in the other synagogue?"

"That synagogue!" replied the Jew, growing very excited. "Let me tell you something—I wouldn't be caught dead in that synagogue!"

The second story comes from the old comic strip "Pogo the Possum," created by Walt Kelly. Albert the Alligator and the Bear, the two biggest and most ferocious animals in the swamp, were sworn enemies, always fighting. One day, however, the Bear suggested that their constant war was foolish and counterproductive. If they cooperated instead of fighting, they could rule the swamp unchallenged. Albert agreed, and so they set out to divide the swamp and its inhabitants into their respective spheres. But this division led to many quarrels over who got what, with Albert insisting, for example, that since the Bear was half a head taller than he, all the animals under Albert's rule had to be half a head taller than the Bear's animals. Finally the Bear said in disgust, "You know, I used to enjoy having you for an enemy—but I hates having you for a friend!"

These two stories can be used to illustrate the theory and history of international politics, particularly a view long dominant and still prominent among political scientists and historians: the so-called realist view. According to this view international politics is essentially a competitive, conflictual struggle over power and scarce resources. The primary goal of the players, especially the main ones, must be to achieve security against threats, to protect and advance their own interests, and to make gains over their competitors. The competitive power struggle can be balanced and to some extent moderated and controlled, but it can never eliminated or transcended.

The story of the Jew on the desert island might not seem to illustrate this (he faced no objective threat). Yet it fits the "realist" perception that groups and societies constitute themselves and establish their identity in competition with others, distinguishing and separating themselves from outsiders and opponents, and that this is a root cause of violence. Nationalism, for example, is seen as rooted in xenophobia, hatred of the foreigner. Albert the Alligator and the Bear illustrate how even genuine efforts to end hostility by mutual agreement and cooperation usually break down into quarrels over the spoils and relative gains. Considerable international theory and history seem to support this. Alliances between dominant powers, for example, frequently fail for these reasons; victorious coalitions usually dissolve into rivalry after wars.

But these two stories can equally well illustrate a different view of international politics, called idealism or liberal institutionalism. Broadly speaking, this view holds that international politics can change; it is not structurally bound to remain a game of power politics. Individuals and groups, including nations and states, can learn collectively from mistakes and disasters and develop ideas, norms, rules, and institutions to govern their conduct and avoid major violence and conflict. One source of inspiration for liberal institutionalism has been the political philosophy of Immanuel Kant, and these stories fit his ideas about the "asocial sociability" of human beings. They are "asocial," meaning self-centered, egoistic, prone to seek their own interest at the expense of others. Yet this is an asocial sociability—human beings need each other; they can only realize themselves and acquire their individual identity within society. The same rational capacity that they use to advance their particular or group interests in asocial ways can enable them over time to widen their horizons, learn from failure and disaster, and change their conduct, even in international affairs. The Jew on the desert island was so incurably social that he constructed a whole village on his desert island, even including a place for his opponents, though he would not set foot in it. Albert and the Bear did learn that it was better to get along than to fight, even if they hated the process of doing so.

This essay, without denying the important truths and insights found in realism, takes the side of the liberal institutionalists. International politics is not condemned to be a game of competitive power politics. Leaders and peoples can learn and can change their practices so that there is ground for hope and efforts toward a new, different, and better international order. This assertion, of course, is commonplace, almost a cliché. It will be backed up, however, with something less common: an argument that this hopeful outlook on international politics can be based not on theory, current events, or recent favorable world developments and trends but on the very evidence usually cited as grounds for pessimism and despair—the long history of European and world international politics since about 1500. Just as the stories of the Jew on the desert island and the animals in the swamp may appear to illustrate a realist, pessimistic view of international politics but may really fit another view better, so, this essay argues, the long history of international politics may appear to contain little but violence, crime, and folly (and there is surely plenty of these) but actually gives evidence of enough change, evolution, development, and progress to justify hope and further effort. The hope engendered, however, must be of a sober, disenchanted kind, free of utopian expectations. The gateway to international peace bears a sign on it like Dante's on the gates of hell: "Abandon all Utopian hope, ye who enter here."

To explain this proposition (a real exposition or proof is out of the question here) requires painting an overall picture of the long history of European international politics and the international system—an overview so broad and general that it may seem to come not from a mountain top but from outer space. Historians are by profession rightly suspicious of such sweeping generalizations. Yet if the purpose of the overview is understood—not for conveying historical information but for illustrating a certain historical outlook—and some extreme oversimplification and compression is accepted, it may do more good than harm.

Any educated person, asked to name some great achievements of European civilization, could list many things—art, literature, music, architecture, science, technology, industrial and economic development, and so on. Few if any would put international politics on the list. This field seems obviously Europe's great failure and curse—a long, depressing record of crises, wars, conquests, arms races, imperialism, and destruction, still continuing. Nonetheless, I propose to place international politics firmly on that list of great constructive achievements, such as capitalism or organized religion, which also have their dark side.

The reason is that at the core of the admittedly violent and conflict-ridden relations between European governments over centuries lies one of the most profound, inescapable, and difficult problems of modern society: how to reconcile general peace and tolerable order with diversity, independence, and freedom in a multistate community. Over the centuries the struggle with that problem, instead of proving futile and self-defeating, has led to an international state system, which now offers a realistic prospect of a durable solution or management of it.

The problem can be defined as follows. Assume the existence of a number of sizable, permanent communities, each organizing its own government, occupying a defined territory, living in direct contact or close proximity to other similar communities, and engaging in regular, important interactions with them (trade, travel, communications, and exchanges of all kinds). Now ask the question, How can such a group of communities maintain relations of tolerably peaceful and stable coexistence if (as is the case) they differ from each other in various ways (religion, language, race, social and political structure, customs, ideology, and the like), are in competition with each other for vital scarce goods (territory, population, natural resources, waterways, markets, strategic assets, and so on), and all insist on their individual autonomy (independent self-rule) and sovereignty (recognition as the sole source of law and authority within their territorial bounds)?

This is the core problem of peace and order in a multistate world, and the theoretical answer to it is simple: the problem is insoluble. The great strength of realism as a theory and an approach to international politics has been to recognize this—to see that while there are many different causes for individual wars and conflicts, the essential cause of war is the very existence and character of a multistate system as described. Structured by anarchy, it engenders competition and conflict over scarce resources and virtually compels relationships to rest primarily on power. Although various units may gain freedom in the sense of individual autonomy and sovereignty through this system, this gain will always be at the cost of self-defense and the risk of war and possible extinction.

Hence this kind of multistate system cannot in theory provide real, durable peace. For that, the multistate system must be supplanted by empire, with one unit establishing its authority and power over all others or over all those with which it has important contacts. This answer fits history as well as theory. Peace and order through formal and informal empire have obtained for considerable periods over large areas of the globe—witness the Roman Empire, the Chinese, the Mogul in India, the British Empire, or the American Empire in the Western Hemisphere. Nor does peace through empire necessarily imply imperialism of the crude, old-fashioned sort. All past and current schemes for peace through world government or world law represent in the last analysis different ideas for achieving peace through empire and are incompatible with a system of multiple coordinate states.

In medieval Europe, from which the multistate system emerged, the prevalent concept of peace and order was that of empire. The reigning idea of the right political relations among its many different communities was a feudal Christian version of the Roman Empire. Peace and the rule of law were supposed to derive from a single source of authority, God, which then flowed through the Holy Roman emperor down to lesser rulers and orders in society in a grand hierarchical network of authority, privileges, and fealty or obligations embracing everyone down to the lowliest peasant. The ideal was of course never realized in actual politics, and in practice it had clearly broken down by the late fifteenth century. Yet so strong was the grip of this concept on people's minds, especially in the absence of any other convincing principle of authority, that much of the international history of the sixteenth and seventeenth centuries and its wars can be seen as a desperate struggle somehow to preserve and realize this ideal of a single Christian commonwealth in Europe or find something to substitute for it. To be sure, by the mid-seventeenth century it had collapsed to the point that it ceased even to be the reigning concept or ideal, though it still retained adherents. Its breakdown is easy to understand and in retrospect massively overdetermined and inevitable. Major intellectual and social developments—the Renaissance, the Reformation, the Age of Discovery, even the scientific revolution—undermined its belief structure. No state in Europe proved strong enough to assume and enforce the role of imperial hegemon, though certain ones tried.

Some larger territorial states emerged, growing in power and capturing the loyalty of subjects and elites. Above all, the religious wars seemed to make the ideal of a single res publica Christiana impossible and intolerable. In any case the vital point is that in time the very ideal of empire, of universal monarchy, would be regarded as not simply unrealizable but also wrong. A concept that had once united educated Europeans and given them a sense of common identity—the idea of a universal Christian commonwealth held together by a common religion and a common law and authority—now came to be seen as anti-European, a threat to the independence, values, and way of life of the political units constituting Europe. Europe now meant only a family or collection of independent states.

The traditional date for the end of this great crisis of religious and political law and authority is 1648, when the Treaties of Westphalia ended the Thirty Years' War and supposedly founded a new state system based on individual state sovereignty. This state system supposedly lasted until 1945, in some ways until the present day. This conventional view is sound enough, so long as one understands that this so-called Westphalian system, far from solving the basic question of the source and nature of authority and order in international politics or even trying to, actually answered the question only in a negative way, by recognizing that the problem could not be solved by restoring a Christian commonwealth, which was what the Spanish and Austrian Habsburgs had in a sense tried to do. Even after 1648 and the failure of this Habsburg effort, Louis XIV's effort to get himself and France recognized as the leaders of Christendom was made not solely to establish his own glory and French security and power (though these were for Louis doubtless the dominant motives) but also to reestablish some kind of order and hierarchy in Europe against the prevailing anarchy. According to much recent scholarship Louis XIV's quest for glory and hegemony thus represented a kind of perversion of Cardinal Richelieu's earlier notions of collective security under French leadership.[1] After Louis XIV also failed, balance of power competition became the unquestioned rule of eighteenth-century politics, but this too left the question of achieving tolerable peace and order in a multistate system unanswered, or rather confirmed the theoretical negative answer.

All this seems to prove a case opposite from the one promised. The system and its structure explain Europe's constant wars and predict more of the same for the future. Change can occur on the unit level but not on a structural level. Great powers rise and fall and arenas shift, but a struggle among competing units for power and scarce resources goes on much the same.

Yet precisely here my view as a historian of international politics diverges. In theory, perhaps, the history of international politics should reflect this unchanging structure; in fact, it does not. The "realist" paradigm of international politics may work in certain respects for purposes of political science or international relations theory but not for the broad, long sweep of international history. It has three main shortcomings. First, it explains war but not peace—and peace more so than war needs explanation in the history of international politics. Second, it cannot deal adequately with certain vital elements of international history, particularly the reality of change and development in international politics and the international system. Finally, the paradigm takes account of the struggles for power involved in international politics but overlooks the quest for order, stability, and peace and what has emerged from that quest. While taking seriously the central problem of the contradiction between state sovereignty and the rule of law, it does not take equally seriously the efforts of states, leaders, and peoples to solve, manage, or rise above that contradiction and dismisses too readily the possibility of learning and achieving some form of success in the quest. An interpretation of international politics that overlooks this quest for order or dismisses it as futile thereby not merely underestimates one side or aspect of international politics but also distorts the whole by missing a vital dimension. In seeking order, international politics shows its kinship with other kinds of politics—domestic politics, business politics, academic politics, and the like. Without doubt it involves struggles for power and competition for scarce resources, as they do; but, like them, it is also a profoundly human enterprise involving collective learning and problem solving, and over time it has produced development through learning and problem solving.

It would take far too long here to try to prove these three propositions, but I can at least try to clarify them. Peace needs historical explanation more than war does because in the kind of system realists describe, structured by state sovereignty and anarchy, war and conflict are natural outcomes, and peace, in theoretical terms, is exceptional and artificial. The point is generally accepted by theorists. Yet far fewer wars and violent conflicts have occurred and more peace has arisen in history than should have under these assumptions. This is not an abstract academic point but a concrete phenomenon scholars cannot ignore. It is debatable whether over time the tendency of states to resort to war as a means of solving international problems has been increasing or declining. Experts disagree, and the answer depends on many variables difficult to appraise and quantify; hence, the sophisticated statistical and quantitative studies of war that have addressed this question have not settled it decisively. But this concentration of attention on the incidence of war has led scholars to overlook and underrate a major, undeniable development in international politics over the centuries, namely, a massive growth of peace. Since 1500 the number, scope, variety, and importance of peaceful, law-bound, cooperative, and mutually beneficial international transactions among states have grown exponentially. This growth in peace has come in areas where intense international competition once prevailed, where competition for scarce, valuable resources has been and still is keen, and where armed conflict was once a normal and virtually unavoidable means of settling questions.

The most obvious example of this growth in peace, one that continues at an accelerated rate today, concerns trade. Interstate commerce was until relatively recently (roughly the late eighteenth century or so) mainly a zero-sum game, a continuation or extension of war by other means. Its goal in international politics was to beggar one's neighbors—to invade their markets while protecting one's own, acquire their gold and silver for one's own goods, ruin their industries to gain monopoly positions for one's own, acquire colonies for similar purposes, and so on. Overseas trade was especially ruthless, in practice almost indistinguishable from regular war. Portuguese, English, Dutch, and French trading companies fought wars on land and sea in the Indian Ocean and South Seas from the sixteenth century through the eighteenth century while their governments were nominally at peace. Spanish, Dutch, and English trading practices in the Caribbean represented so inextricable a combination of commerce, piracy, and outright war that one can hardly tell which was which. Trade was of course a main cause and motive for interstate wars. For example, between 1652 and 1672 three Anglo-Dutch wars were fought not over religion, territory, national rivalry, ethnic hatred, prestige, honor, security, or other common motives but solely for trade.

International trade is still highly competitive and more important than ever in international politics. Yet today unimagined volumes of international trade proceed almost routinely in peace, regulated by treaties negotiated among states (often large numbers of states simultaneously) rather than imposed by force. No developed country any longer thinks of going to war to seize an enemy's markets or colonies, destroy its merchant fleet, or force it into trade concessions; interstate commerce is widely seen as a win-win rather than a win-lose proposition. This has happened not because commerce has been taken out of international politics but because commerce has been taken out of war and into the realm of peace through international politics. The same trend to peace is apparent in many aspects of international life—foreign travel, communications of all kinds, and the dissemination of ideas, information, technology, and culture.

The obvious reply to this line of argument—that even if war and the danger of war persist, peace has clearly grown exponentially and represents a phenomenon that a purely power-political, conflictual view of international politics cannot adequately explain—would be that such changes and peaceful gains as these in international affairs are peripheral to the system and also temporary, conditional, and reversible. They remain at the mercy of a permanent balance of power competition, making great wars always possible. Impressive growths in "peace" have been swept away by war before—think of 1914—and another great war today would repeat the story on a far worse scale. The growth of peace in the interstices of the system and the gaps between wars therefore do not alter the history of international politics. The main story remains a ceaseless, unchanging balance of power competition and the cyclical rise and fall of great powers.

Many historians agree with this view.[2] Nonetheless, on simple empirical grounds it is an unsatisfactory way to understand the history of European international politics. The perception of unchanging power-political competition, as well as the cyclical alternation between balance of power and hegemony that it includes, represents an optical illusion, an artificial pattern imposed on the facts. The actual course of international history is one of ongoing change—uneven, zigzag change backwards and forwards, with periods of stagnation or reversal and sudden breakthrough, yet long-range, directional change all the same. For example, the fundamental causes of war have not remained the same in different regions and eras because of the structural anarchy of the state system and the balance of power but have differed in each era and region, and international politics has constantly changed to cope with them. To say that the underlying condition of international politics is structural anarchy and that this is the root cause of wars is a bit like saying that the underlying condition of all human life and activity is mortality and that this is the root cause of death. It is true in a sense, but also unhelpful, irrelevant, and essentially meaningless. Historians doing demographic history or the history of medicine know that all persons are mortal and discount the fact as irrelevant for their purposes, which are to explain why birth and death rates, life expectancy, and specific causes of death vary so greatly in various eras and regions and how the effort to conquer disease and prolong life contributes to this change. The same principle holds for international history, and similar changes in its patterns and character can be shown. A sound theory and history need to explain these; the conventional view does not.

Once again, only a detailed historical account could demonstrate this, showing how the specific problems of international politics and the main causes of wars have changed irreversibly from era to era.[3] Since this is impossible here, I must be content with the assertion that international politics has continually changed to meet new conditions and problems. The permanent, unchanging reality in international politics is change.

This leads to the proposition that history also includes problem solving and collective learning and demonstrates progress in problem solving and collective learning. Of the three propositions, this one is likely to arouse the greatest skepticism because it sounds like the kind of naive sentiments entertained in Europe before 1914, now rendered untenable by two world wars and other twentieth-century horrors. This point therefore requires more discussion, starting with an attempt to deal with the negative proposition that recurrent wars and failures have rendered the notion of cumulative learning in international politics unbelievable.

Certain qualifications need to be stated. Admittedly, the learning process has been very uneven, mixed with much wrong learning and many failures or refusals to learn. Setbacks and reversals have been commonplace; even right, sensible approaches often fail. Greed, selfishness, ignorance, evil, and crime have persisted and have got in the way. Yet once this is accepted as the normal way human beings learn in all kinds of social or collective enterprises, it is as obvious that there have been learning and progress in international politics as that there has been learning in, for example, making the capitalist system or liberal representative democracy work better in economics or civil government. It was impossible for these systems to work at all in the seventeenth century; by the late nineteenth and twentieth centuries they had become feasible in some but not all parts of the world, and they remained liable to great failures and setbacks. Even today they face huge risks. Yet most scholars would not deny that progress has been made in learning how to make a market economy or a representative democratic system work since the seventeenth century. The history of international politics tells the same basic story. Through collective learning, it improved from the sixteenth to the seventeenth century, from the seventeenth to the eighteenth, and especially from the eighteenth to the nineteenth.

The twentieth century, to be sure, looks like a great retrogression, a descent into barbarism—or at least it did until a few years ago. Yet not even the two world wars and other twentieth-century horrors negate this pattern. The notion that 1914, 1933, 1939, and 1945 together constitute some kind of year zero, forever negating the notion of progress in history, is an understandable reaction but not sound historical judgment. World War I, instead of proving that leaders had learned nothing about conducting international politics, demonstrates only that they had forgotten or rejected some earlier lessons, especially from 1815, and tried some wrong answers for new problems, which is normal. It mainly proves that the learning had been too slow, so that whole peoples and individual leaders became overwhelmed by the escalating problems of international politics in a new industrialized, modernized, nationalized, and imperialized world. The learning curve lagged behind the curve of events. The failed peace settlement after World War I proves the same thing—not that leaders and peoples had learned nothing from the war but that the pace of learning was too slow and uncoordinated. In the 1920s much was learned, and the seeds of many of the progressive developments of the post-1945 era were planted then—only to be trampled on in the Great Depression. Even World War II, for all its unspeakable horrors and crimes, does not prove progress in international politics an illusion. Historians and the public have tended to miss the significance of the fact that this was in a special sense Hitler's war, and his only.[4] Many dangerous, militarist, aggressive, imperialist governments were in power in 1939, notably those of Fascist Italy and Imperial Japan.[5] Yet even these, though opportunist and expansionist, were not out for major war. Only one government, one leader, had not learned the great lesson that another great war was too costly and dangerous to serve as a rational means for conquest. Even the German people, though they overwhelmingly supported Hitler, had learned that lesson from 1914 to 1918. That one such leader was capable of plunging Europe into war does not negate the evidence that collective learning was occurring.

All this is only a defense against the supposition that the recurrence of war disproves collective learning. There is a more powerful positive argument in the form of concrete historical evidence that international politics has over the centuries been transformed through collective learning. It can be illustrated by two examples: the Congress of Vienna and the history of alliances and associations. In 1814–15 the Congress of Vienna established the most successful and durable peace settlement of all time. It is common today to call the period since 1945 the "long peace," because since then no major wars in Europe have occurred. Yet in certain respects the expression is misleading. Europe since 1945 has constituted only one part of the world system, not usually the main part, and world international politics since 1945 has witnessed the intense arms competition of the cold war, some dangerous crises and threats of nuclear war, and much hot war and major conflict and violence in other parts of the world. In contrast, in 1815 Europe represented for practical purposes the only international system there was, and it contained all the important international players. The settlement of that year pacified and stabilized the whole system all at once and kept it peaceful and stable for decades. There were not only no wars between European states for many years but also no serious crises or threats of war, no arms races, and no dangerous ideological or economic competition in Europe and beyond. Instead, there was a surprising amount of great-power cooperation across alliances and ideological blocs to regulate change, enforce norms, and preserve peace. Even outside Europe, European colonial and commercial competition moderated and ceased to threaten the peace in Europe and, incidentally, entailed a less exploitative kind of imperialism toward native peoples than in earlier and later eras.

For a long time historians and other scholars have argued that this "long peace" occurred because the rulers of Europe were all conservative monarchs exhausted by war, fearful of revolution, territorially sated, and above all held in check by the balance of power restored at Vienna. They have thereby not explained it but explained it away. These conditions cannot account for this "long peace"; most of them have existed at other times and have characterized other peace settlements after great wars without ever producing the same effects. More important, a central element in this explanation of peace under the Vienna settlement, the restoration and operation of a balance of power, is factually incorrect. Presumably this notoriously slippery and malleable term *balance of power* means here what it usually does and should, namely, a roughly equal distribution of power among the major states that works to keep all states relatively secure against threats from or domination by any of the others. One may doubt in general that such a distribution of power ever produces general security and stability; but in any case it demonstrably did not prevail in the post-Vienna era.

Two world powers, Great Britain and Russia, dominated the system. Both were more powerful and invulnerable than any of the others by a wide margin; the other major powers, France, Austria, and Prussia, were much weaker and more threatened, while Europe's many smaller states had no significant power and gained no security from the so-called balance of power. All the smaller German states, for example, were militarily at the mercy of Austria and Prussia, partners in running the German Confederation and supported by Russia in doing so. The Italian states were in the same position vis-à-vis Austria. If balance of power politics means (as it does in theory) that one state's or alliance's power checks that of other states or groups through confrontation or blocking coalitions, then one can easily show that from 1815 to 1848 alliances and alignments did not generally work in this way. That is, they did not operate as a means of countervailing power, for purposes of deterrence, and by implicit or explicit threats. Instead, the normal way to deal with threats was the concert method—to restrain states that seemed to pose a danger by grouping them within the general European alliance and by restraining them through particular alliances with their friends. Austria, Prussia, and Russia restrained and managed each other in their so-called Holy Alliance; Britain and France normally restrained each other in their liberal entente. Only if these concert and grouping methods failed were stronger measures to be used—isolation from the general alliance, a blocking coalition, and, as a last resort, force.

In other words (the key point here), the Vienna system was a system of solidarity, not balance of power. It resulted from collective learning in how to solve acute and hitherto insoluble problems. A generation of constant war and failure taught European leaders that eighteenth-century balance of power politics led to intolerable levels of war and imperialism, above all under Napoleon, and that unless a new politics of solidarity were achieved not only would individual thrones and states be overthrown, but Europe itself as a community of independent states would not survive. They therefore abandoned their old game of high-stakes, winner-take-all poker, which under the French Revolution and Napoleon had turned into Russian roulette, and devised a new game of contract bridge. Put less metaphorically, they finally recognized the fundamental flaws and dangers of their old system of politics, reached consensus on a concrete definition of peace and a program to achieve it, devised specific remedies and answers to the problems and obstacles in its path, and implemented this program. This clearly demonstrates the reality and importance of collective learning and problem solving in international politics.

A second proof of evolution and development in international politics comes from the history of alliances and associations. If, as seen earlier, the central problem of peace lies in the clash between individual state autonomy and sovereignty and the rule of international law, and if, as hinted earlier, all attempts to meet this problem by establishing world government or a super-state international authority able to enforce international law are impractical and dangerous and would entail worse violence and more coercion and tyranny than they were supposed to prevent, then only one rational hope remains for meeting this problem lying at the heart of international politics. The hope must be that voluntary alliances and associations among states can develop, so powerful and durable that while preserving the independence of their members, they will also unite them in vital peaceful pursuits (mutual security, conflict resolution, democracy, civil rights, wider trade, freer communication, and the like). To put it another way, if ordinary balance of power competition does not reliably promote peace and can actually promote war, and

if world government and enforceable international law are not practical
or even desirable remedies, then only voluntary associations and alliances
among states and other international actors, such as international bodies
and nongovernmental organizations, can possibly do the job.

The question is whether this theoretical possibility is utopian or whether
there is concrete historical evidence that alliances and associations in international politics can be developed over time in the desired direction.
Such evidence clearly exists; even a rough thumbnail sketch of the history of alliances and associations in Europe over the last 350 years suffic-
es to show it. In the seventeenth century it was simply impossible to form
durable, reliable alliances for any purpose, no matter what the effort or
cost. Even Louis XIV's power and wealth were insufficient to keep his allies in line. In the eighteenth century it became possible to build fairly
reliable alliances but only for brief periods and for strictly power-political
purposes. Allies would normally fulfill their alliance obligations only to
the letter and only so long as loyalty to the alliance paid off in cash, territory, or other concrete goods. When an alliance failed to do this, the
sensible and normal course, if one could get away with it, was to defect
from the alliance and perhaps seek a profit on the other side. In the nineteenth century not only did alliances become considerably more reliable
and durable, but also the Vienna era, as shown earlier, brought a significant change in the main purposes and character of alliances and associations. The Vienna system proscribed alliances for conquest or territorial
aggrandizement in favor of ones for maintaining peace and the legal status quo, and these alliances served mainly to enable the alliance partners
to restrain and control each other and manage common political problems. When the Vienna system broke down in the mid-nineteenth century and later, balance of power competition returned, wrecking these
restraints and reviving the old-style alliances for military security, competitive advantage, and territorial expansion. With this return to power
politics, paradoxically, the very stability and reliability earlier gained by
nineteenth-century alliances turned from an asset into a critical threat to
the international system and a principal cause of World War I. If one had
to state in one sentence why a crisis in June–July 1914 turned into general war whereas many earlier crises had not, this would be it: this time
every major state acted on the principle that its alliances had to be maintained even at the cost of general war.

Yet this was not the sole line of development taken by alliances and
associations in the late nineteenth century and early twentieth. The era
also produced many ideas and efforts at wider international associations
for general peace and collective security, especially after World War I.

These failed, it is true, and World War II seemed to discredit and bury them along with much else. Yet according to the normal pattern of evolution in international politics—usually two steps forward and one backward, sometimes two steps backward and one forward—they left behind seeds. These have taken root and emerged since World War II in a dramatic, irreversible turn in the evolution of alliances and associations. Such alliances and associations as NATO and the European Union have been formed and have become so durable that they have lasted for decades and actually have outlived their original targets and purposes; so useful and flexible that they have united and integrated their members in purposes far transcending their original ones of defense or economic cooperation; and so attractive that their members no longer seriously consider defecting, while former enemies now beg for admission. Many more compelling examples of the recent evolution of alliances and associations could be cited. If this history does not demonstrate change and progress in international politics and the reality of collective learning and problem solving, nothing can.

This historical perspective and these insights ought to influence citizens' attitudes and outlooks regarding international politics today. They could, for example, help introduce a sense of the limits of the possible and a dose of sober expectations into current debates that often fluctuate wildly between euphoria and cynical despair. When one reads, for example, that NATO is in crisis because it cannot decide just how or when to admit the East European countries to membership, or that the European Union is in decline because monetary union has been postponed, or that both of these associations along with the United Nations have proved their cowardice and worthlessness by failing to stop the civil war in Bosnia, it would be useful to ask some questions. When in previous eras could associations like NATO and the European Union even have been conceived, much less brought into existence and maintained to the point that they now face problems born of their own success? How many crises and problems worse than these have they not already survived and solved or managed? In what previous era of European history could one have seriously called on the great powers of Europe and the world for military intervention to stop a civil war in the Balkans? Had someone proposed in 1950, or even in 1980, that a multinational force including Germans and Italians be sent to the former Yugoslavia, the suggestion would have been rightly condemned as a bad joke at best, a good way to promote a great-power confrontation and general war. War crimes trials of the perpetrators of aggressive war and genocide have been held before, following World War II; but they were made possible only by the total defeat of one side in the conflict and thus inevitably had certain aspects of victor's justice about them, especially the trials at Tokyo. Today they not only rest on a far sounder and more widely accepted juridical basis but also are being held and pushed through as a part of a diplomatic and political settlement of an ongoing conflict. When in past times would this have been possible? To counter the common dismissal of the new world order as a sham and an illusion and the claim that current world conditions are more chaotic and dangerous than ever, one need only ask, Would any sane person really want to exchange the current world order, with all its uncertainties and dangers, for that of any previous period up to 1985?

Yet the main purpose of insisting that real change, development, evolution, and progress have occurred in the history of international politics is not to counter the currently fashionable cynics and prophets of doom but to provide grounds for rational hope and action.[6] It makes a difference if one realizes that international history has never been, and is not now, simply a recurrent cycle of power-political struggle erupting at intervals into great systemic war but has always been a human activity like many others, a process of meeting change and challenges, solving and managing problems, and collectively learning how to do so better. Over history, at great cost, the world community has become more knowledgeable and better equipped to meet the challenges of peacemaking.

This hope, however, calls for unremitting effort, not relaxation. Although many of the past's supposedly insoluble problems of international politics have now been solved or are on the road to solution, many more still loom on the horizon or below it. Whether these can be met by the old means and methods or demand new ones, we cannot tell. In all likelihood new and unexpected changes and solutions will be necessary for emerging problems that almost anyone can foresee but few can define— those of the global environment, population pressures, uncontrolled urbanization, unstable governments, ethnic and religious conflict, and more.

The historical perspective urged here thus offers no guarantee that even the new and better system of today will ensure durable peace. It does, however, strongly suggest what has to be avoided—a return to the discredited power politics of the past—and what has to be continued— progress on the road that has brought us this far toward durable, relative, general world peace (important adjectives), which is the road of international politics. There are more obstacles to continuing on that road than the obvious ones: aggressive state ambitions; hunger for power; national passions; ideological, ethnic, and religious hatreds; and struggles over resources, security, status, autonomy, and so on. Utopian ideas and expectations about international politics are just as dangerous: the belief that the international system can and ought to produce goods that it cannot, the demand that it do so right now, an insistence on pursuing unrealistic goals by impossible means, and the cynical or despairing rejection of politics born of failed utopian hopes. Utopianism in international politics takes many forms and guises, both realist and idealist, spanning the political and ideological spectrum. Reactionary and conservative utopias compete with liberal and radical ones. Yet three main sources of utopianism can be distinguished, dominating notions about peace over the centuries. The first is the one mainly criticized here, the utopianism of so-called realism, of peace through power: the seductive notion that the right distribution of power, in the right hands, held and used by the right countries, balanced in the right way, will ensure peace. The second, less discussed here, is the utopianism of legalism, of peace through law: the notion that a certain structure of law, drawn up and agreed on by all the world's civilized countries, enforced and upheld by them against any and all lawbreakers, will guarantee peace. The last, in some ways most subtle, attractive, and deceptive, is the utopianism of one kind of morality and religion, peace through justice: the notion that satisfying the legitimate claims of various peoples and groups, harmonizing and guaranteeing human rights and needs, promoting procedural and distributive justice throughout the world, will ensure peace.

None of these utopian concepts of world peace has ever worked or ever can. An understanding of history is a prophylactic against them, or ought to be. They are utopian not simply because they have repeatedly been tried and have failed for structural reasons and not simply because they portray partial elements of peace as the whole or as sufficient means for the whole. What makes them utopian and unhistorical is their vision of peace as some sort of condition to be reached at some point in time and then preserved. International peace must be seen not as an end or condition but as a political process. Power will always be a major element in it, as will law and justice. But none of these and no combination or arrangement of them will constitute peace or guarantee it. Peace means the process of peacemaking and peacekeeping—controlling and limiting power and its uses, extending the influence and bounds of law, harmonizing and satisfying to the best practical degree the innumerable conflicting and overlapping rights and claims of international life. The right and only word for this process is *politics*.

Thomas Jefferson said, "Eternal vigilance is the price of liberty." That axiom is wrong or at least very incomplete. Eternal vigilance against the enemies of liberty—tyrants, unscrupulous politicians, big government, whatever—is not enough to ensure domestic liberty. A purely negative defense of liberty that concentrates solely on limiting governmental power and defending individual rights can actually undermine it by making more difficult or impossible the kind of active, free government under law needed to sustain liberty. The British political theorist Bernard Crick has corrected Jefferson: "Eternal politics is the price of liberty." The same holds for international affairs: eternal politics is the price of peace.

Notes

This essay was presented as the Twenty-seventh Annual Joe Paterson Smith Lecture at Illinois College on November 15, 1994.

1. See, for example, Hermann Weber, "Dieu, le roi et las chrétienté: Aspects de la politique du Cardinal de Richelieu," *Francia* 13 (1985): 233–45; and Karl Otmar von Aretin, *Das Reich, Friedensgarantie und europäisches Gleichgewicht, 1648–1806* (Stuttgart: Klett-Cotta, 1986).

2. A noted example is Paul M. Kennedy, *The Rise and Fall of the Great Powers* (New York: Alfred A. Knopf, 1987).

3. I have tried to show this for the eighteenth and nineteenth centuries in *The Transformation of European Politics, 1763–1848* (Oxford: Clarendon, 1994). Another work arguing for long-term, irreversible change, although from a different standpoint, is David Kaiser, *Politics and War: European Conflict from Philip II to Hitler* (Cambridge, Mass.: Harvard University Press, 1990).

4. A point emphasized by Donald Cameron Watt, *How War Came: The Immediate Origins of the Second World War, 1938–1939* (New York: Random House, 1989).

5. On Mussolini in particular, I accept the view of him as a genuine, if incompetent, imperialist, as argued by MacGregor Knox, *Mussolini Unleashed, 1939–1941* (Cambridge: Cambridge University Press, 1982); and Denis Mack Smith, *Mussolini: A Biography* (New York: Alfred A. Knopf, 1982), against the (to me) apologetic views of such scholars as Renzo De Felice, Rosario Romeo, and Ennio di Nolfo.

6. For a good analysis of the cynics and prophets of doom, at once amusing and convincing, see John Mueller, "The Catastrophe Quota—Trouble after the Cold War," *Journal of Conflict Resolution* 38, no. 3 (1994): 355–75.

7

Peacekeeping in Somalia, Cambodia, and the Former Yugoslavia

Paul F. Diehl

The emergence of a "new world order," with the collapse of the cold war and superpower rivalry, has raised expectations that U.N. peacekeeping operations can play a major role in addressing threats to international peace and security. The apparent end of the superpower stalemate in the Security Council and the emerging norm that international intervention is justified, even though it is contrary to traditional conceptions of sovereignty,[1] are powerful evidence that some aspects of international relations have been fundamentally altered. Nevertheless, the persistence of regional conflict in the Middle East, South Asia, and elsewhere suggests some elements have remained constant. Other problems of the new world order, primarily ethnic and nationalist conflict, have reemerged after being relatively dormant since World War II. These continuing challenges are particularly disturbing because they involve purely civil or internationalized civil conflict, exactly the types of challenges with which the United Nations has had so much difficulty in the past.[2]

In this essay the success of U.N. peacekeeping operations is evaluated in three of the most prominent operations of the early 1990s: the United Nations Transitional Authority in Cambodia (UNTAC), the United Nations Operation in Somalia (UNOSOM I and II), and the United Nations Protection Force (UNPROFOR) in the former Yugoslavia. These three operations are good tests of the United Nations in the new world order because they reflect different situations and involve a variety of tasks for the peacekeeping forces, including some nontraditional roles. In that sense they can be considered "second-generation multinational forces."[3] The Cambodian operation occurred following a peace agreement among all relevant parties. In contrast, deployment of U.N. peacekeeping forces in the former Yugoslavia took place during an internationalized civil war, with only periodic (and often fleeting) cease-fire arrangements. Finally,

UNOSOM faced a situation in which no host state government existed, and it may provide lessons for future U.N. intervention in "failed states."[4] The range of assigned roles also varied, with U.N. personnel in Cambodia responsible for quasi-governmental tasks and election supervision and the U.N. peacekeepers in Somalia and Bosnia focusing on humanitarian relief operations. In the light of the peacekeeping operations since the end of the cold war,[5] election supervision and humanitarian assistance are likely to constitute a disproportionate share of new U.N. peacekeeping efforts.

The history and purpose of each of the three new world order peacekeeping operations, as well as some judgments about its success, are briefly outlined. Evaluating the prospects for conflict resolution is particularly difficult, given ongoing mediation efforts and the lack of historical hindsight to evaluate any of the peace agreements. Nevertheless, each of the operations has experienced problems, each has had some achievements, and each can be evaluated at least in a preliminary fashion according to its ability to promote conflict abatement and conflict resolution.[6]

After assessing each operation, the next step is to examine such factors as neutrality, geography, third-party state behavior, and subnational actors that might help account for the relative success or failure of the mission.[7] The result not only helps us test our ideas in the context of new world order peacekeeping operations but also provides insight into recent policy successes or tragedies of the United Nations and its leading member states. We thus gain insight into the limits for U.N. peacekeeping in the post–cold war era.

United Nations Operation in Somalia

The problems in Somalia extend beyond those normally associated with a civil war. When President Siad Barre fled the country as rebel troops approached the capital of Mogadishu in January 1991, no other group or individual was powerful enough to take his place. As a result, the national government ceased to exist, and most forms of social and political order broke down. Meanwhile, the civil war between different factions raged on. Further complicating this was the widespread famine, especially in the countryside, that threatened a large portion of the Somali population. Somalia was thus beset by the twin problems of civil war and mass starvation and lacked any effective governmental structure to handle the human disaster that the population faced.

More than a year after the overthrow of Barre, the United Nations established UNOSOM I. Faction leaders had agreed to abide by a cease-fire in the capital city and to allow the distribution of humanitarian assistance. UNOSOM was supposed to supervise that cease-fire, provide protection for U.N. personnel in the capital, and escort humanitarian relief shipments in the immediate area. Only five hundred U.N. personnel were ultimately deployed for this purpose. In the summer of 1992 the prospects for peace were favorable as factional leaders signed a declaration laying the groundwork for a political solution to the civil strife. Hopes were soon dashed, however, as the scope of the humanitarian crisis became apparent. The rural areas were not being properly serviced by the United Nations and other relief agencies. Accordingly, the mandate of UNOSOM was expanded to include areas beyond the immediate outskirts of Mogadishu.

Despite a special emergency program in the early fall of 1992, UNOSOM was largely ineffective in stabilizing the situation and ensuring the delivery of relief supplies. Peacekeeping forces regularly came under attack by factional troops and bandits in the rural areas, making the distribution of food very inefficient if not impossible. Relief organizations had to resort to bribery and other techniques to ensure that some portion of the humanitarian assistance got to the populace. Even in the capital city, warehouses storing supplies were looted, and food was diverted to the black market. The lull in the fighting following the initial agreement ended. It should be noted, however, that despite repeated cease-fire violations, full-scale war did not recur after the U.N.-sponsored agreements; neither did war resume after final troop withdrawal. The first phase of UNOSOM might be judged a failure insofar as significant violence occurred during its deployment and humanitarian relief operations experienced severe problems despite the presence of U.N. peacekeepers. Of course, we must not forget that the violence lessened for a period of time and that some aid was delivered to starving people, even though the mission fell far short of its goals.

With the worsening of the situation, the United States agreed to send military troops to protect humanitarian relief shipments, and in December 1992 the U.N. Security Council authorized (in Resolution 794) states to use "all means necessary" to provide a safe environment for the relief operation. Twenty-eight thousand American troops, supplemented by those from several other countries, were deployed. The military operation was generally successful in halting the fighting and increasing the amount of humanitarian assistance that reached populations in areas distant from the capital city. Within five months the American-led operation had made enough progress to turn over the mission to the United Nations, and UNOSOM II was created. UNOSOM was given an expanded mandate that could include enforcement actions and provided for the disarming of Somali militias. Disarming them would take away much of the power of the warlords, and not surprisingly they resisted efforts to hand over their weapons. In June 1993 Pakistani peacekeepers were ambushed, and twenty-five of them were killed. Sniper attacks increased, and it was often difficult for the peacekeepers to fire back without jeopardizing the lives of innocent civilians. In response the Security Council called for an investigation into the attacks and the arrest of those responsible. Evidence indicated that General Mohammed Aideed and his followers were responsible for the attack.

U.N. troops led a number of unsuccessful raids against suspected Aideed hideouts and strongholds, although some of his associates were captured. American forces took over Aideed's Mogadishu headquarters, attacked some of his other bases, and raided suspected arms depots. There was a significant backlash from this strategy, not only from the portion of the population loyal to Aideed but also from some U.N. members. Italy, for example, objected that the hunt for Aideed had transformed the mission from a purely humanitarian one to an enforcement operation. The commander of the Italian contingent, General Bruno Lois, refused orders from the United Nations, and the Italian government refused to relieve him of his command. Tensions also rose between the secretary-general and the United States over strategy and international command of forces. This tension became acute with the death of several U.S. soldiers.

Just as the solidarity of key U.N. members was cracking and the hunt for Aideed was becoming increasingly frustrating, local opposition to the U.N. force intensified. The Somali people had initially welcomed foreign intervention. Now, at the instigation of General Aideed, many Somalis objected to U.N. and U.S. actions. Sniper attacks on peacekeepers increased, relief shipments were ambushed, and most dramatically eighteen U.S. troops were killed in a clash with Aideed supporters in October 1993, and the body of one American soldier was paraded through the streets. These incidents prompted President Clinton to send fifteen thousand more American troops as reinforcements, but this only masked the erosion of American popular and congressional support for the operation. A target date of March 31, 1994, was set for the withdrawal of the American contingent from the U.N. operation.

General Aideed made several offers to observe a cease-fire and resume negotiations if the warrant for his arrest was rescinded and his captured aides released. In November 1993 the Security Council finally abandoned efforts to capture Aideed and in a face-saving gesture requested that a special commission investigate the deaths of the peacekeepers, which had prompted the manhunt in the first place. The end of 1993 saw Aideed join the peace negotiations, and several prominent contributing countries (the United States, France, Germany, and Italy) actually withdrew or began preparations to withdraw some or all of their troops.

Early in 1994 Secretary-General Boutros Boutros-Ghali proposed a shift in strategy for UNOSOM II, away from disarming the factions and keeping order in Mogadishu back to assisting refugees and protecting humanitarian relief efforts. The United Nations also authorized the release of some aides to Aideed in the hopes of promoting reconciliation and jumpstarting the peace talks. Peace talks apparently bore fruit in March when Aideed and Ali Mahdi agreed to a cease-fire and to procedures for facilitating a transition to democratic elections and the reestablishment of a functioning government in Somalia. Optimism continued with reports that the effects of the famine had been largely eliminated through relief efforts; data on vaccinations, schools, and deaths all documented the success of the United Nations and the web of nongovernmental agencies assisting in the effort.

Although the humanitarian crisis subsided, progress on halting the fighting and achieving a diplomatic solution did not materialize. Periodic attacks on U.N. peacekeepers continued, and Ali Mahdi and Aideed could not agree on the "final" reconciliation talks that would put Somalia on the path to normalcy. The United Nations came under increasing criticism for its performance in the fall of 1994, some of it from within its own ranks. Mohammed Sahnoun, the former U.N. special representative, was sharply critical of Boutros-Ghali's actions in Somalia. Jeopardizing the United Nations' reputation further, the organization refused to release the report of its special commission that had investigated the deaths of peacekeepers almost a year earlier, fearing that it might complicate the achievement of a peace settlement. With the hopes of a peaceful resolution fading, the Security Council voted in November 1994 to terminate the whole operation, citing the inability of the force to achieve reconciliation and reestablish an indigenous government.

The last few months of UNOSOM, in late 1994 and early 1995, saw some renewed violence amid preparations for the departure of the peacekeeping force. Perhaps symbolically, forces loyal to General Aideed seized what had been U.N. headquarters in Mogadishu on February 1 after the last remaining peacekeeping contingent evacuated to the airport. Led by the United States, the withdrawal of U.N. peacekeeping forces took place throughout February amid continued fighting in surrounding areas and was completed at the beginning of March 1995.

UNOSOM had mixed success in moderating the armed conflict and safeguarding humanitarian assistance. Certainly, the mission contributed to improving the lives of many Somali citizens, especially those suffering from drought in the rural areas. Nevertheless, it made little progress in finding a resolution to the civil war. Several factors account for these problems in what was supposed to be a benchmark operation for nation-building in the post–cold war era.[8]

The successes and failures of the Somali mission are clearly tied to the situation the peacekeepers faced but also to some unfortunate choices made by the United Nations and the leading states in the peacekeeping operation. First, the geography of delivering humanitarian assistance proved to be very difficult for the peacekeepers. Working with U.N. and private relief agencies, the peacekeepers had to ensure that food and other aid were transported from the capital, Mogadishu, to outlying refugee camps and other areas of greatest need. This was extremely problematic. The small peacekeeping force was not well suited to guarding the warehouses where the supplies were kept, and the supplies were frequently stolen by armed groups and even indigenous personnel working for the United Nations. Transporting the supplies left the peacekeepers in vulnerable positions from the port throughout the trek in the countryside. It was not surprising, then, that the peacekeepers were frequently attacked or hijacked by bandits seeking food for the black market. Providing humanitarian assistance is very difficult over a broad area, and the initial deployment of a few hundred personnel in UNOSOM I was woefully inadequate to the task, even with the assistance of nongovernmental organizations.

A second difficulty was the lack of cooperation by subnational actors. Although various factions and faction leaders expressed their support for the humanitarian assistance, there were built-in incentives for various groups to disrupt the shipments. Beyond the desire to prevent food and supplies from going to enemies or those of another ethnic group, there was a powerful profit motive in stealing the supplies. Stealing the provisions not only meant more food for one's own forces but also enormous profits from selling the food on the black market. Furthermore, many of the armed groups operating in chaotic Somalia were no more than informal armed gangs not under the control of any faction or organization. Anarchy makes promises of cooperation by identifiable subnational actors ineffective in practice. A peacekeeping force is ill-equipped to establish the law and order necessary when full cooperation from all relevant actors can be ensured only by deterrence or coercion.

This brings us to the third consideration, the appropriateness of the peacekeeping option instead of the enforcement option. In some sense the UNOSOM operations reflected varying mixes of these strategies at different junctures. The initial small operation was largely carried out under traditional U.N. principles, albeit modified by the new functional role of humanitarian assistance. The U.S. military intervention was primarily an enforcement action, which cannot really be labeled a part of the U.N. operation at all. After the withdrawal of many of the U.S. troops, the operation reverted to the U.N. peacekeeping forces, although they too undertook some subsequent enforcement actions. Generally, the peacekeeping aspects of the mission were failures, and the enforcement component (with a notable exception discussed below) was more successful in delivering food and other aid.

The peacekeeping strategy seems largely inappropriate to the tasks required in humanitarian assistance. Even given reinforcements, however, a small peacekeeping force of lightly armed troops that could fire only in self-defense could not function effectively under the conditions in Somalia. The local groups and bandits were certainly not as well armed as the Bosnian Serb army, but they could effectively match or exceed the firepower of the U.N. peacekeepers, and snipers were a persistent source of danger. In contrast, U.S. marines had greater firepower and the authorization to use whatever means necessary to secure areas for food distribution. This is not to say that they did not have problems with snipers. Nevertheless, they had the training and the weaponry to meet most circumstances they faced. More important, in the early stages their show of force had a deterrent effect on the local population and therefore made the apparent costs of attacking food convoys greater than the perceived benefits. The military aspect of the food distribution was thus better handled by military forces than by peacekeeping troops.

UNOSOM II had more success than its predecessor but perhaps not as much as a pure military operation. A continuing problem was the failure of the U.N. operation to disarm the various factions (this mandate was disputed by several states that disagreed with Secretary-General Boutros-Ghali's assignment of this task). That it was not achieved not only complicated the mission but also remained an obstacle to the stability of any political settlement. In any case such a mandate is more suitable for a military force and goes well beyond the arms verification role (where peacekeepers supervise a consensual agreement by all parties) that U.N. peacekeeping forces might play.

Another problem with UNOSOM II was that it violated the canon of neutrality that has been the centerpiece of the peacekeeping strategy. Admittedly, U.N. forces did come under attack, and the faction led by General Aideed was judged to be responsible. Nevertheless, the shift in U.N. policy, supported by the major powers, to arrest Aideed and those responsible inherently removed the force from an impartial position. U.N. troops became embroiled in the local conflict as they searched for Aideed and his lieutenants. Furthermore, Aideed supporters rallied to his aid, conducting demonstrations in the capital city and clashing with U.N. personnel. The number of violent incidents, sniper attacks, and casualties (both civilian and U.N. personnel) escalated during this period. Those supporting Aideed regarded the U.N. force as a tool of the United States or at least foreign invaders; the troops were no longer the humanitarian saviors they once were, and nationalist or tribalist appeals resonated within this group.

The U.N. attempt to capture General Aideed was a miserable failure in several respects. Most obviously, the United Nations was unable to capture the factional leader, the goal of the new mandate. Second, the United Nations complicated its ability to find a political solution to the chaos. It might be credibly argued that the United Nations had few choices other than to try to punish Aideed for his actions, but this still undermined the peace process, and U.N. peacekeepers were ill-equipped to perform this task. Third, the loss of life and the injuries increased as a result of the manhunt. Finally, and perhaps most important, the operation undermined the support of U.N. initiatives by several key U.N. members, including the United States and Italy. American public opinion, in particular, became less supportive of U.S. participation in or leadership of U.N. operations after seeing the body of an American dragged through the streets by an angry mob. It was probably no coincidence that the level of violence diminished after the United Nations abandoned its policy of capturing General Aideed in favor of trying to find a negotiated solution involving even the Aideed faction.

The final difficulty of the Somalia operations was the relatively low priority given to efforts at conflict resolution. Of course, this is partially understandable because in the face of thousands of people on the brink of starvation, initial efforts had to address their suffering. Nevertheless, Somalia posed some unique problems for the United Nations in the short and long run. The absence of governmental authority meant not only that were there no viable structures to build on in a peace settlement but also that the actors with whom to conduct negotiations were less defined. Nevertheless, even if the United Nations were able to halt all the fighting in the country and provide for the basic human needs of Somali citizens, then what? Could the United Nations continue to play that role indefinitely? Should it assume such a role?[9] Does the United Nations even aspire to such a role? The United Nations has successfully convened peace conferences even at the height of fighting, but the various factions have been unable to reach agreement, and there has been criticism of U.N. mediation efforts. The consequences of failure at conflict resolution are much greater here than in such traditional peacekeeping operations as the United Nations Force in Cyprus (UNFICYP), where a tolerable stalemate has resulted. In Somalia the failure to get a peace agreement means not only that civil war could erupt again but also that the United Nations, in conjunction with private agencies, may have to provide many relief services again if there is a renewal of widespread starvation. This is an expensive and risky prospect.

The world community initially enthusiastically greeted UNOSOM I and II as blueprints for peacekeeping operations in the new world order. The operations, however, were handicapped by the inherent constraints posed by the geographic scope of their duties and incentives for subnational actors to disrupt the distribution of humanitarian aid. Moreover, the United Nations damaged its own peacekeeping effort by using offensive military actions and doing so ineffectively. The Somali experience illustrates the difficulties peacekeeping forces experience and suggests that some missions may be better performed by traditional military groupings, even though the political will of the member states may be lacking for such endeavors.

United Nations Protection Force

The origins of ethnic conflict in Yugoslavia might be traced back several hundred years, but the present troubles stem from the decisions of Croatia and Slovenia to declare their independence from the Yugoslav federation in 1991. Serbian-dominated Yugoslavia resisted these efforts, and long-standing enmities between ethnic groups were rekindled. The net effect was to plunge the area into a bloody civil war and drive many people in the region to become refugees in neighboring territories (the alternative too often was to be killed).

European states attempted to mediate the conflict by sending their own representative, Lord David Owen, but the key European powers—Germany, France, and Great Britain—could not agree on what to do. These peacemaking efforts were joined by Cyrus Vance, the special representative appointed by U.N. Secretary-General Perez de Cuellar. Some progress was made in the initial diplomatic overtures, and a cease-fire was achieved in late 1991. This cease-fire was very short-lived, however, and was only the first step in a pattern of repeated cease-fire agreements and broken promises.

Finally in early 1992 the United Nations authorized (in Resolution 743) the United Nations Protection Force (UNPROFOR). The force was initially designed to enter Croatia and set up "United Nations Protected Areas," ensuring the creation of demilitarized zones and protection of the local population. UNPROFOR's responsibilities expanded when Bosnia and Herzegovina held a referendum on independence, which was approved by an overwhelming majority (although it was boycotted by Bosnian Serbs). Fighting between Bosnian Serbs and Muslims intensified, and the United Nations turned its attention to this part of the former Yugoslavia. The peacekeeping operation's mandate was expanded to include security for the airport at Sarajevo and the delivery of humanitarian assistance to that city and the surrounding areas. U.N. peacekeepers were sent to Macedonia at the end of 1992 in response to a request by that territory's president to ensure that the war not spread to new environs.

The U.N. force, especially in Bosnia, ran into difficulties almost from the outset. "Ethnic cleansing" campaigns, disproportionately carried out by the Bosnian Serbs, led to the slaughter of civilians, whose only crime was to be of a different ethnic group. Various other human rights violations, including concentration camps, rape, and torture, became frequent. Despite numerous cease-fire declarations, the fighting was rarely halted for more than one day, and the United Nations seemed powerless to put a stop to the killing. Efforts at humanitarian relief were no more successful. Relief convoys were directed toward Muslim areas, but Serbian military commanders often refused to stop shelling or fighting around Sarajevo and other cities so that supplies could get through. U.N. food convoys frequently had to travel hundreds of miles over dangerous roads to reach locations that would have been easily accessible (a few miles away) had the disputants cooperated in the operation. Furthermore, Serbian women and children were mobilized to block roads and stop the convoys. An attempted airlift of supplies (with no guarantee of who would get the supplies) proved to be an inadequate substitute.

Things were relatively quiet in the Croatian and Macedonian portions of the operation, and Bosnia continued to occupy the center stage. Negotiations continued among various parties with an apparent breakthrough agreement, the Vance-Owen Plan, which was signed by parties to the conflict and endorsed by the Serbian government of the former Yugoslavia. It appeared the United Nations was on the brink of facilitating the end of the conflict, but the agreement legitimized territorial gains by military force, violating principles of international law long established and reiterated in various U.N. resolutions. Even though the Bosnian Serb leader signed the accord, he could not get his supporters to endorse the pact, and it collapsed. Bosnian Serbs and Croats continued the war to gain more territory and cleanse more villages, whereas the Muslims had the poor choice of continuing to fight or accept widespread losses of territory and political rights.

NATO or U.N. threats to carry out air strikes or enforcement actions to lift the sieges of Sarajevo and other areas proved to be empty. Ironically, it may have been the placement of peacekeeping troops that, in part, made some states unwilling to support the use of military force. Some European states whose nationals served as UNPROFOR peacekeepers feared that air strikes would prompt Serbian retaliation against those troops, and they therefore did not heed the American call for military action. When a bombing in a marketplace in Sarajevo stimulated more U.N. outrage, leaders of the NATO-member states did conduct a few air strikes, and the shelling stopped around Sarajevo. Similar circumstances later led to the de facto safe area around Gorazde, which theoretically had been under U.N. protection for some time. Nevertheless, the Bosnian Serb military took every advantage that it could and was coerced only at the last minute to observe U.N. edicts. Even as it withdrew from around Sarajevo, it intensified its campaigns elsewhere in Bosnia.

The United Nations' inability to keep the peace continued, but things took a turn for the worse in 1995. Several cities in Bosnia came under siege, and the U.N. policy of maintaining safe havens threatened to crumble under Serbian assaults. Most critically, Bosnian Serbs seized heavy weapons that had been under the control of U.N. peacekeeping forces, which were almost powerless to stop the seizure. As the United Nations and NATO threatened air strikes to halt the sieges, Bosnian Serb troops took U.N. peacekeepers hostage. The Bosnian Serbs threaten to harm the hostages if air strikes were launched against them, and they even placed the hostages in locations that would be the most likely targets of those strikes. The United Nations largely backed down from this confrontation, and it seemed likely the war in Bosnia would drag on indefinitely.

The rest of 1995 would see dramatic changes in the Bosnian war and UNPROFOR's mission. Croatian forces began to be successful in pushing Bosnian Serb troops out of disputed territories along the Bosnian-Croatian border, which was one of the first times in the war that the Bosnian Serbs suffered defeat and relinquished territory. One consequence of this was their greater willingness to accept a negotiated settlement to the war. In the fall the United States attempted to broker a peace agreement between the warring states and factions. With intense diplomatic pressure, the Dayton Peace Accords were signed in late November. The governments of Croatia, Bosnia (the Muslim-dominated government), and the former Yugoslavia agreed to end the war and divide

Bosnia into a Muslim Croat federation and a Serb republic, with the entities receiving, respectively, 51 percent and 49 percent of the territory. A central government would be maintained in Bosnia for foreign relations and other matters, but these two entities were granted significant autonomy. The agreement also provided for a reunified Sarajevo and contained various provisions for assisting refugees and holding democratic elections. To ensure the peace, NATO would provide sixty thousand troops for this new peacekeeping effort. These troops effectively replaced UNPROFOR, whose mission was abandoned in favor of the NATO operation. Since the agreement there has been sporadic violence, but it is less organized and at a far lower level than during the war. Significant disagreements between parties to the agreement have existed, but none as yet has undermined the accords.

Overall, there appears to be quite a contrast between U.N. and NATO peacekeeping efforts, although NATO's track record is limited. It might be argued that the trip-wire troops in Macedonia kept the war from spreading, but it is not clear how important their role really was. In Bosnia UNPROFOR was not always effective in delivering humanitarian assistance. Most successes, if we can call them that, in sustaining cease-fires and safe havens were fleeting and small in relation to the killing that occurred. NATO troops have been far more effective in maintaining the cease-fire and putting an end to the genocide and waves of refugees (except for a few instances).

Unlike previous peacekeeping operations, peacemaking efforts in the former Yugoslavia have been a high priority for the United Nations, and almost continuous efforts have been directed toward a long-term cease-fire and a lasting agreement resolving major disputes. Yet, other than the aborted Vance-Owen Plan, the United Nations has been hampered by disagreement among its leading states and, more important, by the intransigence of the disputants. The incentives for the Serbs, and in some instances the Croats, to keep fighting were great, and empty threats at retaliation have not changed this calculus. Even the Bosnian Muslims held out some hope that things could improve beyond what they could gain at the bargaining table; in their view, things could not get much worse. Successful efforts at negotiating a peace agreement came about after an intensification of fighting, not as a result of any stability provided by the presence of U.N. peacekeeping troops. NATO has thus far benefited by having the luxury of being deployed after a peace agreement. Whether the peacekeeping force will play a major role in ensuring long-term conflict resolution in Bosnia is not yet clear. The reasons for the failure of UNPROFOR in Bosnia and UNOSOM in Somalia are similar, but some features make UNPROFOR's case unique and some offer important lessons for conducting humanitarian operations in the future.

The geographic layout of Bosnia complicated the ability of peacekeepers to complete their missions. The peacekeepers were responsible for supervising large cities and transporting humanitarian assistance across great distances. Safe havens could not be guaranteed when military units took positions in the hillsides surrounding Sarajevo and repeatedly shelled targets there. At various junctures this also complicated the ability of assigning responsibility for those attacks; the safe havens were thus not effective in separating the combatants or in aiding with assigning blame once violations were detected. Transporting humanitarian aid through war zones put the peacekeepers at constant risk. Furthermore, U.N. food convoys could be easily stopped by blocking or seizing key roads leading into relief areas. Finally, the weather in the country complicated efforts. Heavy snow sometimes made transportation difficult, and dense cloud cover hampered the ability of NATO planes to monitor (or launch air strikes against) Serbian military positions. It is thus not surprising that U.N. officials repeatedly asked their membership for an increase in troops, requests that went largely unheeded. In contrast, the size of the NATO peacekeeping operation was more than twice that of UNPROFOR, even though the NATO forces did not have to operate in war conditions.

UNPROFOR was deployed without first having a stable cease-fire. The problems that this occasioned were more severe than those in Somalia. The weaponry in Somalia was not very sophisticated; a typical group was armed with a pickup truck retrofitted with a machine gun. In Bosnia the Serbs had access to the most sophisticated weaponry of the former Yugoslavia. This dramatically increased the danger for U.N. troops delivering humanitarian assistance. It also meant the task of monitoring the actions of the various disputants was very complex. Even after the Serbs agreed to remove weaponry from around Sarajevo and Gorazde, the U.N. forces discovered caches of arms hidden in the exclusion zones. The destructive capability of the weaponry also made every failed cease-fire very costly. Once again lightly armed peacekeepers were wholly inappropriate for deployment during war, especially one as ferocious and destructive as this one. In contrast, NATO peacekeepers have adequate numbers and are equipped and organized more like a traditional military force than a typical peacekeeping one. More important, the NATO force benefits from being deployed after a peace agreement. NATO peacekeepers are thus better suited to their mission and operate in a more hospitable environment than did UNPROFOR.

UNPROFOR also suffered from the incentive structure that led disputants to disrupt humanitarian shipments. The war in Bosnia and to a lesser
extent in Croatia involved explicit strategies by one ethnic group to kill
or drive out members of another ethnic group. Placing a blockade around
a city and shelling it were among the tactics employed. For those pursuing such actions, it would be incongruous to allow relief agencies access
to those areas so that food and medical supplies could be provided to the
besieged population. Military commanders also feared that arms might
be smuggled in with the aid. In their minds the aid only helped prolong
their enemies' resistance. When ethnic cleansing campaigns are legitimized by a given ethnic group, moral appeals for providing food and
medical care to the enemy are unlikely to have much impact. The distribution of humanitarian aid can be problematic during any civil war, but
it becomes almost impossible when strong incentives exist for local actors to prevent or disrupt such programs.

Beyond some common problems with the UNOSOM operation,
UNPROFOR suffered from a series of other difficulties. Perhaps none was
more important than the actions of third-party states and subnational
actors. The former Yugoslavia or Serbia assisted its ethnic comrades in
Bosnia by supplying troops and arms, and that state moved to undermine
U.N. efforts at every juncture until the Vance-Owen accord. Serbia endorsed that agreement and announced after its failure that it would no
longer support the Bosnian Serbs in their efforts to carry on the war.
Nonetheless, U.N. sanctions against the rump Yugoslavia continued, evidence that Serbia persisted in arming Serbian elements in Bosnia. Although Serbia bears some responsibility for undermining UNPROFOR, it
has been critical in facilitating the Dayton Peace Accords and their implementation. Serbian pressure persuaded Bosnian Serb leaders to initial
the accords, and Serbia has been a continuing source of pressure on the
Serbs to cooperate with the implementation of their provisions.

Russia was also not always fully supportive of U.N. actions designed to
put pressure on the Serbs. For domestic political reasons Russia favored
supporting its fellow Slavs, the Serbs. The Russians were at times reluctant
to support U.N. efforts to bomb Serbian targets or take any action that would
compromise the Serbs' position. This not only undermined U.N. efforts but
also lessened the credibility of U.N. threats because the Bosnian Serbs rightly
felt that Russia would protect them from the most severe punishments of
the international community (although Russia did support a NATO ultima-
tum on lifting the siege of Gorazde). Some political groups in Russia even
called for lifting sanctions against Serbia, a call that was at odds with the
position of all other leading states in the global organization. Serbian ac-

tion was clearly deleterious to the U.N. peacekeeping force, and the Russian actions may have done some damage as well. The absence of full Russian cooperation probably harmed the mission. Perhaps more Russian pressure on the Serbs would have induced a lessening of the atrocities or facilitated a peace agreement earlier. Croatia also complicated the U.N. mission. Croatians were guilty, although perhaps to a lesser extent, of many of the same war crimes attributed to the Serbs. They were involved in a significant portion of the fighting, alternately supporting Serb and Muslim positions as it suited their own interests.

Beyond third-party states, subnational actors undermined UNPROFOR efforts. The major parties in Bosnia worked against the efforts of the peacekeeping force, and even the Muslims, who bore most of the brunt of the war, were occasionally uncooperative. What may be less apparent is the behavior of the Bosnian Serb military, which repeatedly continued the war, despite cease-fire agreements or promises made by the Bosnian Serb political leadership. As an effectively autonomous actor, the Bosnian Serb military appears to have defied the United Nations at almost every step and backed down only when the consequences of further actions were immediate, severe, and highly likely. U.N. threats rarely met this standard.

Unlike many peacekeeping missions, UNPROFOR had command and control problems that seriously hindered its mission. Troops in the operation remained under national control, as did most operations. Adding to this layer of command was NATO, to which some troop-contributing states belonged. Beyond this, the United States, within and outside NATO, was a key actor. Finally, the special representative of the U.N. secretary-general was given a decision-making role beyond what has been accorded U.N. personnel in the past. Before the United Nations took action, even such simple actions as returning fire had to be approved by the U.N. representative as well as some of the major states or NATO. These actors did not always agree, and the process inherently led to delay when quick, decisive action was required. The United States and some other NATO members were especially critical of the special representative's reluctance to authorize military actions even in the face of bold violations of agreements by Serbian forces. The claim that the U.N. operation in Bosnia was one in which "everyone is in charge and therefore no one is in charge" has some validity. Although it had to integrate some East European forces, the central command for the current NATO operation has been much more efficient, not surprising given the organization and training of NATO, which is quite unlike the ad hoc character of most U.N. peacekeeping missions.

The attempts to combine peacekeeping and enforcement actions in Bosnia illustrate the difficulty, if not the incompatibility, of the two options. By choosing to send peacekeeping troops, the United Nations limited its options for enforcement actions; contributing states were reluctant to support coercive actions because they feared retaliation against those troops. The neutrality of the U.N. personnel was also called into question when the organization was imposing harsh sanctions on Serbia and setting up a war crimes tribunal, threatening air strikes against Serbian military positions, and delivering food and other supplies to Bosnian Muslims. It was unreasonable to expect that U.N. peacekeeping personnel would be perceived as impartial in this context. Combining elements of enforcement and peacekeeping here (admittedly inadequate efforts on both counts) produced no better an outcome than in Somalia.

The peacemaking efforts of the United Nations were ambitious in Bosnia, but general failure here may not be attributable to the organization, although its nonneutral stance and the behavior of some of its leading members did not help. Finding a way to resolve the crisis was difficult because, as noted earlier, both sides had incentives to keep fighting (at least the Serbs did until a successful Croatian offensive), and it was not clear that agreements made by political leaders would hold on the battlefield.

Once again, U.N. diplomatic efforts cannot engender peace when the parties involved do not want it or when their demands are fundamentally irreconcilable. As in the Middle East, other actors may be more effective than the United Nations in facilitating conflict resolution; the breakthrough in Bosnia was a U.S. initiative, with only minimal U.N. involvement.

The UNPROFOR operation was a case of a peacekeeping force being placed in the nearly impossible situation of a brutal civil war and expected to perform its mission without the cooperation of the warring parties, subnational actors, and key third-party states. It is perhaps not surprising that the mission encountered so much difficulty. Whatever benefits that were gained from the operation were perhaps negated by the lost opportunities and problems created by its presence. The NATO-based peacekeeping operation has thus far been far more successful, owing to its large size, adequate military capability, and, most important, its deployment following a settlement of many of the major disputes between the warring sides.

United Nations Transitional Authority in Cambodia

A legacy of the Vietnam War was that Cambodia would suffer through years of civil conflict in which, according to some estimates, one-quarter of the population was killed. In 1991 representatives of the major actors in the conflict—the Vietnamese-backed government, Prince Norodom Sihanouk and his supporters, and the Khmer Rouge (rulers of Cambodia before their overthrow in a Vietnamese invasion)—signed a peace agreement that provided for an end to the civil war and set up the mechanisms for peaceful democratic transition in the country. Facilitated by U.N.-sponsored negotiations, the agreement represented one in a series of diplomatic triumphs (including the Soviet troop withdrawal from Afghanistan and the 1988 Nobel Peace Prize) for the organization.

The United Nations had an extremely ambitious mandate, of which UNTAC was a central part.[10] The United Nations was charged with supervising the cease-fire, disarming the various factions, repatriating refugees, maintaining law and order, conducting some governmental functions, and, most significant, organizing, conducting, and monitoring democratic elections. UNTAC was not alone in this endeavor. The operation included administrative components that were to construct an electoral system, register voters, and conduct the election. A civilian police component also helped maintain law and order, supervise local police, and investigate human rights violations. In all, UNTAC was supplemented by seven thousand U.N. personnel performing tasks essential to the election and the mandate.

Prior to the actual time of the election, the prognosis for a successful election was probably not good. As Brian Urquhart notes, the United Nations had had two notable failures in fulfilling its mandate.[11] It did not do a very good job in performing some of the governmental functions, and during the election campaign violence and harassment of some opposition parties occurred. More important, UNTAC was unable to disarm 70 percent of the disputants' military forces. The threat of violence was significant, and the Khmer Rouge in particular threatened to disrupt the election, especially in the areas it controlled. A series of incidents also indicated that U.N. forces were not operating efficiently. U.N. personnel came under attack at different points, and the Khmer Rouge accused the peacekeepers of supporting the interests of the Vietnamese-backed party of the extant government and failing to ensure that all Vietnamese troops were withdrawn from the country.

The Khmer Rouge became increasingly hostile toward the U.N. operation. Beyond its refusal to disarm and turn over administrative control to the United Nations, the Khmer Rouge threatened at several points to pull out of the peace process and renew its armed struggle. Just before the election this looked likely, and it was unclear what would happen when the voting took place. To the surprise of many, the response of the

Cambodian people was overwhelming. Approximately 90 percent of eligible voters ended up voting, including those in areas of Khmer Rouge support. That faction perhaps decided that it could not disrupt a process with such widespread popular support, and it decided not to carry through with its threats. The election was judged to be free and fair and a resounding success. A Cambodian government of unity was then formed based on the election results.

Although the mandate was not fully achieved and significant problems with the U.N. operation arose, the election went smoothly, with few allegations of irregularities. In that sense the UNTAC operation could be considered a success, just as the United Nations Transition Assistance Group (UNTAG) was before it in performing election supervision.

Of the three operations UNTAC might be considered the most successful, partly because peacekeeping forces were deployed following a peace agreement between the warring parties. This action had a number of advantages. First, it set out specific tasks for the peacekeeping force to complete and ensured broad, although not universal, acceptance by the parties involved. There was therefore less chance that one of the disputants would object to the U.N. presence, especially because the disputants signed the accord authorizing the operation. Second, the peacekeeping force had legitimacy in conducting operations in the country and would not necessarily favor the interests of the host government, something other peacekeeping operations in civil disputes might be prone to do. Third, the agreement provided for a set timetable and the endpoint for the operation, preventing UNTAC from lingering in Cambodia for years, as other peacekeeping operations have done in Lebanon and Cyprus.

Another reason for the success of the operation was the unprecedented support given the agreement by the major powers. The United States, Russia, and China strongly backed the agreement and pressured their allies in Cambodia to make peace and abide by the provisions of the pact. Had the major powers taken the opposite position, it is unlikely a peace agreement would even have been signed. Even given agreement, actions against the election process by those states might have led one of the flashpoints during the operation to escalate and sabotage the election. It was also important that Vietnam did not take any actions that directly threatened the election. Its behavior is in marked contrast to the actions of the former Yugoslavia in the UNPROFOR operation and those of Belgium in U.N. operations in the Congo.

Although UNTAC is generally regarded a success, it was not without problems. As in the other operations involving civil disputes, geography hampered UNTAC's ability to perform its monitoring and disarmament duties. The operation and its personnel were too often confined to the capital city of Phnom Penh. Sections of the countryside remained under the control of the Khmer Rouge, which was less than cooperative with the peacekeeping force. The rural character of Cambodia and the lack of governmental control limited the United Nations' ability to operate in all areas, even with the largest U.N. peacekeeping force in history and a sizable contingent of administrative personnel.

The most complicating factor for UNTAC was the opposition of the Khmer Rouge. Despite its assent to the peace agreement, the guerrilla group continued its opposition. The electoral prospects for the Khmer Rouge were not promising, and its numbers were small. Its influence in the political process had been a function of its military prowess and the territory it controlled. The peace agreement would disarm it and remove much of its power. The election would probably lead to the end of its domination of certain areas and a relatively minor role in a new government. It is significant, however, that the strong support of the Cambodian people, even in Khmer Rouge areas, led the organization to back down on its threats to disrupt the election, and it ended up acquiescing in the process at the most critical time, during the actual voting. This illustrates the point that opposition by subnational groups can be harmful but not necessarily fatal to a peacekeeping operation and must be weighed against the group's level of popular support and its capacity for disruption.

Technically, peacemaking was not an issue for UNTAC because the operation followed a peace agreement instead of preceding it. Nevertheless, despite the free and fair election and the establishment of a unified Cambodian government, the Khmer Rouge started military activity again in early 1994, and the peace agreement and the election have not fully solved the internal conflict of that state. Thus, even under the best of circumstances, the United Nations and its peacekeeping operations may not be able to facilitate or impose peace in the long run.

Conclusion

Three recent peacekeeping operations (UNOSOM, UNPROFOR, and UNTAC) share the common characteristic of facing civil conflict, which is the most difficult context in which the United Nations operates. Furthermore, many of the new functional roles (e.g., humanitarian assistance and election supervision) of peacekeeping operations are evident in these recent cases. So too are the dangers about nationalistic or ethnic conflicts, particularly in Bosnia.

The early returns from the post–cold war peacekeeping operations are not strongly favorable and clearly do not meet the raised expectations of the global community. Many positive trends, including cooperation among the major powers on many security issues and a wave of democratization, are sweeping certain regions of the world. Yet at the same time the new challenges faced by the United Nations include a broader geographic range of conflicts (with the end of superpower spheres of influence), and many long-standing rivalries have been rekindled. Only UNTAC can be considered a success among the three cases here, and this might be primarily because of its deployment following a peace agreement and its assumption of a new role (election supervision) most conducive to the peacekeeping strategy. The other two operations performed a task (humanitarian assistance) that may be inappropriate for lightly armed peacekeepers, and they did so under the most difficult conditions of an ongoing war. Furthermore, geographic considerations and the behavior of third parties caused problems for all the operations.

Although these three cases may not be indicative of peacekeeping in the twenty-first century, they do suggest that peacekeeping operations will not necessarily be more effective in the post–cold war era than they were in the previous forty-five years, even though the number and scope of those operations may greatly increase (subject, of course, to looming financial constraints). Peacekeeping operations are also not a suitable substitute for fully developed enforcement operations. They may be politically substitutable, given the reluctance of U.N. members to authorize enforcement actions, but practically they cannot achieve the same goals. The peacekeeping strategy will still be a viable one in many contexts, but the early failures of the post–cold war era suggest that the United Nations must construct new mechanisms to meet its challenges, much as the peacekeeping strategy was born in response to new challenges and realities in the face of superpower rivalry.

Notes

1. Michael Barnett, "The New U.N. Politics of Peace: From Juridical Sovereignty to Empirical Sovereignty," *Global Governance* 1, no. 1 (1995): 79–97.

2. For a discussion of peacekeeping and civil conflicts, see Thomas Weiss, "The United Nations and Civil Wars," *Washington Quarterly* 17, no. 4 (1994): 139–59; and Alan James, "Internal Peacekeeping," *Peacekeeping and the Challenge of Conflict Resolution,* ed. David Charters (New Brunswick, Nova Scotia: Centre for Conflict Studies, 1994), 3–24.

3. John Mackinlay and Jarat Chopra, "Second Generations Multinational Operations," *Washington Quarterly* 15, no. 3 (1992): 113–34.

4. Gerald Helman and Steven Ratner, "Saving Failed States," *Foreign Policy*, no. 89 (1992–93): 3–20.

5. United Nations, *United Nations Peace-Keeping* (New York: United Nations, 1993).

6. For details on this evaluation scheme, see Paul F. Diehl, *International Peacekeeping* (Baltimore: Johns Hopkins University Press, 1993). For a critique of these criteria, see Robert Johansen, "U.N. Peacekeeping: How Should We Measure Success?" *Mershon International Studies Review* 38, no. 2 (1994): 307–10.

7. Diehl, *International Peacekeeping*.

8. For a fuller analysis of the UNOSOM operations, see Samuel Makinda, *Seeking Peace from Chaos: Humanitarian Intervention in Somalia* (Boulder, Colo.: Lynne Rienner, 1993); Mohammed Sahnoun, *Somalia: The Missed Opportunities* (Washington, D.C.: United States Institute of Peace, 1994); and Paul F. Diehl, "With the Best of Intentions: Lessons from UNOSOM I and II," *Studies in Conflict and Terrorism* 19, no. 2 (1996): 153–77.

9. For arguments that the United Nations should assume such roles, see Helman and Ratner, "Saving Failed States."

10. For details, see Janet Heininger, *Peacekeeping in Transition: The United Nations in Cambodia* (New York: Twentieth Century Fund, 1994).

11. Brian Urquhart, "Who Can Police the World?" *New York Review*, May 12, 1994, 29–33.

8

Conflict Resolution and International Intervention in El Salvador and Cambodia

Gerardo L. Munck and Chetan Kumar

As the cold war has receded, it has left behind a world system characterized by two divergent trends. On the one hand, as the two superpowers have withdrawn their security umbrellas, ethnic and territorial conflicts have sprouted around the globe. On the other hand, as former rival blocs now create alliances, international mechanisms for the peaceful resolution of contentious issues have proliferated. A central concern of our times, then, is whether, and under what circumstances, these new mechanisms will be successful in dealing with the disorderly aspects of the new world "order."

This essay contributes to this ongoing debate by focusing on the United Nations and examining, through a detailed comparison of recent developments in El Salvador and Cambodia, the conditions for successful U.N. intervention in conflict resolution. In these two cases U.N. intervention has played an important role in attempting to resolve long-standing civil conflict, specifically through its instrumental role in brokering both countries' peace accords. After the breakthroughs that allowed for the signing of these accords, however, these two countries have fared quite differently in their efforts to move beyond negotiations to the actual implementation of the accords. While steady progress has been made in El Salvador following the signing of the peace accords, the Cambodian peace process has faced considerably greater obstacles.

To account for the divergent developments in El Salvador and Cambodia, this essay stresses four factors: the number, inclusiveness, and cohesion of the parties to the peace accords; the number and interests of external parties; the transitional institutional framework; and the peace signatories' perceptions of their electoral chances. The core of the analysis thus seeks to show how this combination of domestic and external factors provides an explanation of the two cases. By studying the interaction among these four factors, this essay also advances a systematic assessment of the role of international intervention and a sober view of the its possibilities and limits. An argument concerning the precise conditions under which future U.N. intervention is likely to be successful in resolving conflicts is also provided.

Rationale for the Comparison

Before presenting our analysis, we should explain the rationale for comparing the two cases. Methodologically, it is valuable to compare two cases having different outcomes but many similarities in the sequence of events and the form of international intervention that led to the signing of peace accords. The chronological sequence of events is remarkably similar. Civil war started in early 1979 in Cambodia and in early 1981 in El Salvador, and in both cases it continued throughout the 1980s until peace accords were signed in October 1991 in Cambodia and in January 1992 in El Salvador.[1] The timing of the move toward peace was not coincidental. Indeed, similar forces appeared to be at work.

Both El Salvador and Cambodia are cases of civil conflicts that, because of their international security ramifications, elicited more than passing interest from both regional and global actors during the 1980s. With the retrenchment of both the United States and the former Soviet Union after their cold war engagements, several of the conflicting parties in Cambodia and El Salvador could no longer serve as the superpowers' proxies.[2] The easing of cold war tensions was thus a crucial factor improving the conditions for peace inside both countries. Moreover, changes in the U.S. foreign policy establishment, associated with the cooling of cold war tensions, allowed the United States to support a greater U.N. role in resolving civil conflicts. In sum, these two cases are quite representative of both the challenges and opportunities for international intervention brought about by the end of the cold war.[3]

With the superpowers' increasing willingness to allow the United Nations greater initiative, that body assumed an important role in brokering peace accords in El Salvador and Cambodia. It did so effectively, primarily by containing the mutual distrust of the parties that had long sought to defeat each other militarily and by presenting proposals that the warring parties could accept. Because of its image as an impartial body, the United Nations facilitated cooperative relations among the parties to a stalemated conflict, lowering the risks of entering and remaining in the peace process. The United Nations thus played a crucial role in the October 1991 signing of the so-called Paris Peace Accords, which represented the culmination of negotiations aimed at settling the Cambodian conflict, and in the January 1992 signing of the Final Agreement on Peace, which represented a similar landmark for El Salvador.[4]

The Cambodian accords had some fairly unusual aspects because they attempted something never before tried: to revive a failed state by placing the United Nations in charge of the administration of a country. Specifically, the U.N. operation in Cambodia, formally known as the United Nations Transitional Authority in Cambodia (UNTAC), set up the Supreme National Council (SNC), which would administer Cambodia until new authorities were put in place through free and fair elections conducted directly by the United Nations. In addition to taking over the day-to-day functions of administration, UNTAC would oversee the complete withdrawal of foreign troops, as well as supervise a cease-fire and the demobilization and cantonment of the various warring factions. After organizing elections for the Constituent Assembly, set for May 1993, UNTAC would remain in charge of the country during a three-month constitution-drafting period. When the Constituent Assembly finished drafting a new constitution, it would transform itself into the Legislative Assembly, which would appoint a new government. Only at that point would the U.N. mission be complete.[5]

According to the Salvadoran peace accord a formal cease-fire was to come into effect immediately, and thereafter U.N. observers would conduct an arms inventory leading up to the destruction of all the insurgents' weapons in the final two weeks of October. By October 31, 1992, the demobilization of the FMLN (Farabundo Martí Front for National Liberation) guerrilla force and its transformation into a legal political body was to be completed. The army, which had increased from 16,000 to 56,000 during the 1980s, would be reduced by half over a period of two years, while several of its units would simply be dissolved. In other steps envisioned by the peace plan, officers guilty of human rights abuses would be purged; a new national civil police, which former guerrillas were eligible to join, would be created; and land occupied by peasants in rebel-held areas would remain in their hands. Because elections had been held throughout the 1980s, the existing electoral schedule was maintained. The former military adversaries would first meet in an electoral contest in March 1994.[6]

As significant as these parallel developments may be, whereby both Cambodia and El Salvador moved from civil war to the signing of peace accords, the divergence between the two cases in implementing the peace accords is very striking. In El Salvador progress toward completing the steps mandated by the accords was relatively smooth and steady throughout 1992. Not surprisingly, certain resistances, disputes, and delays emerged along the way. From the outset it was apparent that the schedule for various reforms was unrealistic and that certain delays were inevitable. In addition recriminations were regularly exchanged over a series of issues. But progress continued to be made on key parts of the accords, especially for demobilization of the FMLN. The biggest crisis came between late October and late November 1992 over the issue of purges in the army. This issue was significant because it served as a reminder of the weakness of the civilian government and the security risks for the FMLN in turning in its weapons. If the transition from a military to a political approach to conflict was fraught with risks and tension, the irreversibility of the process was never seriously questioned, and despite continued action by death squads no violations of the cease-fire were registered. Fortunately, outside forces committed to the peace process and able to have a positive effect stepped in during the most critical moments. The United Nations' role in rescheduling the peace plan and extending the deadline for the FMLN's full demobilization from the end of October to mid-December and U.S. pressure on the Salvadoran army were crucial in averting the crisis over the military purges. Thereafter things moved swiftly toward the formal end of the war, and the so-called period of armed peace, begun with the February cease-fire, was brought to a close in mid-December. Throughout 1992, then, the touchiest military aspects of the peace plan were completed, and the peace process continued to advance with clear momentum. Finally in April and May 1994 elections were held, and though the right-wing ARENA (National Republican Alliance) party retained power, the elections also confirmed the FMLN as a legitimate political actor. The FMLN had transformed itself into the second strongest political force in the country. When a new government was installed on June 1, a new phase in El Salvador history began.[7]

This positive assessment of progress in El Salvador does not mean to brush aside its more problematic aspects. There were some clear violations of the peace accord during 1992. On the part of the government, President Alfredo Cristiani delayed the purge of those military officers identified as having violated human rights beyond what he had agreed to, in effect violating the peace accords. On the part of the guerrillas, evidence emerged that they had stockpiled weapons, also in violation of the accords. A series of problems persisted well into 1994. The United Nations' secretary-general, Boutros Boutros-Ghali, informed the U.N. Security Council in May 1994 that aspects of the peace accords pertaining to public security, land reform, the recommendations of the U.N.-appointed Truth Commission, and programs to reinstate former combatants in civilian life remained to be implemented fully. The peace process therefore continued, and the U.N. mission to El Salvador (ONUSAL) was extended for six months beyond its original June 1 expiration. What is most important, however, was the attitude of key actors. As with the well-documented irregularities during the electoral process in 1994, a key sign of the progress toward peace was that the leftist parties did not seek to make too much out of these problems, fearing that they would overshadow a broader gain: they had finally become an accepted actor in El Salvador's electoral process, and the new government was seen as legitimate by all sectors of Salvadoran society.

In contrast to the pattern in El Salvador, the peace process in Cambodia ran into serious difficulties by mid-1992. The most serious problem was that the Khmer Rouge first refused to accept the peace accords' demobilization schedule and subsequently decided to boycott the U.N.-sponsored elections planned for May 1993. Added to this was the systematic violence carried out by the pro-Vietnamese forces of the old regime led by Hun Sen against the main opposition party led by Prince Norodom Ranariddh, Prince Norodom Sihanouk's son. On the positive side, despite Khmer Rouge attempts to intimidate U.N. observers, the United Nations did manage to hold a largely successful election, with a large popular turnout, in May 1993. In this sense the Cambodian operation was partially successful. The election, however, led to the formation of a government in a circuitous manner. When faced with a victory by the opposition party of Prince Ranariddh, the Hun Sen faction refused to accept the election results and threatened to partition the country. Only Prince Sihanouk's great personal standing prevented disaster; he was able to persuade both factions to accept equal membership in a coalition government that he led. In formal terms, then, the very manner in which the government was formed effectively negated the U.N.-sponsored election results. Even more important, a year after the election and the establishment of a new government, the civil war continued, as an intransigent Khmer Rouge persisted in its attacks on the national coalition government headed by Prince Sihanouk. In Cambodia, then, the process of implementing the accords ran into various difficulties that, to the extent they were resolved, were managed outside and not within the guidelines of the U.N.-sponsored accords. Even more damaging, the peace process in Cambodia failed to produce any genuine reconciliation, and the conflict between the Khmer Rouge and the government established through the U.N.-sponsored election continued to be a militarized one. The civil war in effect continued.[8]

Despite initial government successes in its military campaign against the

Khmer Rouge, the Khmer Rouge rebounded and captured the major regional center of Pailin. In the face of this important military comeback, the Cambodian government was forced to turn to the West in search of aid. An associated problem was that the overall ineptitude of the government and the infighting between the royalist FUNCINPEC (United National Front for an Independent, Neutral, Peaceful, and Cooperative Cambodia) party and its Hun Sen partners paralyzed the new government. Corruption and administrative chaos were endemic among both the bureaucrats and the military, and little was left of the United Nations' efforts to create some accountability for human rights abuses, particularly by the army and the security forces. This lack of accountability was primarily responsible for generating grass-roots support for the Khmer Rouge in some rural areas.[9]

This contrasting level of success in the implementation of El Salvador's and Cambodia's peace accords calls for an explanation. The aim of this essay is to explain why El Salvador and Cambodia have fared quite differently as they moved beyond negotiations to the actual implementation of their peace accords. In other words, this essay tackles two central questions: What accounts for the steady progress of the peace process in El Salvador in contrast to the very limited success in Cambodia? What lessons can be drawn from them about the conditions for international intervention in civil conflicts?[10]

Implementation of the Peace Accords

The divergent paths of El Salvador and Cambodia can be explained primarily by four factors that a comparative analysis of these countries points to as key in affecting the continued cooperation of the parties to the peace accords, which is critical in implementing a peace accord.[11] Each of these factors contributes to the successful implementation of a peace accord by strengthening or weakening the continued perception by the parties to the accord that the peace process will lead to a win-win outcome, an outcome in which both parties are winners.[12]

A first factor is the number, inclusiveness, and cohesion of the parties to the peace accords. This factor is central inasmuch as disputes are more easily coordinated between two broadly inclusive or representative parties that can exercise firm control over their followers. In other words, the smaller the number of parties and the greater their inclusiveness and cohesion, the more likely the perception of a win-win outcome will be maintained.[13]

Second, the number and interests of external parties affect the prospects of successful implementation inasmuch as the greater the number of external parties, the harder it will be to maintain the balance that allows for the signing of the peace accords.[14] In addition to the coordination problems produced by more external actors, changes in the interests of external actors can alter the initial conditions that allowed for the signing of the accords, strengthening the perception of one of the signatories that a win-lose outcome in its favor is possible. This type of perception is bound to destabilize the peace process.

Third, the transitional institutional framework provided by the peace accords affects the role of the intervening party as well as that of the parties to the conflict. When the envisioned international intervention is fairly limited and linked with very pointed objectives, there is greater likelihood that the intervening party will be seen as impartial, a prerequisite for effective international intervention. In addition, the implementation of a peace accord is more likely to be successful when the institutional mechanisms provide for regular contact between the signatories. This allows for containing and gradually overcoming the natural distrust among parties, reinforcing the guarantees provided by international intervention that no party will be worse off. Both points are crucial inasmuch as they determine the ability to make midcourse corrections, which can help resolve unforeseeable problems in a way that prevents the derailing of the entire peace process.

Finally, the peace signatories' perceptions of their electoral chances affect the prospects of successful implementation of a signed accord because the security of the major actors, in terms of not feeling condemned to the position of a permanent outsider in electoral politics, reduces the volatility of the situation and increases the likelihood of institutionalizing conflict.[15] Of course, ultimately the success of international intervention for peaceful conflict resolution can be seen in the institutionalization of conflict through the consolidation of a democratic system. Success, in other words, removes the initial need for international intervention.

In addition to these four factors some secondary factors have traditionally affected the success of conflict resolution operations by the United Nations and other international organizations. These include the geographic terrain on which the peacekeeping forces operate, the adequate resolution of logistical problems, and coordination among the various parties contributing to the operation.[16] The subsequent analysis focuses on the four primary factors, for the sake of theoretical parsimony and because of their direct link to the conflicting parties' inclination to continue cooperating.

Number, Inclusiveness, and Cohesion of the Parties

One of the first clear contrasts between El Salvador and Cambodia is the number, inclusiveness, and cohesion of the parties to the accords. In El Salvador the peace process revolved around an essentially dyadic dispute. The two parties to the conflict were broadly inclusive, representing the most relevant interests in the country. The various rebel factions that made war against the government had entered the negotiation process under one banner, the FMLN, and subsequently maintained this common identity.[17] The two signatories also retained a high degree of cohesiveness and ability to control their membership. Although the government complained that FMLN backers were illegally taking over land during the implementation process, the main problems arose from the government's lack of cohesion and its inability to control its army. Only when the government was able to force the army to comply with the mandate of the accords was a major crisis in the implementation of El Salvador's peace accords averted.

In Cambodia, however, the situation was far more complex. When the United Nations brokered the peace accords, there were two parties to the negotiations: the Phnom Penh government and the Coalition Government of Democratic Kampuchea (CGDK), a tripartite body that gathered the Khmer Rouge; Prince Sihanouk, former ruler of Cambodia; and Son Sann, a U.S.-favored moderate.[18] Subsequently, however, the CGDK collapsed because of Khmer Rouge intransigence and the withdrawal of U.S. support. As a result, the United Nations ended up having to deal with four factions with disparate goals and strategies. Not surprisingly, the configuration of relationships among the factions at the time of the signing of the accords changed rapidly. As the Son Sann and the Sihanouk factions broke their alliance with the Khmer Rouge, the Khmer Rouge began to lose confidence in the peace process and decided to retain its capacity to use military force. Soon thereafter, as Sihanouk's popularity increased, initial attempts at cooperation between his faction and the former Phnom Penh government were undermined partly because of the latter's inability to control its own extremists, who launched attacks against the party of Prince Sihanouk's son.

While in El Salvador such key parameters as the number, inclusiveness, and cohesion of the parties to the peace accords remained more or less constant after the accords had been signed, in Cambodia the parameters changed rapidly, with destabilizing consequences. It is possible to conclude, as other studies have argued, that international intervention is more likely to contribute to maintaining the uncertain equilibrium of a win-win solution in instances involving disputes between two broadly representative parties that can firmly control their membership.[19]

Number and Interests of External Parties

In El Salvador the number and interests of external parties were quite simple and straightforward. There was one overwhelmingly important external actor, the United States, which remained committed to the peace process. To make the point, top brass of the U.S. armed forces visited El Salvador to pressure those elements in the Salvadoran military that were voicing opposition to the planned purges of human rights violators. The United States also assured the FMLN that no aid would be given to El Salvador if the government violated the peace accords. The Salvadoran peace process thus clearly benefited from the stabilizing influence played by only one main external actor committed to the process.

The situation in Cambodia was radically different. Not only were more external actors involved than in El Salvador, but also their interests fluctuated more. China's renewed involvement with the Khmer Rouge in the aftermath of the signing of the peace accords contributed to the Khmer Rouge leadership's notion that it might be able to prevail on the battlefield after all. The perception of a stalemate among the warring parties, one of the first conditions for international intervention in support of a win-win solution, was thus weakened. The Khmer Rouge's sense of the renewed viability of the military option was further strengthened by developments on the Thai-Cambodian border. In a masterly stroke of transnational diplomacy, the Khmer Rouge sold lucrative franchises in timber and gems to dozens of Thai companies that enjoyed connections with the Thai military and influential sections of the country's political elite. Using these connections, the Khmer Rouge was able to retain its bases in Thailand and thereby escape the purview of the U.N.-sponsored demobilization programs. The Thai trade also provided the Khmer Rouge with a vital economic lifeline and was instrumental in bolstering its perception of being able to win.

The contrast between El Salvador and Cambodia is thus quite marked. Developments in Cambodia after the signing of the accords led to some serious deviations in the implementation of the accord. The different role played by key external actors altered the initial conditions that allowed for the signing of the peace accord, strengthening one signatory's perception that it could win. In sum, some crucial difficulties that emerged in implementing the peace accords in Cambodia originated in the greater number of external parties involved, which led to greater coordination problems and the modification of the equilibrium that allowed for the signing of the accord, as well as in the interests of external parties, which were not in keeping with the stabilization of the peace process.

The Transitional Institutional Framework

A third factor worth considering is the nature of the transitional institutional framework provided by the peace accords. In El Salvador the United Nations' role was quite limited. The peace accords called for forming the National Commission for the Consolidation of Peace (COPAZ), alongside the established government, to formally supervise the implementation process. COPAZ was distinctive because it was made up of two representatives of the government, two FMLN leaders, one military representative, and one representative from each of the parties in Congress. In other words, it functioned as a consensual body bringing together all major political forces in the country. The U.N. role on the ground—the U.N. Observer Mission in El Salvador (ONUSAL)—was thus clearly a supporting one, centered mainly on demobilizing the guerrilla forces.[20] In its limited role the United Nations retained its image as an impartial overseer in the eyes of both the government and the FMLN. Having pointed out abridgments of the peace accords by both the government and the FMLN, the U.N. secretary-general was able to intervene with great success. In particular, when delays in meeting various deadlines appeared to threaten the entire process, U.N. intervention was crucial in generating consensus for a new and more flexible scheduling. Limited and to the point, U.N. intervention was highly effective.

In Cambodia the U.N. role was quite different. The size and degree of its involvement was dramatically larger than in El Salvador. Under the Cambodian peace accords, a twelve-member Supreme National Council (SNC) was created in Phnom Penh to provide a formal expression for Cambodian sovereignty until elections were held. But it was the United Nations Transitional Authority in Cambodia (UNTAC) that, in addition to supervising the implementation of the peace accords, was the de facto administrator of the country.[21] This institutional mechanism of international intervention had several significant consequences.[22]

The diversion of UNTAC energies and resources to essentially government roles had a series of negative effects. Because it faced a shortage of personnel and money in its attempts to administer the country, UNTAC decided to allow some of the key administrative staff members of the former Phnom Penh government to remain in their positions during the implementation of the peace accord. This step invited charges from the Khmer Rouge that the U.N. presence provided tacit support for the former Phnom Penh government, charges that gave the Khmer Rouge a pretext for not adhering to the accords.[23] That the United Nations took over the task of rebuilding the economy also meant that a substantial inflow of cash entered Phnom Penh. This trend created a web of corruption in an already unmotivated bureaucracy left over from the days of Vietnamese domination, thereby widening the gap between the city dwellers and the vast majority of the malnourished peasantry. The Khmer Rouge was quick to capitalize on this urban-rural gap by distributing some of the wealth it had accumulated from transboundary smuggling activities to the peasants, on the one hand, and by seeding discontent against the United Nations and the entire UNTAC operation, on the other. The Khmer Rouge also capitalized on the fact that the speed with which merchants and traders of Vietnamese origin used U.N. aid to restore their economic fortunes created resentment among the Khmer population and roused old ethnic animosities to the point that the United Nations was seen as being at the center of a Vietnamese conspiracy to control Cambodia. When the United Nations opened itself to accusations of partiality, its bridging function and capacity for initiative declined considerably.

Aside from providing a justification for continued Khmer Rouge military action, the transitional institutional framework in Cambodia provided no mechanism for the signatories to interact regularly and express their views on the way the accord was being implemented. The absence of a body like El Salvador's COPAZ was in many ways an outgrowth of the manner in which the accords had originally been negotiated. In El Salvador the formation of COPAZ resulted from a bargaining process in which the parties to the conflict played an important role, negotiating over key issues in a way that gradually narrowed the differences separating them. In Cambodia the warring parties had less input in the peace accords. There, the United Nations more or less presented a full proposal to the parties, which could either take it or leave it.[24] The United Nations did not subsequently provide any mechanism whereby the parties to the conflict could interact on a regular basis. Given this vacuum, old fears and distrusts were left to fester.

It is important to stress that what progress was made toward peaceful reconciliation in Cambodia resulted from the quite haphazard actions of the local parties, which were able to reach some crucial compromises despite the United Nations. In particular it was the intervention of Prince Sihanouk, going outside the formal steps outlined in the peace process, that at least partly saved the U.N. operation. In El Salvador the transitional institutional framework did allow the United Nations to assist in the on-going bargaining process between antagonistic parties and retain its role as an effective intermediary.

Peace Signatories' Perceptions of Elections

Finally, there is a clear contrast between El Salvador and Cambodia in the peace signatories' perceptions of their electoral chances. In El Salvador certain key leaders who were part of FDR-FMLN (Democratic Revolutionary Front–Farabundo Martí Front for National Liberation), the leftist political-military front that fought the Salvadoran government, decided to move into the electoral arena. When the newly formed Democratic Convergence participated in the electoral process in March 1991,[25] before the signing of the peace accord, and was able to gain significant representation in the unicameral national legislature, the move toward electoral competition gained great momentum. Since the FMLN's former allies were already participating in elections, its decision to face the ballot box would not be a jump into a vacuum. Moreover, with polls taken throughout 1992 showing the FMLN would emerge as the second most popular political force, the former guerrillas were increasingly perceived as able to transform themselves from a military to a political force.[26] On the other side, the good performance of the government party, ARENA, in the 1988, 1989, and 1991 elections gave the Right great confidence in its ability to operate successfully in a future democratic system. In sum, the key actors on both sides had a positive assessment of their electoral chances, and this perception reinforced their determination to see the peace accords implemented.

In contrast, important obstacles to the electoral institutionalization of conflict rapidly became evident in Cambodia. From the beginning the Khmer Rouge never really had an agenda on which to construct a political party. Its ability to transform itself from a military to a political force was doubted from the outset, and the breakup of the CGDK coalition only reinforced this perception. As the Khmer Rouge saw its electoral possibilities diminish, it reneged on its promise to participate in the political process and began taking steps to undermine a process in which it would inevitably end up a loser.

Making matters even worse, the Son Sann faction diminished in importance after the breakup of the CGDK, while the Sihanouk faction developed a strong standing. Moreover, as the United National Front for an Independent, Neutral, Peaceful, and Cooperative Cambodia (FUNCINPEC in its French acronym), the royalist party led by Prince Ranariddh, emerged as the likely winner of the May 1993 elections, the former Phnom Penh government forces led by Hun Sen were put on the defensive. The rising popularity of FUNCINPEC led Hun Sen and his allies to doubt their electoral prospects and to resort to force. A series of attacks on FUNCINPEC personnel and offices, widely attributed to the Hun Sen faction, were launched.[27]

In sum, the diminished chances of success by two key signatories to the Cambodian peace accord, the Khmer Rouge and the former Phnom Penh government forces, led to actions on their part that were clearly threatening to the peace process, while the greater security of the major actors in El Salvador helped reduce the volatility of the situation and increased the prospects for institutionalizing conflict. In other words, the prospects for successfully implementing the peace accords appear to increase when neither party to the accord perceives itself as a permanent outsider in electoral politics. When any party to the accord is highly uncertain about its electoral prospects, however, it is likely to obstruct progress in implementing a peace accord.

Conditions for Successful International Intervention

This analysis of El Salvador and Cambodia appears to strengthen the argument that the four highlighted factors do take us a long way in explaining the divergent paths these two countries followed as they attempted to implement their peace accords. The two cases display significant and consistent differences in terms of the four factors, which are closely linked to the steady progress of the peace process in El Salvador, in contrast to the very limited success in Cambodia. If this is so, the next step is to draw from this study lessons about the conditions for international intervention in civil conflicts.

It is crucial to stress the possibilities and the limits of international intervention that affect such actors as the United Nations. As the comparison of El Salvador and Cambodia makes starkly clear, whatever accomplishment the signing of peace accords may represent, the mere signing does not necessarily guarantee the long-term success of a peace process. Implementing a peace accord can be as complex and difficult as negotiating it. What is at stake is reproducing the initial conditions that enabled the signing of the accord, that is, the emergence of a win-win solution that made a cooperative strategy among previously warring parties possible. Stated negatively, what is at stake is avoiding a renewed perception on the part of one or more of the actors that a win-lose solution can be obtained. The role of international intervention should be assessed in this regard.

The first point that emerges from this study is that the possibilities of international intervention in implementing peace accords are linked to the nature of the transitional institutional framework. Such multilateral agencies as the United Nations have considerable ability to shape events.[28] But international intervention appears to be more successful when it is carried out on a fairly limited scale and is associated with very pointed objectives. This is so because intervention of this sort reduces the likelihood that the perception of the United Nations as an impartial body, a prerequisite for effective international intervention, will be tarnished. A second important point is that an institutional mechanism that regularizes contact between signatories to a peace accord further enhances the prospects of success. Implementation can be seen as a transitional phase, during which the initial contacts between the warring parties that led up to the signing of an accord become more frequent and less contentious but are still constrained or managed by such a body as the United Nations. Both of these features are important because they determine the ability for midcourse corrections, which can help contain and resolve unforeseeable problems in a way that prevents the derailing of the entire peace process, and because they represent important steps in the process of institutionalizing conflict, the ultimate goal in peaceful conflict resolution.

This assessment of the possibilities of international intervention notwithstanding, the limits of such intervention must also be stressed. The most crucial point here is that other factors besides the nature of the transitional institutional framework have a strong impact on the peace process and that a body like the United Nations can do little to affect these factors directly. This study shows that the number, inclusiveness, and cohesion of the parties to the accords affect the peace process. As a general rule, the smaller the number of actors, the greater their inclusiveness or representativeness of the population as a whole, and the greater their control over their membership, the more likely a peace accord will be successfully implemented. The number and interests of external parties are also shown to play a role. The greater the number of external parties, the harder it is to maintain the balance that allowed for the signing of the peace accords, for greater coordination problems make matters more complicated and less manageable. The changing interests of key external actors can also alter the initial conditions that allowed for the signing, strengthening the perception of one of the signatories that a win-lose outcome in its favor is possible. This type of perception inevitably destabilizes the peace process.[29] Finally, the peace signatories' perceptions of their electoral chances are likely to affect the peace process. The governing body must feel confident that its vital interests will not be threatened in the future, and the challenging force must be able to transform itself from a military to a political force if the peace process is to progress smoothly.

While the United Nations may be a key actor in peaceful conflict reso-lution, students of international relations and conflict resolution should not ignore the impact of these other factors. This lesson obviously applies as strongly to international agencies themselves. If there is a lesson in the cases of El Salvador and Cambodia, it is that the United Nations must view its role in relation to these other factors while stressing those aspects over which it has most control, that is, the nature of the transitional institu-tional framework provided in different peace accords. The United Nations is likely to obtain the greatest returns on its commitment of financial and other resources, a concern that it must take to heart if it is to prove to the diplomatic leaders of the major powers that it should be entrusted with a greater role in the emerging new world order.

Notes

The authors would like to thank Stephen P. Cohen and Paul Diehl for helpful comments on earlier drafts of this essay.

1. On the Cambodian civil war and the negotiation process leading up to the signing of the peace accords, see Michael Vickery, *Kampuchea: Politics, Economics, and Society* (Boulder, Colo.: Lynne Rienner, 1986); John McAuliff and Mary Byrne McDonnell, "Ending the Cambodian Stalemate," *World Policy Journal* 7, no. 1 (1989–90): 71–105; David P. Chandler, *A History of Cambodia,* 2d ed. (Boulder, Colo.: Westview, 1992); and Michael Leifer, "Power-sharing and Peacemaking in Cambodia?" *Sais Review* 12, no. 1 (1992): 139–53. On the Salvadoran civil war and the negotiation process leading up to the signing of the peace accords, see Enrique Baloyra, *El Salvador in Transition* (Chapel Hill, N.C.: University of North Carolina Press, 1982); Enrique Baloyra, "Salvaging El Salvador," *Journal of Democ-racy* 3, no. 2 (1992): 70–80; William M. LeoGrande, "After the Battle of San Sal-vador," in *Understanding the Central American Crisis,* ed. Kenneth M. Coleman and George C. Herring (Wilmington, Del.: Scholarly Resources, 1992), 111–38; Terry Lynn Karl, "El Salvador's Negotiated Revolution," *Foreign Affairs* 71, no. 2 (1992): 147–64; Joseph Tulchin and Gary Bland, eds., *Is There a Transition to Democracy in El Salvador?* (Boulder, Colo.: Lynne Rienner, 1992); and Gerardo L. Munck, "Be-yond Electoralism in El Salvador: Conflict Resolution through Negotiated Com-promise," *Third World Quarterly* 14, no. 1 (1993): 75–93.

2. Michael Haas, *Genocide by Proxy: Cambodian Pawn on a Superpower Chessboard* (New York: Praeger, 1991); Daniel S. Papp, "Soviet and American Peacemaking Efforts in Regional Conflicts in Asia: Afghanistan and Cambodia," in *The End of Superpower Conflict in the Third World,* ed. Melvin A. Goodman (Boulder, Colo.: Westview, 1992), 93–137; Jack Child, *The Central American Peace Process, 1983–1991* (Boulder, Colo.: Lynne Rienner, 1992); Jan S. Adams, *A Foreign Policy in Transi-*

tion: Moscow's Retreat from Central America and the Caribbean, 1985–1992 (Durham, N.C.: Duke University Press, 1992).

3. James Rosenau, *Turbulence in World Politics: A Theory of Continuity and Change* (Princeton, N.J.: Princeton University Press, 1991); James Rosenau, *The United Nations in a Turbulent World* (Boulder, Colo.: Westview, 1992).

4. For the entire text of the accords, see United Nations, *Agreements on a Comprehensive Political Settlement of the Cambodia Conflict,* United Nations, DPI/1180-92077-January 1992-10M (New York: United Nations, 1992); and "Acuerdos de paz de Chapultepec," *Revista del Pensamiento Centroamericano,* no. 214 (1992): 32–82.

5. For more details on the U.N. role and the Cambodian peace plan, see Steven R. Ratner, *The New U.N. Peacekeeping: Building Peace in Lands of Conflict after the Cold War* (New York: St. Martin's, 1995), chapters 6–8; and Yasushi Akashi, "To Build a New Country: The Task of the U.N. Transitional Authority in Cambodia," *Harvard International Review* 15, no. 2 (1992): 34–37.

6. For more details on the U.N. role and the Salvadoran peace plan, see Munck, "Beyond Electoralism in El Salvador," 83–84; and David Holiday and William Stanley, "Building the Peace: Preliminary Lessons from El Salvador," *Journal of International Affairs* 46, no. 2 (1993): 415–38.

7. On the implementation of the peace accords and the 1994 elections, see Munck, "Beyond Electoralism in El Salvador," 84–86; Holiday and Stanley, "Building the Peace"; Joseph G. Sullivan, "How Peace Came to El Salvador," *Orbis* 38, no. 1 (1994): 83–98; Alvaro de Soto and Graciana del Castillo, "Obstacles to Peacebuilding," *Foreign Policy,* no. 94 (1994): 69–83; George Vickers and Jack Spence, "Elections in El Salvador: The Right Consolidates Power," *NACLA Report on the Americas* 28, no. 1 (1994): 6–11; and Richard Stahler-Sholk, "El Salvador's Negotiated Transition: From Low-Intensity Conflict to Low-Intensity Democracy," *Journal of Inter-American Studies and World Affairs* 36, no. 4 (1994): 1–59.

8. On the 1993 election and its aftermath, see Julio A. Jeldres, "The U.N. and the Cambodian Transition," *Journal of Democracy* 4, no. 4 (1993): 104–14; Sheri Prasso, "Cambodia: A Heritage of Violence," *World Policy Journal* 11, no. 3 (1994): 71–77; Terence Duffy, "Cambodia since the Election: Peace, Democracy, and Human Rights?" *Contemporary Southeast Asia* 15, no. 4 (1994): 407–32; and Julio A. Jeldres, "Cambodia's Fading Hopes," *Journal of Democracy* 7, no. 1 (1996): 148–57.

9. For a detailed critique of UNTAC's strategy of focusing primarily on holding elections to the detriment of other peacekeeping goals, see "Cambodia: Elections in the Killing Fields," in *Life, Death, and Aid: The Médecins sans Frontieres Report on World Crisis Intervention,* ed. François Jean (London: Routledge, 1993), 79–86. On the advances of the Khmer Rouge and the response of the government, see Nate Thayer and Nayan Chanda, "Things Fall Apart," *Far Eastern Economic Review,* May 19, 1994, 16–18; and Philip Shenon, "U.S. Considers Supplying Arms to Help Sihanouk in Cambodia," *New York Times,* May 15, 1994. Although occurring too late to be analyzed in this essay, the July 1997 coup by the Cambodian People's party leader and co–prime minister Hun Sen against his coalition partner, Prince Ranariddh of the royalist FUNCINPEC party, further supports our argument that the

Cambodian peace accord failed to resolve the country's civil war. On the coup, see "A Coup in Cambodia," *Economist,* July 12, 1997, 33–34.

10. The term *civil conflict* as used in this essay refers to a violent conflict between two or more parties within the boundaries of the same state, in which the goals of the conflicting parties are stated in the context of that particular state's polity. The 1983 U.S. intervention in Grenada, for example, would not be an instance of civil conflict. This definition, however, does not preclude considering cases where civil conflict has transboundary ramifications or where one or more of the conflicting parties is performing proxy roles for external agents.

The term *international intervention* refers to a multilateral intervention or an intervention by a regional or global international organization in a civil conflict. The intervention's expressed purpose should be to obtain a negotiated resolution of the conflict, not the forceful imposition of the goals of any one of the intervening parties. Conflicts that are "resolved" or terminated through one party's military victory are not considered here. Good examples of the kinds of intervention encompassed in the definition are the U.N. interventions in Cambodia, El Salvador, and Namibia, as well as the multilateral West African intervention in Liberia. This definition would preclude, for instance, the 1989 U.S. intervention in Panama or the 1991 Indian intervention in the Maldives, as well as all other unilateral interventions. However, an exception would be made in those instances where the purpose of unilateral intervention is to restore peaceful conditions and where the intervention is carried out in collaboration with, or the support of, various international bodies. A good example of such intervention is Italy's role in brokering the peace accords in Mozambique.

11. El Salvador and Cambodia were used to pinpoint which factors were likely to encourage the conflicting parties to continue cooperating and to formulate some initial hypotheses concerning the role of these factors. On the use of case studies in the development of theory, see Arend Lijphart, "Comparative Politics and the Comparative Method," *American Political Science Review* 65, no. 3 (1971): 682–93; Harry Eckstein, "Case Study and Theory in Political Science," in *Strategies of Inquiry,* ed. Fred I. Greenstein and Nelson W. Polsby, vol. 7 of *Handbook of Political Science* (Reading, Mass.: Addison-Wesley, 1975), 79–137; and Alexander L. George, "Case Studies and Theory Development: The Method of Structured, Focused Comparison," in *Diplomacy: New Approaches in History, Theory, and Policy,* ed. Paul Gordon Lauren (New York: Free Press, 1979), 43–68. The four factors we focus on have also been highlighted in the literature on conflict resolution, as well as in other complementary bodies of literature. See, for example, Paul F. Diehl, "When Peacekeeping Does Not Lead to Peace: Some Notes on Conflict Resolution," *Bulletin of Peace Proposals* 18, no. 1 (1987): 47–53; Mark Hoffman, "Third-Party Mediation and Conflict Resolution in the Post–Cold War," in *Dilemmas of World Politics: International Issues in a Changing World,* ed. John Baylis and N. J. Rengger (New York: Oxford University Press, 1992), 260–86; and Thomas Princen, *Intermediaries in International Conflict* (Princeton, N.J.: Princeton University Press, 1992).

12. Gerardo L. Munck and Chetan Kumar, "Civil Conflicts and the Conditions

for Successful International Intervention: A Comparative Study of Cambodia and El Salvador," *Review of International Studies* 21, no. 2 (1995): 159–81; Dean G. Pruit, Jeffrey Z. Rubin, and Sung Hee Kim, *Social Conflict: Escalation, Stalemate, and Settlement,* 2d ed. (New York: McGraw Hill, 1994); Saadia Touval and I. William Zartman, *International Mediation in Theory and Practice* (Boulder, Colo.: Westview, 1985).

13. As stressed in bargaining theory, particularly as applied to corporatist pacts, the existence of well-defined collective actors with a leadership able to speak for the rank-and-file membership and to enforce agreed upon conditions is a precondition for any negotiation to take place and for the resulting agreements to be enforced. In this essay we are concerned with characteristics of the actors that affect the likelihood of the signed accord being implemented. The reason dyadic disputes are more amenable to resolution is that an increase in the number of parties to a dispute leads to an increase in the number of conflicting interests that need to be coordinated. The destabilizing tendencies are correspondingly increased. This type of argument has been made in the context of international intervention and conflict resolution by Paul F. Diehl and Chetan Kumar, "Mutual Benefits from International Intervention: New Roles for United Nations Peacekeeping Forces," *Bulletin of Peace Proposals* 22, no. 4 (1991): 369–75. For a reference to the corporatism literature, see Peter Lange, "Unions, Workers, and Wage Regulation: The Rational Bases of Consent," in *Order and Conflict in Contemporary Capitalism: Studies in the Political Economy of Western European Nations,* ed. John Goldthorpe (Oxford: Oxford University Press, 1984), 106–8.

14. The term *external party* is used to refer to the outside parties that were initially involved in the conflict, not to the mediating party. For example, while in Cambodia the external mediator is the United Nations, the external parties include China, Thailand, and Vietnam.

15. The democratization literature has also argued that the process of pact making sometimes calls for extending guarantees to certain parties in return for their willingness to negotiate with their opponents and to back political solutions to conflictive situations. See, for example, Guillermo O'Donnell and Philippe Schmitter, *Transitions from Authoritarian Rule: Tentative Conclusions about Uncertain Democracies* (Baltimore: Johns Hopkins University Press, 1986), 28–32, 69. Of course, electoral laws and constitutional structures also determine whether power sharing and respect for minority rights are likely to result and whether the losing party will have a realistic chance of coming to power at a future date. Matthew S. Shugart, "Guerrillas and Elections: An Institutionalist Perspective on the Costs of Conflict and Competition," *International Studies Quarterly* 36, no. 2 (1992): 121–52.

16. John Gerard Ruggie, "Wandering in the Void: Charting the U.N.'s New Strategic Role," *Foreign Affairs* 72, no. 5 (1993): 26–31.

17. The unification of the FMLN came about in October 1980, more or less at the insistence of Fidel Castro. A condition for his offering any assistance to the rebel forces was that they have a clearly identifiable head. The five main guerrilla factions at the time therefore came together in the FMLN. In May 1994, when

the Legislative Assembly was sworn in, a dispute between two wings of the FMLN broke out, and the FMLN splintered. The formal split in the FMLN in late 1994, however, came at a time when the major obstacles to peace had been overcome.

18. Even though the individual members of the coalition signed the accord separately, the CGDK had acted as a unified body.

19. See, for example, Diehl and Kumar, "Mutual Benefits from International Intervention."

20. The United Nations was also helpful in resolving another key problem in El Salvador, the existence of a big rural refugee population. In initiating and promoting the resettlement of refugees, ONUSAL's operation followed the lead of the various Salvadoran organizations that already existed for the purpose, including the National Coordinator of Repopulation, a nongovernmental organization representing the displaced; the Salvadoran government's commission on the displaced (CONADES); and the Christian Committee for the Displaced (CRIPDES), a church-sponsored nongovernmental organization. The United Nations' cooperation with these agencies helped restore and strengthen civil society after years of warfare, thereby allowing the peace process to gain a positive momentum that had a chance of continuing when the United Nations eventually withdrew.

21. On the surface the assertion that UNTAC would administer Cambodia appears to contradict the U.N. Charter, which prohibits U.N. trusteeship of a member state (Article 78) and bans any U.N. intervention in matters that are considered within the domestic jurisdiction of any state (Article 2/7). The United Nations, however, got around these limitations by creating the SNC, defined in the Paris Peace Accords as "the unique legitimate body and source of authority in which, throughout the transitional period, the sovereignty, independence, and unity of Cambodia are enshrined." The SNC, which elected Prince Sihanouk as head, then "delegate[d] to the United Nations all powers necessary to ensure the implementation of this Agreement." (The Security Council could have ordered an enforcement action under chapter 7 to restore international security, as happened in the Gulf War, but this was not considered practical for Cambodia.)

22. On the U.N. role in implementing Cambodia's peace plan, see Jeldres, "The U.N. and the Cambodian Transition," 106–9; and Ramses Amer, "The United Nations' Peacekeeping Operation in Cambodia: Overview and Assessment," *Contemporary Southeast Asia* 15, no. 2 (1993): 211–31.

23. Nayan Chanda, "Easy Scapegoat: People Blame the U.N. for All Their Woes," *Far Eastern Economic Review,* October 22, 1992, 18.

24. Jeldres, "The U.N. and the Cambodian Transition," 107.

25. The Democratic Convergence was made up of important FDR politicians previously aligned with the FMLN who came together to form a new coalition representing a leftist agenda following the signing of the Esquipulas II accord in August 1987. Obviously, this decision was only possible in the first place because the electoral arena had continued to operate with restrictions during the period of the civil war in the 1980s. In the March 1991 elections the Democratic Con-

vergence gained 12 percent of the vote and eight out of eighty-four seats in the unicameral national legislature.

26. "FMLN Close on ARENA's Heel," *Central America Report* 14 (August 1992): 235–36.

27. "Cambodia: Human Rights before and after the Elections," *Asia Watch* 5 (May 1993): 9–12.

28. There are important limits, however, that restrict the ability of the United Nations or other such bodies to shape the nature of the transitional institutional framework. Specifically, as the negotiation process in both El Salvador and Cambodia shows, the United Nations' ability to shape the ideal transitional institutional framework is limited by such preexisting factors as the willingness and ability of the warring parties to have input into the making of the peace accord. Although the United Nations can influence the disposition of the warring parties, this factor remains to a large extent exogenous.

29. This role of external actors also affects the contribution of international intervention in the negotiation phase. The end of the cold war and the increasing willingness and interest of major powers to allow for greater U.N. initiative have made it possible for the United Nations to take advantage of these opportunities and to offer its services as a broker in Cambodia and El Salvador. Where the degree of interest on the part of both regional and global actors to see "something done" is much lower, as in Sudan or Tajikistan, this lack of attention impedes a peace process from the start.

9

Conflict Management in East Central Europe

Carol Skalnik Leff

In the early phase of Gorbachev's new thinking, the foreign policy adviser Georgy Arbatov conveyed to his Western colleagues what Dmitry Trenin calls "Arbatov's Curse": "We are going to do something really terri-
ble to you. We are going to rid you of your enemy."[1] In some respects this
has indeed been a curse. The end of the cold war was also the end of a
relatively stable bipolar security architecture in Europe. The NATO–Warsaw Treaty Organization (WTO) confrontation in the heart of Europe did
freeze the Soviet sphere of influence in Eastern Europe, but even in the
throes of cold war disputation over the balance of military power, both
camps accrued some acknowledged payoffs from the institutionalized
standoff. Chief among them was a diplomatic and negotiation space that
decades of relative stability in the alliance structure afforded. In 1990, even
after the collapse of communism, President Václav Havel of Czechoslovakia would assert the interim value of the existing security institutions
as a framework for arms control negotiations. In the shadow of bipolar
stability the Helsinki process—an inclusive consensual apparatus dubbed
the CSCE (Conference on Security and Cooperation in Europe)—functioned as a floating forum to respond to mutually felt needs for recognizing the integrity of national boundaries and for establishing transparency and confidence-building measures in the security area.[2] In its genesis
and operations CSCE was not so much a harbinger of a future European
order as it was a creature of the cold war context. Such an inclusive process was then possible only under the overarching umbrella of tighter
WTO-NATO alliances that underpinned a more predictable, negotiable
security environment.

In one way or another most scholars and participants in European security matters acknowledged the positive features of an enduring and
expensive confrontation—John Gaddis's "long peace"—that nonetheless

was institutionalized below the threshold of overt violence. A corollary to this understanding of the cold war framework was the way in which it tended to freeze regional conflict, even as it institutionalized continental tensions. The cold war alignment forced cooperation among states with traditional historical antagonisms and imposed the status quo on states with serious internal divisions (either directly or, as in the Yugoslav case, in solidarity against external pressures). This was the peace of the political graveyard, inasmuch as conflict was suppressed rather than resolved. However, the freezing of overt conflict in Eastern Europe undeniably benefited Western European states because it insulated them from the necessity of responding to Eastern European instabilities as they had perforce done throughout the previous century. In effect, in dividing Europe and "pacifying" the east, the cold war alignment cut through the controversies that had generated two twentieth-century world wars. The stabilized cold war system was not, of course, a system of conflict resolution; particularly in Eastern Europe it was a system of regional conflict suspension or deferral. Nonetheless, for decades it cleared the security agenda of some of its most pressing previous problems. There is no little merit to James Mayall's pungent comment, "If war has been the midwife of history, the cold war was its taxidermist."[3]

This selective survey of the status quo ante 1989 is important in considering post–cold war security issues and regional conflict resolution because it establishes some of the stakes of the transition period. The collapse of communist power in the region that had been demarcated with the political label Eastern Europe was not merely a series of simultaneous, mutually inciting domestic transformations but also a deathblow to the stabilizing features of cold war security architecture. The following analysis explores the consequences of this momentous change in two related areas: the reconfiguration of the security agenda—that is, the sources of regional conflict—and the reconfiguration of European security architecture in response to these new demands for conflict resolution.

What were these new demands? Asked what the Western European stakes were in the new Eastern Europe, Prime Minister Margaret Thatcher replied, "Refugees, terrorism, Balkan wars drawing in other countries, and worse."[4] Politicians can afford to be pithier than political scientists, and some elaboration is called for, particularly since Thatcher designated certain unwelcome consequences without specifying the conflict situations from which they might flow.

It is clear what the West wishes to avoid in the East—the spillover effects of weakness and instability. This is hardly a new desideratum; it dates in recognizable form from the period of Western concern with the instability of Eastern empires in the nineteenth century. It is the context that has changed. Until 1945 Eastern instabilities played into divisions in the West, where the major powers were almost perpetually at odds with one another. After 1945, as a workable and relatively inclusive Western European economic and security order emerged, the character of the threat posed by Eastern instability altered. Although it could still be divisive, the consequence was unlikely to be war among the Western European states. In fact the attractiveness of the Western model to new Eastern European regimes was rooted in that successful reordering of older Western European antagonisms into an increasingly integrated system that permitted economic growth and political stability. Incentives the West could offer in turn rested on good behavior to win inclusion in that order.

This was clearly a more benign international environment for the resolution of Eastern European security problems than that which had obtained in the first period of East European independence between the two world wars. In that period Eastern Europe was beleaguered by the fragility of the larger continental security arrangements and hemmed in by Bolshevism and quarreling Western neighbors. After 1989 the former Soviet Union posed no immediate threat of coordinated external aggression; rather, it threatened by its weakness, generating instabilities in successor states that all too frequently crossed the threshold of violence, with unpredictable spillover effects. Westward, however, lay a better integrated and more stable alignment positioned to be part of the solution rather than part of the problem. The major threat that loomed from the West was that of exclusion.

The specific roots of regional conflict in Eastern Europe were therefore largely internal. They flowed from several convergent sources. Foremost is the reconfiguration of longstanding national identity questions that have haunted the ethnically diverse and complex East European states for more than a century. The explosiveness of this issue, however, is due not merely to its considerable primordial power but also to the context in which it reemerged after 1989.[5] This context was the disintegration of the restraining security regime, on the one hand, and the open field of expression for national disputation in democratized electoral and media politics, on the other.[6] More broadly, however, what Claus Offe has styled the "triple transition" itself tended to generate potentially destabilizing conflict.[7] His characterization of the transformation agendas of the East emphasizes the problematic dynamics of simultaneous efforts to democratize political institutions, to marketize and privatize the socialist economies, and to reconstruct national identities. The internal dynamics of triple transition have put a heavy burden on internal politics. As Daniel Nelson notes,

"The entire east-central half of Europe is a 'threat-rich' environment, composed of weak (low-capacity) political units."[8] In turn the adequacy of domestic conflict resolution capabilities has become an international question to the extent that chronic economic dislocation and cycles of political instability threaten to create vortices that drain European resources and generate out-migration that is particularly threatening to Western states already struggling with the economic and identity questions raised by foreign workers from southern Europe and North Africa.[9] Because these contextual elements raise the core issue of relationships between external and internal political factors, some elaboration of this nexus is necessary before considering regional conflict resolution.

Domestic and International Linkages

The most important feature of post–cold war dynamics in dealing with regional conflict is the extent to which domestic issues are embedded in international politics in Eastern Europe. This was, of course, equally true of the Soviet era. Much of the literature on alliance formation treats or even defines alliance behavior as a set of converging sovereign choices based on calculations of reciprocal benefit for or self-defense of the member states. Such an approach can be useful in many cases, but it does not adequately capture the special dynamics of such a highly constrained hegemonic alliance as the Soviet dominance of its Eastern European allies. The Soviet "mandate" for alliance cooperation entailed the imposition of key domestic structures patterned on the Soviet model; the parallelism of domestic systems was a major component of the Soviet rationale for alliance—the protection of socialism.

After 1989 this tight nexus between domestic and international politics meant that the change in domestic political regime was also in a sense a "national liberation movement" that fatally undercut the alliance structure.[10] Timing of the collapse (not to be confused with its deeper reasons) was closely tied to the weakening of the Soviet hegemon and the reduced threat of Soviet retaliation against domestic innovation in Eastern Europe. Inherent in the collapse of communist power in individual regimes, therefore, was the collapse of the alliance structure, Soviet efforts to maintain it in some form notwithstanding. The dismantling of the communist alliance apparatus was not instantaneous and generated some very delicate negotiations in line with the continuing need to avoid unduly alarming the floundering Russian state. Nonetheless, 1991 marked the demise of the bloc's economic institution, the CMEA (Council for Mutual Economic Assistance), and the Warsaw military alliance. The withdrawal of Soviet troops from the region, a more logistically complicated issue, was completed in Hungary and Czechoslovakia in 1991 and in Poland and Germany in 1994. The dissolution of the former bloc structures left a security vacuum in the region that has yet to be adequately filled.

A second important proposition is that the linkage between domestic and international balances of power remained pivotal in the postcommunist transition period. One sense in which this is true relates to the multinational complexity of Eastern Europe. A series of earlier experiments in national self-determination as a regional stabilizing factor had failed to resolve tensions arising from this complexity; it spilled over borders not only where there were strong cross-boundary ethnic ties but also where internal tensions first threatened existing states and then succeeded in destroying them. A striking feature of this spillover effect is that it has thrown into relief the essential ambiguities and contradictions of some of the fundamental premises of the international state system. Such theorists as James Mayall have systematically analyzed some of these inconsistencies. The problem of meshing a theory of state sovereignty with the increasingly acknowledged right to self-determination lies precisely in the fact that while these two principles may be mutually reinforcing in some cases, they are completely at odds when an ethnonational movement within a state seeks international priority for its own claims to statehood.[11] The postcommunist period has presented the international community with a plethora of such painful clashes between principles; the West has stumbled repeatedly in trying to accommodate them.

The domestic-international linkages were also partly a legacy of communism because postcommunist domestic projects entailed transforming socialist economic and political institutions to be consonant with Western models. In essence the new agenda entailed unraveling the web of interlocking logic—international and domestic—that had tied the Soviet bloc together as a core of "socialist states." The new projects centered squarely on what was understood to be a "return to Europe." The path to stability and prosperity thus defined led through the European Union (EU) and through NATO; from their inception domestic transformation projects incorporated a generalized but compelling strategy of integration with Western Europe.

Just as the Soviet alliance created an interlocking web of domestic and international imperatives, so did the postcommunist matrix of relationships. The new Eastern European regimes were supremely sensitive to the goal of establishing their credentials as good "Eurocitizens," and this orientation subjected the entire domestic agenda, as well as the foreign policy agenda, to international scrutiny. The implications of this proposition are explored in greater detail later, but the central point is that this "return to Europe" is a fundamental element of the strategic environment within which postcommunist conflict resolution in Europe must be analyzed. The theorist's maxim that "the domestic and the international [levels of security] are becoming much less insulated from each other" is embraced by practicing Europoliticians as well and forms part of their basic approach to core issues of internal organization and policy.[12]

This linkage is a very important element in the framework for conflict resolution because it provides an incentive structure for "good" Eastern European behavior, including the aversion to or resolution of destabilizing conflict. Eastern European stakes in conflict resolution are broader than the direct damage that conflict itself may inflict on a given state; unresolved conflict carries the risk of impeding Western European support for economic and political transformation.

In making this assertion, I do not wish to imply that Western European desires regarding Eastern European behavior necessarily represent Eastern Europe's best interests in any ideal sense. It need not be assumed—in fact it must not be assumed—that Western prescriptions for good Eurocitizenship and the means of attaining it invariably coincide with optimal patterns of growth and interaction in the region. In very general terms Western expectations do conform to Eastern aspirations for healthy market economies that underpin support for consolidated and nondisputatious democratic regimes. This goal in turn corresponds to the theoretical understanding of existing democratic governments in advanced industrial societies as more inclined to peaceful conflict resolution. There is thus a comity of mutual interest between East and West that is hard to refute at the most general level, one that conforms to our theoretical understanding of a benign environment for conflict resolution. The ways and means of achieving these ends, however, may be very much in dispute, and the process of getting to capitalist democracy may be a much less stabilizing process than the hoped-for end product. In the following analysis I pinpoint the ways in which the fit between Eastern and Western interests is imperfect.

A final proposition concerns what Gregory Treverton has termed the "mismatch between institutions and purposes" in postcommunist Europe.[13] The NATO-WTO axis had evolved to deter large-scale conventional and nuclear war on the continent. Strategy, battle plans, and troop deployment had been designed not only to fight such a war but also, by so preparing, to make such a war unfightable. The radical change of the postcommunist context, however, rendered these security measures—and the elaborate and expensive ballet of deterrence that accompanied them—

largely irrelevant. The Soviet loss of its forward base and its allies destroyed the WTO, but it also hurtled NATO into a profound and prolonged crisis of identity. The new security threats to Europe required capabilities that NATO did not really possess. NATO had no mandate for "out-of-area operations." Nor was it organized to respond to the kind of spot crises that were soon manifest in the postcommunist environment, crises generated by dysfunctions in domestic politics rather than by clear-cut acts of international aggression. These new conflicts required essentially political and diplomatic solutions, the military concomitants of which were generally quite controversial. NATO was a muscle-bound giant with inadequate rapid deployment capabilities and no coherent consensus on how to deploy the capabilities it did possess. In the face of dramatic and radical changes in internal politics that destroyed the existing bloc system, it was not feasible to maintain the institutional status quo.

The "New" Security Threats

It is possible to distinguish roughly between low-level and high-intensity conflict factors in the postcommunist setting, differentiating them by disruptive potential. The limits to this approach lie in the interlocking character of the transformative processes under way in the region. It is therefore useful to look more closely at the tensions and complexities of the interlocking transformative processes of the triple transition and at the external dimensions of these tensions.

These processes interlock in two important respects. The first crosses boundaries and speaks to the significance of simultaneous state transitions across the region. Latin Americanists have found the rough simultaneity of democratic transitions in their region theoretically useful because it offered a set of better matched cases, across which comparisons and contrasts were facilitated by certain commonalities in culture, historical experience, and temporal setting. They were less concerned with the interactive effects as such (what Laurence Whitehead calls "contagion effects" in clusters of cases).[14] In Eastern Europe, however, the launching of parallel transition efforts was significant in a much larger and more pervasive sense.

A hypothetical renegade Eastern European state that proved capable, by some unidentified and unlikely historical conjunction of events, of freeing itself individually and peacefully from the bloc would have gained some clear advantages in reorienting itself to the West. The concentrated attention of Western support on a single target state would have been a pleasant alternative to competing for Western aid, trade, and investment, even as the stable framework of bloc trade would have cushioned the economic reorientation. One might find very partial analogues to this situation in Yugoslavia's earlier balancing act between cold war blocs or in Hungary's and Poland's preferential status in the late 1980s, when the relative economic and political liberalization of these two countries gave them a head start in courting Western economic support (the current PHARE program for specialized assistance to all of Eastern Europe carries this history in its acronym, which stands for Poland/Hungary: Aid for Restructuring of Economies).

However, the point of this thought experiment (hard as it is to contextualize in practice) is to highlight certain stresses inherent in the simultaneous transitions that did occur. To capsulize these stresses, one can point to (1) the collapse of former bloc trade, to which a number of analysts have attributed a substantial part of the post-1989 economic downturn in the region, and (2) the multiplication of needy transitional states, which spread international assistance more thinly over a wider range of recipients and set these countries in competition for shrinking Eastern markets and for the somewhat stagnant Western markets of the early 1990s. The simultaneity of transformation efforts in Eastern Europe therefore not only entailed the loss of some of the distinctive leverage that might have accrued to a single state but also multiplied the economic stress of transition.

The stresses of transition also manifested themselves in the complexities of simultaneous processes in domestic politics—the essence of the triple transition. The social pain of economic transition, the political dilemmas of institutional design and elite-mass relations, and the tormented process of renegotiating an ethnonational bargain in postcommunist states are not separate processes. They interact in ways that seriously magnify social stress. The economic costs of transition—GDP decline, inflation, unemployment—have generated public dissatisfaction with fledgling political regimes, undermining legitimacy and stability. The more open democratic electoral systems are seismometers of this economic dislocation. The electoral arena and the media have become the terrain of political free-for-alls over the logic of technocratically designed economic reform, ventilating grievances and often framing the economic agenda in polarizingly populist terms—nomenklatura and Mafia capitalists siphoning off windfall profits while the population suffers. Small wonder that some political leaders are tempted by a Pinochet-style authoritarian project of economic adjustment.

The simultaneity of democratization and the attempt to resolve intractable ethnonational problems is also a mixed blessing. Moderation and compromise in ethnonational bargaining tend to be undercut in a climate of shrill media and nationalist populism, where fringe parties can outbid the government in making claims for preeminence in the protection of national interests. In short the new democratic arena articulates internal disagreements all too well, and the growth pains of political institutionalization threaten system overload. Regime change, as Donald Horowitz notes, opens a "window of opportunity" for renegotiating important unresolved issues of performance and identity, but precisely in a political climate in which such issues can be most politically delicate and volatile.[15]

These internal dynamics have multiple meanings for internationally relevant conflict. First, by amplifying the difficulties of governance, they also amplify political instabilities and increase system vulnerability to populist appeals that strike resonant chords and oversimplify complex problems, most of them with pronounced international dimensions. This is a common characteristic of democratic systems, but it is more dangerous in fragile transitional states.

Second, the intensity and scope of international linkages to the domestic agenda produce internal political dynamics, dynamics that may be stabilizing or contentious. The international presence does, as we will see it was intended to do, frame domestic issues on nearly every topic relevant to the transition. There is no basic policy or institutional choice to be made about which the international audience is wholly indifferent or for which international models and reference points are wholly lacking. The political discourse is shaped by the need to meet European standards, to behave as "civilized" nations. It is useful to outline how the three elements of the triple transition tend to interact with international considerations, because the way this is played out in domestic politics tends to differ somewhat from one area of policy formulation to another.

This is very evident in the politics of economic transformation, which has its own important international dimensions. Above and beyond such specific foreign policy considerations as trade liberalization, investment incentives, and the courting of aid for fiscal and monetary stabilization, aspirations for EU membership dictate a sustained effort to bring domestic economic institutions and practices into line with EU standards.

This pattern of response to external models and expectations has been increasingly conscious and systematic. Most of the transitional Eastern European states have set up some form of process by which they can ascertain whether new laws and practices conform to EU standards. For example, the Hungarian Parliament established a European Affairs Scrutiny Committee in 1992 to monitor compatibility of legislation with Western standards, and in 1994 such legislative conformity became legally mandatory, as is also the case in the Czech Republic and Poland. Under the auspices of the Polish European Integration Office, Poland also conducted a major survey comparing existing legislation with EU norms and defining the needed changes in the legal system.[16] A 1992 Polish study suggested that some seven thousand laws would need revision to meet EU standards and procedures. Similar commissions have been established in the Baltic states.

Those committed to major economic transformation are likely to invoke international standards for economic integration as a rationale for restructuring. International monitoring and incentive structures are incorporated into the argument for change. To some extent, the constraints imposed by the international setting can even be invoked as a substitute for wholehearted public commitment to economic transformation, whereby outside pressures compensate for lackadaisical pressures from below or even substitute for the absent or disorganized socioeconomic interests of a new entrepreneurial class.

Injecting the performance standards and expectations of the "other" into the political dialogue carries electoral risks, however. There is ample space in the political spectrum for a critique of economic transformation policies, particularly inasmuch as the transformation exacts painful and unequally distributed costs in unemployment and inflation. It is possible to discuss these cleavage structures in electoral politics by referring primarily to domestic policy, rooted in competing economic interests, divergent religious and secular visions of society, and contradictory national claims.

However, none of these contested positions in electoral politics is free of an external dimension. The international dimension of economic transformation can become a weak point in reformer arguments; opposition parties and other reform critics can gain significant electoral leverage from a quasi-conspiratorial reading that paints reformers as the catpaws of foreign interests. Reliance on international economic resources for economic reconstruction and on foreign advice opens governments to charges of selling the "family jewels" to foreigners, subservience to the International Monetary Fund (IMF), and loss of sovereignty. The IMF regimen has for years given play to similar dynamics elsewhere: a government appealing to the necessity of adhering to IMF requirements to give backbone to the case for austerity finds itself vulnerable to attack as the mouthpiece for a foreign organization. Nor is this critique wholly without merit. A serious scholarly debate has been waged over the benignity of strategies dependent on foreign investment and assistance. It is by no means an isolated few who question the validity of the IMF economic prescriptions.

The political dimension of the attempted transformations in Eastern Europe had its own definable external dimension as well, an orientation that was very clear in the dissident community before 1989. This perspective centered on the extended debate in dissident circles over the meaning of central Europe, a construct that placed the communist countries of Eastern Europe squarely in the mainstream of European historical development. In this understanding, particularly among Czech, Polish, and Hungarian intellectuals, their own mainstream European cultures had been "kidnapped" by the East, wrested from the European orbit by brute force of the coercive gravitational pull of the Soviet Union.

A central implication of this view, ever more explicitly articulated after 1989, was that the kidnapped countries were not inferior imitations of the West but genuine participants in Western history and civilization and were no less entitled to membership in that community of states than their more fortunate Western European counterparts. Since 1989 that message, both in its commitment to Western values and in its sometimes aggrieved protestations against Western sluggishness in response, has continued to mark politics in the region. In general, despite the high visibility of foreign advisory missions, the constitutional designs of the new regimes have not been subject to the kind of foreign pressure exerted in the economic sphere. Generally, political institutionalization has been critiqued as a process distorted by foreign influence largely where the underlying issue is ethnonational tension, as was the case with the citizenship disputes in the Baltics.

What makes the ethnonational issue so susceptible to controversial internationalization is the imperfect fit between state boundaries and ethnonational distribution in the region. Even such relatively homogeneous states as Poland and Hungary have substantial communities abroad, and the protection of these communities has entered the policy agenda as a significant foreign policy issue. Cross-boundary ethnic ties have been isolated in several important comparative studies as a significant factor in internationalizing internal conflicts. In addition internal ethnonational conflicts have generated serious international repercussions when they escalate to the level of state disintegration, as they have in Yugoslavia, the former Soviet Union, and Czechoslovakia.

To date, the most serious diplomatic and military tensions in Eastern Europe have stemmed from "internationalized" ethnonational conflict. Efforts to cope with resurgent ethnonational tensions generated a somewhat different external dynamic than was the case for political and economic transformation projects. The existing Western institutions had developed regulatory frameworks for political and economic transactions among themselves prior to, and more or less independent of, developments in Eastern Europe. To join the game, Eastern European countries were encouraged to play by the existing Western rules, amplified and elaborated in the new context. The situation was different in bargaining over national relations in multiethnic states. It was not that the West lacked multiethnic complexity (as in Spain and Great Britain); however, these political complications had not been a major subject of transnational bargaining within regional organizations but remained largely negotiable within national boundaries. In east central Europe, by contrast, cross-boundary ethnonational links and the larger stakes of transition framed domestic issues in an international context almost from the start. In its negotiations with the Romanian government, the Democratic Union of Hungarians in Romania defined the problem of improving internal ethnic relations in a transnational setting: "Relations between Romanians and Hungarians living in Romania cannot be improved very much without revaluing and improving relations between the two countries."[17]

To gauge the problem of national conflict in the region, one cannot merely list the roster of ethnic groups in Eastern Europe and tally the relative numerical weight of minorities in each state. It is not even sufficient to annotate this roster with an accounting of the ways in which such identities have been politicized and the kinds of internal controversies that have ensued since 1989. This accounting process is essential but incomplete, because it fails to take into account the synergistic effects of the multiple ethnonational agendas to which each state must respond.

The Romanian case is an excellent example. Romania faces at least two different identity questions: the definition of the position of its substantial Hungarian minority and the character of the ties that bind Romania to the ethnically Romanian citizens of neighboring Moldova, a former Soviet republic, much of which had been territorially Romanian in the interwar period. These two issues were part of the same interactive politics of identity formation, since Hungarian attempts to consolidate a secure civic status for its own ethnic minority were contingent on a definition of citizenship that transcended ethnonational identity, while Romanian ties to Moldova were based precisely on ethnic affinity. Meanwhile, Romanian relations with Europe paradoxically hinged on the tragic identity politics of the former Yugoslavia, inasmuch as its geopolitical position ensured that Romania's observance of the embargo would be the paramount concern of the West. The Western priority given the Yugoslav crisis temporarily made Romanian performance in supporting the embargo more important than its patchy record handling its own ethnonational agenda. Virtually all Eastern European states were embroiled in such webs of intersecting identity issues; there was no coherent way of processing them separately and giving them equal weight.

The collapse of communism thus unleashed multiple identity issues and spurred an institutional response. As ethnic tensions and disputes became a key factor in generating Eastern political instability within and across borders, the West responded by elaborating institutional expectations of minority group treatment, which were increasingly codified in major European organizations, notably the Council of Europe and the Conference for Security and Cooperation in Europe. The impulse to incorporate protections of national identity, however, did not originate solely in the West. Ethnonational groups with claims sought validation through regional organizations, as did Eastern European governments. By and large the key states in this effort were Russia and Hungary, each facing the problem of protecting its cross-border kin without giving the appearance of unilateral pressure and bullying. The activation of internationally supported minority rights regimes served to "sanitize" the issue of external intervention, lending it a prescriptive and legally normative multilateral character.

The internal dynamics described in this section are worth elaboration because they are central to the development and content of conflict resolution efforts. The political-electoral balance of domestic forces dictates the amount of external leverage for conflict resolution in a given case. Note that this is true not regardless of the processes of economic-political transformation but precisely because of them. Rapid change creates dislocation, and democratization as an electoral phenomenon offers a base from which to challenge international expectations as well as to support them, especially since central conflictual issues are themselves closely tied to sensitive questions of national identity and sovereignty. Western Europe can seem a puissant obstacle to the attainment of Western European levels of development to the extent that it mounts barriers to trade in "sensitive" areas, pleads poverty in response to aid requests, or hesitates to extend security guarantees in the face of threatening Russian instability. Any outside intervention in highly sensitive issues of national identity (such as the treatment of minorities) reinforces a sense of beleaguerment and threat. The Serbian case, in which all external pressures were so consistently defied and an image of Serbian victimization by the world was sustained, is extreme. The dynamics of that resistance, rooted in a heroic electoral appeal to stand up for Serbia's interests against the world, is reflected in lesser measure in postcommunist states throughout the region, as for example in the politics of beleaguerment practiced in independent Slovakia.

There are therefore at least two competing logics to the way in which the interactive domestic and international effects might operate in potential conflict situations. The simplest formulation of the issue, often implicit in Western scholarship, is that conformity to Western models is itself a conflict reduction mechanism. Capitalist democratic nations do not fight each other. Given an international context supportive of capitalist democratization, the postcommunist states responding to that incentive structure are moving toward security in its broadest sense. Internal incentives to democratize and marketize are reinforced by international incentives to do so, and the interests of Eastern and Western Europe march together. Integration into Western European institutions, particularly the European Union, would only cement the process, since, as Laurence Whitehead argues, such integration is "irreversible," setting "in motion a very complex and profound set of mutual adjustment processes . . . nearly all of which tend to favor democratic consolidation."[18]

There is considerable merit to this conceptualization of the relationship. It captures the embeddedness of the domestic transformation process in its international setting and the generally constructive impact that this embeddedness has had. Yet the international dimension has not been purely positive, bolstering heroic domestic reformers and undercutting benighted opponents. A more nuanced picture incorporates an acknowledgment that international interventions can also generate backlash effects and give opponents new and politically potent grounds to challenge the domestic transformation project as a foreign implant with a price tag on national sovereignty. Given the degree of economic dislocation in transition, some form of backlash is almost certain to manifest itself in electoral politics, and the price of cooperation and integration is almost certain to be controversial. Being an advanced industrial society may promote conflict resolution; getting to that point may carry its own conflict.

The Evolution and Dynamics of Conflict Resolution

The defining features of the external response have been its scope and the multiplicity of its intervention agents. The domestic political and economic reconstruction process is framed by extensive and specialized external intervention that provides technical resources and advice. A look at the "input" side of politics, the linkage institutions connecting elites with mass publics, offers an illustrative example. Western research institutions and foundations have bankrolled an infusion of expertise in public opinion polling to improve the quality of surveys of public policy and electoral preferences. Nascent parties have received foreign support for basic equipment (computers, faxes, campaign materials) and for the formulation of programs and tactics. The sources have included official government programs (the U.S. Fund for Democracy, for example), individual Western parties (the Konrad Adenauer Foundation of the German Christian Democrats or the Fritz Ebert Foundation of the German Social Democrats), and international federations of ideologically associated parties. The electoral systems themselves emerged from a process of institutional design that included technical assistance in drafting electoral laws and election monitoring (drawing on, for example, the legal expertise of the Venice Commission of the Council of Europe). Elected legislators have moved into a parliamentary setting that is institutionally reinforced by external training programs and resources for staffs and parliamentarians (from, for example, the Speaker's Special Task Force on the Development of Parliamentary Institutions in Eastern Europe of the U.S. House of Representatives).[19] A similar point could be made about interventions in the economic arena.

The second feature of this matrix of external interventions is its political character. Taken as a whole, external advice and assistance are not neutral. However dispersed the sources and focus of this influence, it is cumulatively directed toward promoting democratization and marketization compatible with the functioning of Western industrialized democracies. Alternative sources are not always coherent in their impact; they focus on a specialized piece of the democratization puzzle, and there may even be professional rivalry in the attempted implantation of French versus American versus British accounting methods, for example. It may even be argued that the clearest primary beneficiaries of any given intervention are the paid foreign consultants, whose fees and expenses frequently absorb a disproportionate share of the technical aid to the East that supports such ventures.[20] Nonetheless, the expert advice being peddled at multiple access points in the new polities does not reflect a free marketplace of ideas. The sources of funding and support and the kinds of expertise available ensure that existing Western approaches and structures will be promoted. External interventions are not designed to locate or develop a third way or even to tailor policy prescriptions to the unique environment of postcommunist transition. This is an environment in which there is no established expertise, only experimental practitioners.

Nor is external intervention solely advisory in character. Transnational organizations play an important validating role in assessing and credentialing the economic and political policies of a state. The IMF seal of approval for a government's economic agenda not only determines the release of IMF loans but also signals potential investors and others of the viability of the economy in question, its readiness to absorb economic investment and trade.

There is no single isolated logic to any given external transaction. For example, the attainment of Council of Europe (CE) membership, a record of cooperation with and responsiveness to a CSCE fact-finding mission, and successful negotiations with the IMF all signal to other international organizations that the state has surmounted hurdles that move it closer to the return to Europe. A state's international status thus depends on not only its domestic performance but also external evaluations of that performance. Each state encounters an ever-intensifying web of external relationships as it promotes the process of internal change. A state's formal long-term commitment to European integration is constantly tested by the immediacy of specific expectations from a multiplicity of external sources. Interdependence is an accurate but rather vague and imprecise way of describing this embeddedness.

Eastern interest in inclusion offered Western European governments a range of incentives to promote conduct becoming a Eurocitizen. Membership and improvised associational relations operated on several levels. At the most basic level, the message was behave and hope to join. But beyond that inducement, membership and other transactions were vehicles for monitoring and modifying Eastern European behavior.

The Council of Europe is an important example. The CE offered membership only to democratic governments. To be certified, states had to undergo an investigatory process that did not cease with admission. Fledgling members were in effect on probation, subject to follow-up evaluation pending eventual unconditional membership.

What is most significant about this feedback cycle is its content. Membership in the CE did entail incurring certain international obligations to fellow members, but eligibility also hinged on a state's internal politics. No state was of course compelled to submit to CE vetting, but those that did so mortgaged parts of their sovereignty and agenda-setting autonomy to the organization. Over the course of its history the Council of Europe has ratified almost 150 conventions binding on its membership, and new members are expected to come into compliance with these conventions. Ratification of CE human rights protocols, for example, entitles individual citizens or groups of citizens in member states to appeal their grievances to the CE Human Rights Committee, thus extending the international monitoring process indefinitely. Membership in the Council of Europe was not a single "carrot" or one-time incentive to behavior moderation but instead an ongoing process of accommodation with that institution's definitions of constructive behavior, both codified and uncodified. Membership was not only a reward but also a normative structure that set standards and a monitoring structure that evaluated compliance with the standards; it was thus a mechanism for encouraging favorable results on a broad range of domestic and foreign policy issues over time.

Estonia's application for membership in the Council of Europe may give a fuller sense of the dynamics of obtaining and holding membership. To qualify, the state underwent a series of eligibility reviews, notably by the human rights subcommittee, which, in approving the application, noted that Estonia's citizenship laws and other practices conformed to international protocols (a result achieved only after revision in accordance with external recommendations), while making recommendations about legislation on criminal justice and journalistic freedom of information.[21]

Attaining good standing with other multilateral organizations entailed a similar process of external intervention in domestic policy. Estonian officials reported having hosted more than a dozen human rights fact-finding missions from the United Nations and European organizations in its first two years of statehood. All such missions were accepted in the interests of certifying the validity of the state's democratic practice. The most prized attainments, NATO and EU membership, raise the challenge of this form of accreditation no less than did the CE. The broad criteria for NATO and EU membership were similar to those of the CE, including a democratic system. In the case of the EU, democracy and a capitalist economy were presumed to be necessary prerequisites to the more specific requirements of system compatibility. NATO follows the rationale that peaceful states are democratic states in imposing a similar requirement of democratic conditionality. In virtually every European institution to which the Eastern states might aspire, therefore, there was a quid pro quo not only in behavior but also in compatible domestic systems.

European Union

The European Union is an important institution in conflict management despite its own inadequacy as a security organization and the underinstitutionalization of its security arm, the West European Union (WEU). This is because the EU has significant trade and aid incentives to offer and because EU membership is one of the most powerful incentives to good behavior that the West possesses. In addition, by strategic decision in the summer of 1989 the European Commission of the EU became the primary body for coordinating aid to Eastern European states (at that time, Hungary and Poland) seeking to marketize their economies.[22]

The transitions of the East have of course taxed the EU's capacity to respond, for it is weakest in precisely those areas that would enhance a coherent response—in the coordination of a common foreign and security policy (CFSP). Divisiveness on the handing of the Yugoslav crisis was evident from the outset in German insistence that a reluctant EU grant prompt recognition to Croatia and Slovenia. More recently the EU hesitated painfully in responding to the need to restore order in Albania following tumultuous popular response to the collapse of several pyramid schemes in early 1997. A range of factors impeded effective response. Sensitive questions about the rules of engagement and the presence of Italian troops in a country occupied by Mussolini's armies in World War II were specific to the Albanian crisis. Response was also constrained by institutional factors, including the lack of a standing WEU military force, the unanimity rule governing CFSP policy initiatives, and the question of how a collegial leadership speaks with one voice for Europe. As Henry Kissinger once said, "When I want to speak to Europe, who do I call?"[23] More generally there is a lack of consensus over the issue of "broadening versus deepening" the organization, which has led to flirtations with the idea of a "two-speed" EU structure, whose inner core would be more tightly integrated.

Paralleling this controversy is a divergence of interests within the EU over the accession of new Eastern members. The poorer members (Spain and Portugal) fear a dilution of their own subsidies and the diversion of EU resources eastward. Germany's staunch championship of Eastern inclusion and its insistence that Eastern European instability is a continental security threat have led to the perception that a united Germany is too dominant in imposing its agenda on the EU. These divisions tend to undercut the incentive structure, insofar as uncertainties about EU's commitment to including some of the postcommunist states weakens the tight linkage between good conduct and the reward of inclusion. To the extent that EU membership is seen as a vague and receding target, its power as an incentive to modulate conduct is diminished.[24]

Nonetheless, there has been sufficient movement toward a clearer timetable for accession to maintain the power of the membership incentive. EU delegations routinely conducted site visits to transitioning Eastern European states from Albania to Hungary to explore needs and evaluate progress toward reform, as have the representatives in the European Parliament for EU relations with the former communist states. The EU negotiated bilateral economic agreements with all the postcommunist states, although Eastern states remain vocally dissatisfied with the restriction on trade in such "sensitive areas" as agriculture and steel, in which they are highly competitive. At a more intensive level the EU concluded the so-called European Agreements with ten postcommunist states that accord them associate member status, proffer a vaguely formulated acknowledgment of their membership aspirations, and include a package of trade and aid agreements. All of these agreements are important not only for what they offer in specific terms but also as stepping stones in an ongoing process of engagement that encourages each postcommunist to preserve stability and promote progress in democratization and marketization.

In December 1994 the EU announced a "preaccession strategy"—a "structured dialogue" to guide the policy choices of Eastern European aspirants to membership. An EU "white paper" followed in May 1995, stipulating the most salient parts of the *acquis communautaire* (EU regulations) to which Eastern Europeans must conform to establish their eligibility to participate in the European single market. This move was accompanied by an aid package designed to help defray the costs of coming into compliance with EU standards. Accession talks with Poland, the Czech Republic, Estonia, Hungary, and Slovenia are slated for 1998. Slovakia and Romania remain in limbo.

Overall, the EU's gatekeeper function in the return to Europe is its strongest card in exerting a generalized influence on Eastern instabilities. The sense of constrained political autonomy is very clearly expressed in the comments of rival Hungarian and Romanian officials, whose dissension on the treatment of the Hungarian minority in Romania does not blind them to the consequences of overstepping boundaries on this contentious issue. As the Romanian foreign minister, more sensitive to international pressures than many of his domestic colleagues, acknowledged in 1992, "The main goal of both Romania and Hungary is to become integrated into European structures. It is clear that neither Romania nor Hungary will be received as full members if they fail to prove that they are able to rise to the level of European dialogue and behavior. . . . Whether we like it or not, and even if this causes a certain amount of antagonistic feelings, a considerable part of Romania's road toward Europe leads through Hungary. Romanian-Hungarian relations are also Romanian-EC relations."[25]

NATO

NATO's capacity to respond to new conflict situations in postcommunist Europe has been hampered by a range of challenges to institutional adaptation. Chief among them is that NATO was conceived as a traditional alliance, designed to deter or defeat aggression. The laboriously crafted nuclear and conventional arms control regimes concluded through WTO-NATO negotiations were of only limited value to post–cold war conflict resolution. NATO was thus ill-prepared to respond to a series of post–cold war crises and hot spots that, despite compelling international dimensions and stakes, originated in internal conflict, often ethnonational in character. The alliance's limitations were brutally clear in the Yugoslav crisis from the outset, and NATO did not subsequently adjust effectively. Its cumbersome relationship with the United Nations in enforcing U.N. mandates was a case in point. NATO's internal divisions on the appropriate strategy of conflict management were also vividly evident in Euro-American disputes: the U.S. refusal to supply ground troops for NATO-directed enforcement of safe zones, European refusal to support U.S. enthusiasm for continued punitive air strikes in Bosnia, and the unilateral U.S. abandonment of enforcement of the arms embargo to permit Bosnian self-defense, and the disputes over NATO deployment following the Dayton Peace Accords of 1995. Such divisions, not unique to the post–cold war period, nonetheless have become more pressing in recent years. Past alliance quarrels over the IMF or sharing the defense burden were very real, but they were conducted in a vacuum; no active conflict situation required a concrete response. The Yugoslav crisis pushed NATO to its consensual limits and intensified the existing crisis of mission by forcing onto the security agenda a conflict that effectively dramatized the alliance's inadequacies.

The most pressing future task in this tragic situation, a task to be continued in the ambit of combined European and U.N. agencies, is the containment of the conflict within its current boundaries. In practical terms this means shoring up the stability of neighboring countries (Bulgaria, Albania, and Greece)—as much a diplomatic mission as a military one—and, problematically, offering the Yugoslav successor states inducements to accord minimally acceptable treatment to their remaining minorities, particularly the Albanians of Kosovo. In each instance the essential element is crisis prevention. The further regionalization of the Yugoslav conflict would provoke a disaster that could dwarf the scale of the previous one.

NATO's broader crisis is a crisis of inclusion, of extending the alliance eastward. In addition to NATO fears of enlarging security concerns by accepting new Eastern members, a true security dilemma lurked behind Western reluctance to antagonize a defensive Russia. Would the extension of security guarantees to central Europe be an extension of the security zone in Europe or a red flag that by alarming Russia could increase tensions in the area? Russian officials depicted the incorporation of new

NATO members as "a mighty armed fist near our border" and argued that NATO expansion was the "West's biggest mistake since the end of the Cold War," threatening to redivide Europe.[26] The Russian leadership continues to pursue a vision of security that is unacceptable to the West: a multipillared blocless Europe in which NATO, the WEU, and Russia (with a special sphere of responsibility in the Commonwealth of Independent States) would broker security threats under the umbrella of the Organization for Security and Cooperation in Europe (OSCE).[27]

The NATO initiatives since 1989 to extend military cooperation and information sharing were designed to hedge this Russian question and the additional questions of undertaking more direct and binding commitments to an unstable area. The initial gesture—the establishment of a North Atlantic Cooperation Council open to virtually all postcommunist European states—was succeeded by U.S. president Bill Clinton's Partnership for Peace initiative in 1993. Both were adjudged half-way measures in central Europe. Most central European governments grudgingly agreed with Estonian president Lennart Meri in his comment that the "Partnership for Peace was the best NATO could at present offer to East European states,"[28] given Russian resistance.

The continuing aspirations of Eastern European governments to achieve alliance membership and security guarantees, despite the costs of bringing postcommunist military establishments into conformity with NATO standards,[29] placed NATO in an awkward position. Like the EU, NATO hoped to respond to Eastern impatience with clear guidelines but was plagued by divisions and doubts. European concerns with appearing to partition Europe were reinforced by the sense that such a move would stunt the development of a separate European defense identity, which might better be served by giving priority to EU expansion and the development of its WEU (Eastern European states and the Baltics were accorded associate membership in the WEU in May 1994). The instabilities of the East thus continue to be framed by an ambiguous security environment, an environment that NATO is reluctant to reconfigure because it fears triggering a "cold peace" (in Yeltsin's words) that might protect the elite states that gained admission while excluding Russia, Ukraine, and other states. It is therefore too simple to think of NATO expansion as extending the scope of deterrence or ensuring other univalent conflict reduction effects. That same act of clarification risks raising tensions and redefining excluded states as outside the protection zone and even as enemies.

Plagued by such concerns, NATO waited until the fall of 1995 to approve an enlargement study on the criteria for accepting new members—criteria that tellingly included democratic governance and a free market economy. This study, however, specified neither prospective members nor a timetable for admission. The first membership cohort—Poland, the Czech Republic, and Hungary—was named at the NATO meeting of July 1997, only after face-saving measures to respond to Russian doubts and insecurities.

CSCE

NATO's dilemma was initially an incentive to look elsewhere for conflict management resources. Despite its organizational weaknesses, the Conference on Security and Cooperation in Europe (CSCE) was a promising forum for conflict resolution for several reasons. It included all parties to potential and actual regional disputes. Unlike the Western European economic and security institutions, the CSCE had from the outset been valuable precisely because it was inclusive; it was designed to be. The looseness of its organization reflected that inclusiveness; tighter contractual arrangements across political systems and cold war boundaries were difficult to envisage. It maintained its inclusive character after 1989, expanding from thirty-five members to fifty-three to include the new successor states of the former communist federations. But the end of the cold war also gave the CSCE an impetus to fuller institutionalization. The easing of the previous dissension over values and the urgency of the task of managing fallout from disruptive state and systemic change produced a spurt of organizational energy.

Above all the establishment of more permanent agencies seemed important to stabilize channels of communication and conferral. These included a permanent secretariat in Prague, the Conflict Prevention Center in Vienna, and the Office for Free Elections (after 1992 the Office of Democratic Institutions and Human Rights) in Warsaw. The apotheosis of its organizational metamorphosis was the renaming of the CSCE in late 1994, when it abandoned its semi-institutional identity as a "conference" for that of the Organization for Cooperation and Security in Europe (OSCE).

If this institutionalization process augmented CSCE conflict resolution capabilities, so too did the partial mitigation of the consensus rule that had previously hamstrung CSCE initiatives. The consensus rule was not in itself discarded, but its application depended on the type of action to be undertaken. Fact-finding missions, for example, could be organized at the behest of as few as five member states. It was resolved in 1992 that agenda items could be open for discussion and CSCE policy declarations made without unanimity, even if the target country itself (Serbia, for example) objected. This modification of the consensus rule, dubbed "consensus minus one," allowed the CSCE to avoid being silenced by the veto of the very member whose behavior was in question.[30]

The CSCE contributed two kinds of initiatives to the pursuit of postcommunist conflict management: the elaboration of norms of domestic and international conduct and the elaboration of intervention mechanisms for monitoring and mediating tensions, particularly those that seethed below the threshold of violence. Both of these initiatives can be illustrated in the CSCE's increasing engagement in conflict prevention in the realm of ethnonational tensions, which has been a landmark in the evolution of the organizational mission.[31] Although the treatment of minorities had been mentioned tangentially in the Helsinki Final Act, the CSCE of 1989 had no institutional mandate to respond to the volatile ethnonational tensions in postcommunist Europe. Spurred partly by institutional helplessness in the face of the Yugoslav crisis and by its ominous implications for the possible escalation of ethnic tensions elsewhere, the CSCE began to discuss ethnonational threats to security in earnest as early as 1990, when the documents of the Copenhagen meeting included a separate chapter on minority issues. This detailed listing of expectations about minority treatment, heavily qualified though they were by concessions to raison d'état, was underscored the following year when the expert conference on national minorities in Geneva resolved that minority issues were of "legitimate international concern and consequently do not constitute exclusively an internal affair of the respective State."[32]

Taken together, these two policy declarations outlined a rough code of conduct and placed it squarely within the province of legitimate international concern. It was in the CSCE above all that a clear reformulation of the limits of national sovereignty regarding individual and group identity issues came into focus, a reformulation that outstripped in clarity and detail any other international human rights regime on national identity questions, including that of the United Nations itself. The CSCE's Moscow conference in October 1991 hammered out a "mechanism" for providing experienced mediators and fact-finding missions to deal with targeted ethnic problems. The final and most practically important step in this process was the establishment, in July 1992, of the CSCE High Commissioner of National Minorities, charged with developing an "early warning" system to identify and help defuse ethnic tensions that might escalate to regionally destabilizing levels. Koen Koch emphasizes the mission of this institution, observing that it was charged with acting as an "'instrument of conflict prevention at the earliest possible stage,' rather than to promote the protection of minority rights per se."[33] Minority rights activists in the region also note a shift in emphasis on ethnic questions "from being a human rights issue" to "a security issue"[34] and profess to welcome it as assurance that the minority question will be taken seriously.

Despite its weakness in the core Yugoslav conflict, the OSCE made vigorous and extensive use of these mechanisms in other settings, including a series of initiatives designed to broker stability in the fringe areas of the conflict. Although earlier intercession in the sensitive Serbian areas of Kosovo and the Vojvodina ceased with the retraction of Serbian permission in 1993, efforts continue in Macedonia, and the OSCE has struggled with the mandate to oversee elections and human rights observance in post-Dayton Bosnia.

The OSCE has also tried to improve the quality of mediation efforts in overt conflicts in the former Soviet Union (Nagorno-Karabakh, Moldova, and Tajikistan); it has been as lukewarm as other international organizations to Russia's interest in anointing itself regional peacekeeper in this area. The Budapest summit of the newly minted OSCE in 1994 approved in principle a breakthrough declaration allowing a contingent of three thousand troops to be sent to Nagorno-Karabakh under the aegis of the OSCE in the event that a local agreement on the termination of armed conflict could be achieved. OSCE engagement in the Baltic states has been particularly visible and pervasive, almost certainly contributing to greater leniency in citizenship laws and to Russian agreements for troop withdrawal from the area.

The value of these mechanisms for investigation and mediation is difficult to assess, though most analysts have been approving but very cautious regarding OSCE capabilities. A target state may abort potential conflict resolution initiatives by simply refusing to cooperate or even to admit OSCE observers. Serbia eventually did this in 1993. The OSCE still has no enforcement capability of its own, although NATO agreed in 1992 to put forces at its disposal on request. It might be argued that OSCE activities are currently most influential in their ability to validate or discredit a state's progress toward Western integration; the organization is a gatekeeper to membership in Western organizations insofar as its evaluation of current and potential conflict situations weighs with the overlapping membership of the EU and NATO. To date the OSCE is a low-cost operation (most expertise is obtained from member states) whose benefits surely outweigh the outlay, but it has failed to meet any stringent test of conflict management.

Although it is helpful to isolate major European organizations for consideration, it is highly artificial to treat Europe's institutional resources for conflict moderation and resolution separately. Characteristically, states with security concerns or grievances have availed themselves of the full range of existing international forums. Facing continuing uncertainty in negotiations with Russia over troop withdrawals, for example, the Baltics states appealed to the OSCE, the United Nations, and the Council of Europe, among others. Russians counterpetitioned the same organizations on the issue of treatment of ethnically Russian Balts. The network of external actors must be regarded as precisely that—a network.

Conclusion

The key features of the setting for international conflict resolution in Eastern Europe are normative coherence and multiplicity of agents engaged in the negotiation of desired behavior. Recent studies of international regimes have emphasized the "prescriptive status" of behavioral norms as a precondition of appropriate behavior.[35] A norm that has acquired prescriptive status will frequently be invoked as a yardstick for evaluating state conduct. Any close reading of the official statements and public disputations of Eastern European political actors would tend to confirm that the norms of international conventions to which they have formally subscribed or to which they aspire to subscribe have generally attained such a prescriptive status. Defense of one's own conduct and the evaluation of others' conduct are routinely couched in the language of international norms. Although quarrels over application and interpretation abound, the mainstream political discourse of Eastern Europe is clearly one that accepts the premises of such international instruments as human rights conventions, norms of peaceful conflict resolution and democratic accountability, and so on. This general normative consensus is embodied in the expectations of diverse external actors, whose prescriptions for appropriate state behavior generally overlap markedly from one organization to another, regardless of the functional specialization of missions.

There are three potential problems with this normative regime. The first is the extent to which prescriptive norms are not a coherent package but a menu from which political actors willfully and selectively choose, a problem that might be illustrated in Romania's continued dodging of the minority rights issue. The second problem is the extent to which the prescriptive norms are a coherent package only in later phases of transformation. Capitalist wealth and stable democracy may be mutually reinforcing in a well-established political regime, but such a virtuous circle does not operate in the early phases of institution building, where fragile new political mechanisms must struggle with the social pain of economic transformation. Attaining the full benefits of the normative package may require more popular patience than a fledgling system can sustain. Finally, normative prescriptions may correspond rather inadequately to behavioral practice. Koch has noted the disturbing extent to which "the international community seems to excel in 'declaratory' diplomacy and 'symbolic politics'" at the expense of practical execution.[36]

Nonetheless, the norms generated by the Council of Europe, NATO, the European Union, and others have been notably consistent in general terms, and some features, such as the "democratic conditionality" attached to membership eligibility in political, military, and economic structures, lend coherence to the pattern of expectations to which the Eastern countries are invited to adhere. Moreover, external norms and expectations correspond roughly to the goals of internal transformation (doubters find external norms a straitjacket and a prescription for protracted economic pain).

A second feature of the postcommunist setting for conflict resolution is that the contemporary "mechanism" for responding to crisis and conflict is a hydra-headed organism lacking any single institutional focus. Each institutional component of the amalgam is greatly deficient in core capabilities. All European military response capabilities currently depend on the support of American airlift and intelligence capacities. The WEU lacks an integrated military command to mobilize Euroforces, and the nascent Eurocorps (with troops from Spain, France, Belgium, and Germany) floats between organizations without autonomous resources to mount a full-scale engagement on its own. All of these, plus NATO itself, lack a clear and articulated mission in the unprotected areas of postcommunist Europe.

The political and economic pillars of a new European security architecture also overlap, exclude, and include in a pattern that gains influence in conflict management through the incentives for cooperation it imposes on the East. It is notable that the corridor of states that had been neutral in the cold war period (Sweden, Austria, Finland) is dissolving into Western alignment with their accession to the EU. Their cold war distance from the European Community (EC) had been framed by the political and security implications of EC membership.

The complex of institutional interrelationships focused on economic security is equally multifaceted. The burden of monitoring, evaluating, and supporting Eastern reform is diffused throughout a network of established institutions (the EU, IMF, G-7, OECD), as well as through a phalanx of newly developed ones specifically devised in response to the channeling of the Eastern economic transformation (PHARE and the European Bank for Reconstruction and Development, for example).

In traditional security and economic arenas the complexity and density of organizational linkages have accelerated in the aftermath of 1989. This intensification and elaboration is surprisingly coherent, however, largely because of the normative consistency across institutions. The result is that feedback cycles are self-amplifying: negative or positive performance by an Eastern country on a given issue tends to resonate throughout the web of relationships, generating proportionate rewards or punishments and tying one area of conduct to external response in a range of others. Although this web was not consciously engineered (many of the key elements predate 1989), the effect has been to align external influences in a uniform way that gives a certain consistency to the stances of Eastern European politicians who play the international card at home.

Consistency, of course, does not mean a clear division of responsibility. In the face of the 1997 Albanian crisis, the complex multilateral institutions displayed a hesitancy that is now characteristic in determining what the appropriate channel of response should be. As the EU deadlocked on sending military forces to secure aid convoys and public order, the United States argued for the coordination of the mission by the OSCE instead. The OSCE in turn brought a proposal to the United Nations, and it was under U.N. auspices that the authorization for the commitment of military forces was made. In other cases a division of labor marks the engagement of the multilateral network. In Bosnia, for example, the Dayton Accords provided diverse roles and responsibilities for NATO, the OSCE, the United Nations, the EU, and the Council of Europe.

What conclusions can be drawn from this understanding of the environment for conflict management and resolution? The tight and multifaceted external constraints on Eastern European domestic policy agendas amount to a gamble that the interlocking logic of democratization, marketization, and ethnonational conciliation will pay off in material wellbeing and security soon enough to prevent a self-defeating cycle of instability that is fed rather than ameliorated by external monitoring and incentives. To illustrate this negative scenario, consider the case of Slovakia, where governments responsive to Western expectations have alternated with combative Meciar governments that have played to internal desires for autonomy and domestic resentments of foreign influence. Slovakia thus remains on the fringes of political eligibility and respectability in Europe and is subject to swings in internal commitment to making the tough decisions about reform. It has paid the penalty by being dropped from the list of favorites for first-round admission to NATO and the EU. All countries in the region have developed some reservoirs of resentment over the slow pace of integration into Europe, the stringent stabilization regimen of the IMF, and the limits of trade liberalization. To date, however, ignoring external expectations has costs that have deterred all the mainstream politicians outside Yugoslavia (even ex-communists returned to power) from any radical rejection of the logic of external expectations. On the whole, then, interconnected networks seem to be serving their intended purposes.

A reasonable argument could be made that the dislocation and stress in the transition and ethnic tensions are manageable under the currently evolving international organizations in all cases where state disintegration was avoided. That is to say that the worst security threat to the post-communist order lies with the former federal states, where exceptionally complex ethnic issues (reflected in the very fact of federalization) led to internal deadlock and explosive disintegration. European institutions were particularly ill-adapted to deal with this situation because of its slippery domestic-international character and the issues raised about territorial integrity and the limits of national self-determination. Where this incendiary situation does not exist (outside the former Soviet Union and Yugoslavia), domestic and international capacities for mediation and negotiation of conflict are probably sufficient to contain it, if not to resolve it. This analysis, of course, may not be particularly comforting, for it offers limited solace to those who must deal with the fallout of the Yugoslav crisis or the continuing flares of violence in the Commonwealth of Independent States.

Where in this welter of crosscutting institutions is the security architecture of the new Europe? Where is this embryonic security regime heading? Toward no immediate tidy conclusion. For the foreseeable future, the process of economic integration is likely to be protracted, and the messiness of the overlapping monitoring and support apparatuses is likely to persist. I would even argue that the ambiguities (calculated or uncalculated) of this messiness are preferable to a clear single track that sets stark boundaries in Europe between haves and have-nots, the protected and the unprotected, the members and the nonmembers. The greatest test of Europe's new security architecture will come when excluded states feel themselves definitively and permanently on the wrong side of a European fence-building project. The current proliferation of access points for consultation and intervention, the multiplicitous though modest aid sources, the improvised associate memberships and interim cooperation agreements, the complex structure of reward, normative standard-setting, and compliance monitoring—all of these bought time for democratization and marketization to work.

Notes

1. Dmitry Trenin, "NATO Faces the Future," *Moscow Times*, November 13, 1994.

2. Transparency measures are efforts to increase security by making sure rival states inform each other of such things as troop movements, troop levels, and other military information. The idea is that making a state's military activities more "transparent" will reassure neighbors that they know what is going on next door, and, for example, will not mistake routine military exercises for more threatening activity.

3. James Mayall, "Nationalism and International Security after the Cold War," *Survival* 34, no. 1 (1992): 19.

4. Quoted in *New York Times*, August 10, 1992.

5. It must be understood that national tensions were not frozen during the cold war period. What was frozen was their constructive acknowledgment. The period between 1945 and 1989 did recontour some of the issues and institutions surrounding the national question. The demographic shifts in the Baltics and the federalization of both Yugoslavia and Czechoslovakia are only examples of the kinds of shifts in the strategic environment of the national question that occurred after 1945.

6. Other important postcommunist regional problems, such as the nuclear proliferation that occurred because the USSR disintegrated, fall outside the core regional focus of this analysis.

7. Claus Offe, "Capitalism by Democratic Design? Democratic Theory Facing the Triple Transition in East Central Europe," *Social Research* 58, no. 4 (1991): 865–92.

8. Daniel N. Nelson, "Security in Europe's Eastern Half," in *East-Central Europe and the USSR*, ed. Richard F. Staar (New York: St. Martin's, 1991), 62.

9. The growing core of foreign residents analyzed by James F. Hollifield, *Immigrants, Markets, and States: The Political Economy of Postwar Europe* (Cambridge, Mass.: Harvard University Press, 1992); Reginald T. Appleyard, *International Migration: Challenge for the Nineties* (Geneva: International Organization for Migration, 1991); and others in France, Germany, and Great Britain posed a knotty political problem well before freedom of movement for East European populations threatened to augment it with new sources of migration. The specifically East European component of this issue has been investigated in F. Stephen Larrabee, "Down and Out in Warsaw and Budapest: East Europe and East-West Migration," *International Security* 16, no. 4 (1992): 5–33; Michael Shafir, ed., "Immigrants, Refugees and Postcommunism," Special Series on Immigration Questions, *RFE/RL Research Report* 3, no. 23 (1994); and Richard Layard, Olivier Blanchard, Rudiger Dornbusch, and Paul Krugman, *East-West Migration: The Alternatives* (Cambridge, Mass.: MIT Press, 1992).

10. Geoffrey Pridham, "Democratic Transitions in Theory and Practice: Southern European Lessons for Eastern Europe," in *Democratization in Eastern Europe: Domestic and International Perspectives*, ed. Geoffrey Pridham and Tatu Vanhanen (London: Routledge, 1994), 15–38.

11. James Mayall, *Nationalism and International Society* (Cambridge: Cambridge University Press, 1990).

12. Eric Herring, "International Security and Democratisation in Eastern Europe," in *Building Democracy? The International Dimension of Democratisation in Eastern Europe,* ed. Geoffrey Pridham, Eric Herring, and George Sanford (New York: St. Martin's, 1994), 89.

13. Gregory Treverton, "The New Europe," *Foreign Affairs* 71, no. 1 (1991/1992): 106.

14. Laurence Whitehead, "Three International Dimensions of Democratization," in *The International Dimensions of Democratization: Europe and the Americas,* ed. Laurence Whitehead (New York: Oxford University Press, 1996), 3–27.

15. Donald L. Horowitz, *Ethnic Groups in Conflict* (Berkeley: University of California Press, 1985), 580–84.

16. "European Economic Integration: The Little White Book," *Warsaw Voice,* November 13, 1994.

17. *Magyar Hírlap,* October 22, 1992, 2, in *FBIS-EEU-92-208,* October 27, 1992, 22.

18. Laurence Whitehead, "The International Dimension of Democratization: A Survey of the Alternatives" (Paper presented at the Fifteenth World Congress of the International Political Science Association, Buenos Aires, July 1991), 16–17.

19. Joern G. Stegen, "The Parliamentary Assembly of the Council of Europe and Its Relations with Central and Eastern Europe," in *Working Papers on Comparative Legislative Studies,* ed. Lawrence D. Longley (Paris: Research Committee of Legislative Specialists, IPSA, 1994), 407–9; Adrian G. V. Hyde-Price, "Democratization in Eastern Europe: The External Dimension," in *Democratization in Eastern Europe,* ed. Pridham and Vanhanen, 191–219; William H. Robinson and Francis Miko, "Parliamentary Development Assistance in Central Europe and the Former Soviet Union: Some Lessons from Experience," in *Working Papers on Comparative Legislative Studies,* ed. Longley, 409–30.

20. See especially Thomas Carothers, *Assessing Democracy Assistance: The Case of Romania* (New York: Carnegie Endowment for Peace, 1996).

21. See Moscow Baltfax, March 31, 1993, in *FBIS-SOV-93-061,* April 1, 1993, 82.

22. Hyde-Price, "Democratization in Eastern Europe."

23. Henry Kissinger quoted in the *Economist,* March 22, 1997, 60.

24. The recent accession of European Free Trade Association (EFTA) states to the EU probably enhances East European eligibility. The EFTA recruits are richer and more developed than the average EU member and thus increase EU's assistance capabilities for new, poorer members.

25. *Népszabadság,* January 4, 1992, 1, in *FBIS-EEU-93-003,* January 6, 1993, 27.

26. *OMRI [Open Media Research Institute] Daily Digest,* no. 33 (February 1997) and no. 56 (20 March 1997).

27. Michael Mihalka, "European-Russian Security and NATO's Partnership for Peace," *RFE/RL Research Report* 3, no. 33 (1994): 38.

28. Press release, quoted in *FBIS-SOV-94-011,* January 18, 1994, 104.

29. This thrust entails developing weapons systems compatible with NATO's, a prospect to which Russia objects not only on security grounds but also because of the probable further erosion of the Russian arms market.

30. On occasion, however, CSCE declarations regarding Serbia were scotched by Russian dissent from the proposed formulation, as was the case with the declaration at the Budapest CSCE summit of December 1994.

31. William Korey, "Minority Rights after Helsinki," *Ethics and International Affairs* 8 (1994): 119–41.

32. This proposition became a formal CSCE decision at the Moscow Meeting of the CSCE Commission on the Human Dimension in October 1991. Konrad J. Huber, "The CSCE's New Role in the East: Conflict Prevention," *RFE/RL Research Report* 3, no. 31 (1994): 31. See also Konrad J. Huber, "Preventing Ethnic Conflict in the New Europe: The CSCE High Commissioner on National Minorities," in *Minorities: The New Europe's Old Issue,* ed. Ian Cuthbertson and Jane Leibowitz (Prague: Institute for East-West Studies, 1993), 285–310; and Konrad J. Huber, "The CSCE and Ethnic Conflict in the East," *RFE/RL Research Report* 2, no. 31 (1993): 30–36.

33. Koen Koch, "The International Community and Forms of Intervention in the Field of Minority Rights Protection," in *Minorities: The New Europe's Old Issue,* ed. Cuthbertson and Leibowitz, 254.

34. Miklós Duray, chairman of the Hungarian-based Coexistence party in Slovakia, cited in Budapest *Koztársaság,* December 18, 1992, in *FBIS-EEU-92-249,* December 28, 1992, 12.

35. Volker Rittberger, ed., *International Regimes in East-West Politics* (New York: Pinter, 1990).

36. Koch, "The International Community and Forms of Intervention in the Field of Minority Rights Protection," 256.

10

Russia as a Regional Peacekeeper

Alexander V. Kozhemiakin and Roger E. Kanet

The rapid disintegration of the USSR into more than a dozen independent states, while avoiding massive violence, has resulted in intense localized conflicts within and between the new republics. The Russian Federation, considering itself the successor to the Soviet Union, has repeatedly declared and acted on its intentions to play an active diplomatic and, most important, military role in ameliorating such conflicts. This policy is clearly manifested in Russian president Boris Yeltsin's assertion that "the time has come for distinguished international organizations, including the United Nations, to grant Russia special powers of a guarantor of peace and stability in regions of the former USSR."[1]

The primary purpose of this study is to examine the determinants of Russian military involvement in the conflicts that have erupted in the former Soviet Union. It is argued that although Moscow lacks a coherent policy of conflict resolution, its decisions to send troops to the strife-ridden former Soviet republics are driven by goals and impeded by constraints that can be identified and examined. As the following analysis suggests, short of any substantial change in the international climate, Russia is likely to continue pursuing an assertive policy as a regional peacekeeper.

Peacekeeping: Why Do Russians Get Involved?

There are several goals that the Russian leadership attempts to advance through its military involvement in the conflicts in the "near abroad" (a term that refers to the other, non-Russian, former republics of the USSR).[2] The general classification of these goals in order of importance is an extremely slippery task because of the normative considerations involved. Moreover, a classification of this sort is not analytically significant, since no such system of ordering exists currently in Russia; each decision maker, whether a member of Parliament or a presidential adviser, classifies the goals of a military mission according to his or her own political views and individual values.

One of the most publicized objectives of Russian military involvement in regional conflicts taking place in other former Soviet republics is the desire to fill the power vacuum that resulted after the collapse of the USSR. Thus, for example, the former commander in chief of the CIS joint armed forces, Marshal Evgenii Shaposhnikov, repeatedly warned of the rising power of such countries as Turkey, Iran, and Pakistan and their potential influence on the developments in the Asian republics of the Commonwealth of Independent States (CIS).[3] Others, especially opponents of Yeltsin's initial pro-Western stance such as Evgenii Ambartsumov, former chairman of the parliamentary Committee on International Affairs and Foreign Economic Relations, expressed concern about the possibility of U.N. intervention or active OSCE (Organization for Security and Cooperation in Europe) involvement in the post-Soviet conflicts.[4] This partly explains their strong opposition to military intervention against Serbia, which might serve as a precedent for future intervention on former Soviet territory.[5]

It is interesting to note that even Andrei Kozyrev, who as post-Soviet Russia's first foreign minister became famous in the West for his liberal, antinationalist orientation, eventually started to refer to the former Soviet republics as part of the Russian "home." For example, supporting the decision to send Russian troops to Georgia on a peacekeeping mission, Kozyrev emphasized that "there is never a vacuum—if we refuse to live up to our geopolitical role, someone else will try and clean up the mess in our home."[6] Although Kozyrev denied any shift in his policies after the 1993 parliamentary elections during which Vladimir Zhirinovsky's ultranationalist party emerged as a qualified winner by gaining more than one-fifth of the vote, Moscow officials, motivated by political survival under conditions of electoral competition, became extremely sensitive to the increasingly powerful domestic nationalist pressures.[7] The "diplomacy of smiles" and the "policy of yes"—that is, Russian support for Western policy initiatives—emerged as favorite targets for the right-wing populist opposition that attacked Yeltsin's government, especially the Foreign Ministry, for "selling out" Russian interests to the West.[8] The primary focus of the most violent criticism of Russian foreign policy was, however, Moscow's moderate position toward other Soviet successor states based on the respect for their sovereignty.[9] As the former vice president and now active nationalist politician Aleksandr Rutskoi put it, "The historical con-

sciousness of the Russians will not allow anybody to equate mechanical-
ly the borders of Russia with those of the Russian Federation and to take
away what constituted the glorious pages of Russian history."[10]

The second objective of the Russian military involvement is therefore
to glue together the remnants of the collapsed union. With the lowering
of the Soviet flag over the Kremlin, Russia's position as a catalyst of the
disintegration processes in the former Soviet region has been rapidly reversed. Regarding itself the principal successor to the Soviet Union and
conscious of its substantial geopolitical resources, Russia has started to play
the role of primus inter pares in the former Soviet republics.

Despite official disclaimers that Russia has no desire to reestablish dominance over the newly emerging states, Russian leaders have had problems adjusting to the new reality in which they are expected to negotiate as equals with independent political elites in Kiev and Almaty rather
than merely issue instructions, as would have occurred in the past. This
is part of a much larger psychological problem of "redefining Russia's statehood and establishing a new concept of Russian identity," in the words
of John Lough.[11]

Military presence in the republics of the "near abroad," combined with
their membership in the Russia-dominated Commonwealth of Independent States, provides Moscow with a perfect opportunity to control domestic processes in the former Soviet region.[12] It is not surprising that
other former Soviet republics strenuously resist Russia's efforts to establish permanent military bases on their territory;[13] only after intensive economic pressure bordering on blackmail do they concede.

Georgia, which is plagued by civil unrest, economic instability, and a
war against secessionist Abkhazia, has been a relatively easy target for
Moscow. The fall of Sukhumi in September 1993 bolstered the strength
of not only secessionist but also antigovernment forces that supported
Georgia's former president Zviyad Gamsakhurdia. Under these conditions,
the Georgian leader Eduard Shevardnadze (a former Soviet foreign minister) had no other option but to cave in to Russian economic pressure.[14]
Until then Georgia had declined to join the CIS because it viewed the
organization as infringing on its sovereignty. However, upon becoming a
CIS member, Georgia received much-needed Russian logistical support
against antigovernment forces. Furthermore, Pavel Grachev, the former
Russian defense minister, and Shevardnadze signed an agreement establishing joint border guard units to protect the borders of Georgia[15] and held
talks on the "creation of three permanent Russian military bases in Georgia
in 1995 on the expiry of the present temporary agreement on the status
of the Russian troops currently deployed there."[16] Shortly afterward Rus-

sian field engineers also began to prepare about twenty-five hundred peacekeepers to be deployed between Georgian and Abkhazian forces.

Not all republics have been so accommodating, however. For instance, despite the ongoing conflict in the predominantly Armenian enclave of Nagorno-Karabakh, Azerbaijan has been reluctant to allow Russian peacekeeping troops in the area because it feared their permanent presence. Azerbaijani authorities have insisted that in a choice between Grachev's peacekeeping plan and the plan developed by OSCE, the latter should be implemented.

Nevertheless, under severe economic pressure from Moscow, Azerbaijan was forced to rejoin the CIS, just as Georgia was. It is worth emphasizing that with these two states' becoming members of the Commonwealth, the CIS now includes all former Soviet republics except the Baltics. In the opinion of some leaders of the newly independent states (e.g., Kazakhstan's President Nursultan Nazarbayev), the CIS is needed to preserve the existing links of interrepublican cooperation mainly in the economic sphere. In the opinion of others (e.g., the former Ukrainian president Leonid Kravchuk), the Commonwealth's sole purpose should be to solve the temporary logistical problems associated with the disintegration of the USSR. For Russians, however, the CIS is primarily a political, economic, and military mechanism to secure the republic's dominant role in the region. Not surprisingly, Russian diplomats have been actively promoting the idea that the Commonwealth should be recognized as a regional and an international organization by such authoritative international bodies as the United Nations and the OSCE.[17] With such a recognition the Russian Federation's peacekeeping operations in the former Soviet Union conducted under the banner of the CIS would be legitimized by the international community, thus institutionalizing Moscow's preponderant role in the region.

By summer 1993, however, little evidence existed that the CIS was evolving into an effective integrative organization, especially in the security area. At a meeting of CIS defense ministers in May, Russia opposed two draft agreements that called for the creation of unified CIS military forces, although five other CIS states supported the proposed security organization. The Russian representative explained part of Moscow's opposition by noting that Russia would have to bear the brunt of the costs of such a force.[18] All pretense at military coordination within the CIS was finally dropped when Marshal Shaposhnikov resigned to take a high-level position in the Russian government. Several days later, on June 15, 1993, it was announced in Moscow that the CIS joint military command had been abolished.[19]

Since the summer of 1993, however, several important developments have occurred in security relations between the Russian Federation and other Soviet successor states, partly within the context of CIS institutions. As noted earlier, an agreement with Georgia resulted in the continued presence of Russian troops in the Caucasus and the establishment of joint border guard units (a similar agreement was also concluded with Armenia). Russia also signed important air defense agreements with a number of CIS states. In Central Asia the Russians have been active in coordinating security-related activities with the countries of the region, especially concerning the civil war in Tajikistan. Russia continues to view the borders of CIS members in the south as Russian borders and has committed the military personnel to defend them.

It is precisely the defense of its own internationally recognized borders, particularly in Central Asia, that constitutes the third objective pursued by Russia through its military involvement in the "near abroad." As emphasized by Colonel General Andrei Nikolaev, the commander of Russia's border troops, Russia cannot effectively guard its borders with CIS states against smuggling or arms and drug trafficking because of the need to maintain the unobstructed exchange of goods within the Commonwealth and the high cost of redeploying the border troops on Russia's new borders. According to Nikolaev, the solution is "guarding the CIS outer borders."[20]

Moscow officials are especially concerned about arms smugglers and drug traffickers who allegedly often come to Russia by penetrating the Tajik-Afghan border. To address this problem, as well as to pursue the other goals mentioned earlier, Russia has been seeking to resolve the civil war in Tajikistan and to secure the Tajik-Afghan border by means of its military presence in the republic. Thus, for example, arguing in support of keeping Russian military bases in Tajikistan, Anatoly Adamishin, the Russian president's special representative to Tajikistan and first deputy foreign minister, has warned that "should we go, the streamlet of drugs will become a river."[21]

The implementation of Russian foreign policy objectives has undoubtedly been helped by the dynamics of Tajikistan's civil war. The fact that Tajik antigovernmental forces have been receiving aid from Afghanistan and that their Afghan supporters have been involved in minor military expeditions into Tajik territory has led other Central Asian states, except for Turkmenistan, to view the ongoing civil war as a danger to the CIS at large. Pressured by its neighbors and confronted with the mounting challenge of opposition forces, the Tajik government has closely aligned itself with the Russian Federation in hope of receiving military aid. In late 1992 an agreement between the Tajik and Russian governments led to the stationing of Russian troops along the Tajik-Afghan border. Currently, some twenty thousand Russian troops are stationed in Tajikistan, where they continue to provide the only effective security support for a government challenged by Islamic opponents.[22]

On April 5, 1994, the Tajik government and the Tajik opposition began talks aimed at bringing an end to the civil war. Because of Russia's military support of the Tajik government, the opposition started to question the impartiality of Russian mediation efforts. Though Russia was reported to have pressured Tajikistan's government into peace talks with the opposition, Russia also warned the antigovernment forces that it would take "whatever steps are necessary to secure the Tajik-Afghan border."[23] Although peace talks have progressed under the eyes of the United Nations, Pakistan, and Iran, it is obvious that Russia has the strongest influence over the Tajik government. Yet after more than four years of sporadic fighting, the military situation in Tajikistan has not been resolved, and antigovernment forces continue to obtain support from forces in Afghanistan.

The fourth major goal of Russian military involvement in the conflicts in the former USSR is the protection of the ethnic Russian or, more generally, Russian-speaking population. Note that this objective is separated from the first three. The "protection of compatriots" is one of the favorite arguments in support of the neo-imperial policies, but there is genuine concern in Moscow about the fate of approximately 25 million Russians who after the collapse of the Soviet Union found themselves in the position of a minority in a foreign country. It should be emphasized, however, that in reality such a separation of goals is extremely difficult—the sincere and the more mercenary foreign policy objectives are often hopelessly intertwined.

For instance, since 1992 the Russian Federation has supported the move toward independence by the Russian-speaking minority located in the Transdniester region of eastern Moldova. Fearful of Moldovan nationalism and encroachments on their linguistic and cultural rights, many Russians in the Transdniester region have come to regard political independence as the only adequate guarantee of their well-being. Russia still maintains troops, the Fourteenth Army, on Moldovan territory. Not surprisingly, the successor to the former Fourteenth Army has actively supported the Dniester republic in its quest for independence. As a sovereign state, Moldova has repeatedly asked that the Russian troops withdraw from Moldovan territory. In response, however, Moscow claimed that the

Fourteenth Army and its successor force have been "playing a peacekeeping role and preventing bloodshed" in the Transdniester region.[24] Russia has linked its troop withdrawal with the issue of sovereignty for the Dniester republic and has attached its own economic and political conditions.

Since late 1992 the Russian Federation has been seeking an agreement to legitimize the presence of its troops in Moldova. Recognizing its weak position vis-à-vis Russia, some members of the Moldovan leadership have suggested agreeing to a treaty for the temporary stationing of Russian troops as preferable to the current "fait accompli of an unregulated, open ended troop presence."[25] Representing the Russian perspective, Lieutenant General Aleksandr Lebed, the former commander of the Fourteenth Army and now important political figure, stated that "to persuade Chisinau [Moldova's capital] of the necessity of granting the basing rights, it is not necessary to use force openly; economic measures are enough."[26] The truth of his statement was proven by 1994, when Russia successfully exerted economic pressure on Moldova, in effect forcing the republic to become a full member of the CIS.

The fifth and the final major goal of Russian peacekeeping in the "near abroad" states is to stop bloodshed in the regions of the former USSR. After all, a significant portion of Russian population still regards the CIS republics as a single, politically and culturally indivisible country. Referring to the conflicts in the former Soviet Union, Andrei Kozyrev summarized the feelings of many Russians by noting that "the people who are killing each other there are not alien to us, we lived in the same country until three years ago and we cannot simply leave them to their fate."[27]

The motivations in Moscow are clear for a more direct and assertive Russian response to what is perceived as growing chaos along—and even spilling over—its borders. Since negotiations have proved to be ineffective in most of the ongoing military conflicts, many Russian political elites, according to a Russian analyst, have come to believe that the bloodshed in "lands which simply can't qualify as 'foreign territories' must be halted, even if it means the direct use of Russian military force."[28]

From a more mercenary standpoint Moscow's leadership is becoming increasingly concerned about the massive flow of Russian, as well as non-Russian, refugees from the zones of conflict into the republic. Given the substantial housing shortage and the severe economic situation in Russia, the arriving refugees create many new socioeconomic difficulties that the Russian government wishes to avoid. Stopping the bloodshed of regional conflicts is one of the ways in which Russia tries to diminish the extremely burdensome influx of refugees from the "near abroad."

Peacekeeping: Let Somebody Else Do It?

Despite multiple objectives that can be effectively pursued by means of peacekeeping, Russia's military involvement in the conflicts entails a number of domestic and international problems. First, Russian peacekeeping missions have been domestically criticized for their high human cost. In the atmosphere of aggressive nationalism that now encompasses many Russian decision-making structures, such a line of criticism fails to gain a broad appeal, however. For example, the Russian policy of bolstering the Tajik government in its war against the opposition came under emotional attack in Moscow when twenty-five Russian soldiers were killed on the Tajik-Afghan border, but instead of curtailing Russia's military presence, this incident had a completely opposite effect. Reinforcements of Russian troops were at once flown into Tajikistan, and Russian missile attacks were mounted across the border into Afghanistan.[29] Russian troops are still occasionally killed in the fighting in Tajikistan.

Nevertheless, the Russian debacle in the secessionist republic Chechnya has the potential of diminishing domestic support for military operations in the former Soviet Union. The human tragedy brought about by the massive use of force in Chechnya has made many Russians wary of imperialist ambitions expressed by nationalist and conservative politicians. In a sense the Chechen conflict can paradoxically foster Russia's chances of escaping from the nationalist trap. By explicitly showing the dire consequences of reckless nationalist policies, Chechnya may inhibit the willingness of Russia's public and elites to support similar policies in the future, not only inside the Federation but also in the "near" and "far abroad."

Second, the financial cost of Russia's military mission has also been criticized in Moscow's policy-making circles. This is not surprising, since peacekeeping is rather expensive, especially for an economically distressed country like Russia. The Russian Defense Ministry estimated the cost of the operation in Tajikistan alone at 2.3 billion rubles in 1992.[30] Still, the notorious Russian affinity for great power politics and the strategic importance of the processes unraveling in the "near abroad" are likely to continue to outweigh financial considerations.

Third, serious resistance to Russia's role as a regional peacekeeper comes from the "near abroad" states themselves. Regardless of Russian motives— and neo-imperialist designs simply cannot be discounted, President Yeltsin's claims notwithstanding—some of Russia's neighbors have responded very negatively to the prospect of expanded Russian military involvement throughout the region. Discussions took place in 1993 concerning the establishment of a common security system for Eastern Europe that would include the former western republics of the USSR and the former central European members of the Warsaw Pact. According to Dmitrii Volskii, a liberal Russian commentator, "The anti-Russian direction of the planned association of East European states is absolutely clear." He attributes the plans to nationalist political forces in Ukraine.[31] Although Volskii is correct that nationalists in some of the new states are motivated by anti-Russian attitudes, high-level Russian officials, including the president, reinforce these attitudes by statements that imply a desire to re-create aspects of the old Russian-Soviet empire. In other words, the leaders of the newly independent states are responding to the views expressed in Moscow—and to Russian behavior patterns that they see as threatening. Calls by political leaders in the Baltics and Ukraine about NATO's expansion eastward to include their countries are examples of this concern.[32]

While the "near abroad" republics lack sufficient power to exert effective diplomatic pressure on the Russian Federation, many of them waste no time appealing to the West and major international organizations in their attempt to protect themselves from what is perceived (often rightly) as Russia's direct interference in their domestic affairs. As a result, Russia's repeated efforts to gain the imprimatur of the United Nations and the OSCE to act as a peacekeeper in the former Soviet region have been largely unsuccessful.

Yet Western countries refrain from explicitly criticizing Russia's military involvement. The United States, for example, moved increasingly toward the idea of "Baltic exceptionalism," according to which the Russians are expected to behave in complete accordance with the norms and principles of international law in Estonia, Latvia, and Lithuania in exchange for an implicit carte blanche in other parts of the former Soviet Union.[33] In general the West perceives Russia's activities in the "near abroad" as largely benign—as a stabilizing factor in a strife-ridden region.[34] Such a position has not gone unnoticed in the Russian Federation, where Boris Yeltsin has repeatedly declared that "the world community" sees Russia as having a special responsibility for keeping peace in the region.[35]

Western countries have not attempted to influence Russian policy toward the "near abroad" by offering (not merely promising) "carrots" either. Immediately after Russia's independence, Russian liberals expected their accelerating rapprochement with the West would result in the blossoming of trade and massive financial aid.[36] Confronted with the discouraging indicators of their own economic performance, however, Western countries have been quite reluctant to extend a helping hand to Russia, thus missing an opportunity to mold Moscow's international behavior.

What emerges from this discussion is the fact that the security interests of Russia—especially since for the foreseeable future they are likely to include the welfare of ethnic Russians in the "near abroad"—will increasingly come into conflict with the interests of at least some neighboring states. In other words, Russia can be viewed, in some cases at least, as a likely contributor to regional conflict, especially given the relative weakness of the government in Moscow and its inability to control the provocative statements and actions of leading political and military figures. Nevertheless, the alternatives to a "special" Russian security role seem very limited because of the apparent intractability of some of the conflicts, the concerns in Russia about their outcome, and the present unwillingness and probable inability of the West and the United Nations or any other international security organization to deal effectively with regional conflict in the former Soviet Union.

Whither Russian Peacekeeping?

The preceding analysis suggests that if the current international climate remains the same, Russia is likely to expand its role as a regional peacekeeper and, by implication, increase its influence over the non-Baltic states of the "near abroad." In other words, barring a Chechnya-style catastrophic performance by Russian troops in the "near abroad" conflicts, only significant international pressure can curtail Russia's military presence in the republics of the former Soviet Union.

Such a situation is fundamentally different from the conditions of a few years ago, when the degree of Russia's military involvement in the conflicts that erupted in the former USSR depended primarily on the balance between Yeltsin's liberal orientation and a much more conservative nationalist vision of Russia's foreign policy. Under present circumstances, however, although there are numerous disagreements among Russia's elites over many other major foreign policy issues, a "tougher" stance on the "near abroad" has been endorsed by virtually all Russian politicians. Referring to the growing domestic dissatisfaction with Russia's declining international status and the popular perception that Russia has been brought to its knees, one prominent analyst of Russian foreign policy has observed that "no government can afford to ignore these domestic features if it wishes to maintain its legitimacy."[37]

The situation in Russia has some similarity to that in the Weimar Republic, in which a deep socioeconomic crisis and the psychological humiliation of losing World War I led to the soaring rise of right-wing forces. For millions of Soviet people who proudly regarded the USSR as their own state and homeland, its disappearance is a disaster. For imperially minded Russians, it is also a "national" catastrophe that is causing a deep psychological trauma.[38] Russian grievances over the collapse of the USSR have been exacerbated by highly publicized accounts that the human rights of those ethnic Russians (or more generally, Russian-speakers) who found themselves outside the boundaries of the Russian Federation were being violated. Various constraints on acquiring citizenship imposed by local authorities, language discrimination, the loss of former privileges, and other explosive issues concerning the rights of Russians in the "near abroad" have substantially radicalized the political process in Russia itself, thus providing fertile soil for the growth of nationalist sentiments.

At the same time, however, because of the concern for electoral support, Yeltsin's government has become extremely vulnerable to nationalist pressures. Although such actions as the crackdown on the rebellious Parliament and the espousal of a super-presidential constitution were intended to relax the impact of internal influences on domestic and foreign policy formulation, the behavior of Yeltsin's Russia has become increasingly reflective of the strength of nationalist sentiment at home.[39] "That which is now taking place," wrote the Russian foreign minister Andrei Kozyrev in *Izvestiya*, "is reminiscent of 1933 in Germany, when some democrats began to adopt nationalist stances."[40]

Implementing a successful foreign policy campaign to defend the "national interest" has become more realistic and much more politically profitable than any attempt, inevitably painful, to resurrect the collapsed economy. Yeltsin himself has been drawn into the competition of "who can be the best nationalist," which might explain the assertiveness of Kozyrev's foreign policy.[41] In January 1996, after engaging in a protracted struggle with conservative forces and realizing that President Yeltsin perceived him as a political liability in the increasingly nationalist environment, Andrei Kozyrev resigned as a foreign minister of the Russian Federation. He was replaced by Yevgenii Primakov, who is widely perceived as more willing than his predecessor to stand up to the West, to reassert Russia's influence in the former Soviet Union, and to defend more vigorously and effectively Russian national interests.[42] At his first press conference Primakov promised he would redirect Russian foreign policy to emphasize relations with CIS and Eastern Europe, a promise he followed up with a series of trips to Tashkent, Dushanbe, Kyiv, Minsk, Bratislava, and Warsaw during the first three months of 1996.[43]

Whether the West needs Russia's "stabilizing" role in the former Soviet region should be decided in policy-making circles. This essay refrains from making any policy prescriptions. Its goal is more modest—to look at the current determinants of the degree of Russian military involvement in the "near abroad" conflicts and analyze the direction of future developments. The conclusion at which this study has arrived is quite clear—short of any substantial change in present international reactions, Russia will continue to play a more active role as a regional peacekeeper.

Notes

An earlier version of this essay was published in *The Soviet and Post-Soviet Review* 22, no. 2 (1995): 165–77. It is included here with the permission of the publisher.

1. Quoted in Suzanne Crow, "Russia Seeks Leadership in Regional Peacekeeping," *RFE/RL Research Report* 2, no. 15 (1993): 28.

2. For a general discussion of Russian peacekeeping, see Roger E. Kanet, "The Russian Federation," in *Coping with Conflict after the Cold War*, ed. Edward A. Kolodziej and Roger E. Kanet (Baltimore, Md.: Johns Hopkins University Press, 1996), 60–86.

3. Radio Rossii, December 11, 1992.

4. Russia welcomes the OSCE logistical, financial, and other "material" support for, but not "supervision" of, its peacekeeping operations in the CIS. See, for example, Vladimir Socor, "Russia Does Not Want 'Supervision' of Its Peacekeeping," *RFE/RL Daily Report*, October 13, 1994.

5. Crow, "Russia Seeks Leadership in Regional Peacekeeping," 28. See also Suzanne Crow, "Ambartsumov's Influence on Russian Foreign Policy," *RFE/RL Research Report* 2, no. 19 (1993): 36–41.

6. Quoted in Leonid Bershidsky, "Georgia Peace Force Riles Duma," *Moscow Times*, June 18, 1994.

7. Celestine Bohlen, "Nationalist Vote Toughens Russian Foreign Policy," *New York Times*, January 25, 1994.

8. Alexei Arbatov, "Russia's Foreign Policy Alternatives," *International Security* 18, no. 2 (1993): 5–43. On one occasion, for instance, Zhirinovsky referred to Kozyrev as a CIA agent and the secretary of the American ambassador in Moscow. See Alex Pravda, "The Politics of Foreign Policy," in *Developments in Russian and Post-Soviet Studies*, ed. Stephen White, Alex Pravda, and Zvi Gitelman (Durham, N.C.: Duke University Press, 1944), 216.

9. Jeff Checkel, "Russian Foreign Policy: Back to the Future?" *RFE/RL Research Report* 1, no. 41 (1992): 17–18.

10. Quoted in *Pravda*, February 20, 1993.

11. John Lough, "Defining Russia's Relations with Neighboring States," *RFE/RL Research Report* 2, no. 20 (1993): 53. See also Lough's earlier article, "The Place of the 'Near Abroad' in Russian Foreign Policy," *RFE/RL Research Report* 2, no. 11

(1993): 21–29; and two essays by Andrei Zagorski, "Russlands Bezienhungen zum 'fernen' und 'nahen Ausland'" and "Die Gemeinschaft Unabhangiger Staaten: Entwicklungen und Perspektiven," *Berichte des Bundesinstiuts fur ostwissenschaftliche und internationale Studien,* no. 46 and 50, respectively (1992).

12. The term *near abroad* is highly nationalist. It can be interpreted to imply that Russia treats other post-Soviet republics as semi-foreign and hence semi-independent entities.

13. The chief of the Russian General Staff, Mikhail Kolesnikov, announced that Moscow was planning to sign bilateral agreements with every former Soviet republic except Ukraine and the Baltic states to establish some thirty military bases throughout the CIS. Quoted in Bruce Porter and Carol Saivetz, "The Once and Future Empire: Russian and the 'Near Abroad,'" *Washington Quarterly* 17, no. 3 (1994): 87.

14. Elizabeth Fuller, "The Transcaucasus: War, Turmoil, Economic Collapse," *RFE/RL Research Report* 3, no. 1 (1994): 57.

15. Bess Brown, "Armenians and Georgians to Serve in Russian Border Troops," *RFE/RL Daily Report,* March 16, 1994.

16. Elizabeth Fuller, "Grachev Visits Georgia," *RFE/RL Daily Report,* June 13, 1994. The security agreements between Russia and Georgia, however, have not yet been ratified by the Georgian parliament.

17. Suzanne Crow, "Russia Promotes the CIS as an International Organization," *RFE/RL Research Report* 3, no. 11 (1994): 33–38.

18. *RFE/RL News Briefs* 2, no. 21 (1993): 21.

19. *RFE/RL News Briefs* 2, no. 26 (1993): 7. See also Stephen Foye, "End of CIS Command Heralds New Russian Defense Policy?" *RFE/RL Research Report* 2, no. 27 (1993): 45–49.

20. Quoted in Vladimir Socor, "Russia Claims to Defend 'CIS Borders,'" *RFE/RL Daily Report,* November 15, 1994.

21. Quoted from *Interfax* News Agency, August 9, 1993, in BBC SWB, Tajik-Afghan Border Situation, Soviet Union 1764 C2/1, August 11, 1993.

22. Keith Martin, "Russians Leaving Tajikistan," *RFE/RL Daily Report,* June 20, 1994.

23. Bess Brown, "Rakhmonov in Moscow," *RFE/RL Daily Report,* May 9, 1994.

24. Michael Shafir, "Grachev Ends Romanian Visit in Clash over 14th Army," *RFE/RL Daily Report,* March 31, 1994.

25. Vladimir Socor, "Moldova to 'Compromise' on Russian Troops?" *RFE/RL Daily Report,* May 19, 1994.

26. Quoted in ibid.

27. Quoted in Leonid Bershidsky, "Georgia Peace Form Riles Duma," *Moscow Times,* June 19, 1994.

28. Arkady Chereshnia, "Big Brother as an Equal," *New Times,* no. 17 (1993): 205–7.

29. Anthony Hyman, "Russian outside Russia," *World Today* 49, no. 11 (1993): 205–7.

30. Crow, "Russia Seeks Leadership in Regional Peacekeeping," 32–38. On the costs of "peacekeeping" in Chechnya, see Andrei Raevsky, "Russian Military Performance in Chechnya: An Initial Evaluation," *Journal of Slavic Military Studies* 8, no. 4 (1995): 681–89.

31. Dmitrii Volskii, "Eastern Europe—Counterbalance to Russia?" New Times, no. 21 (1993): 22. Membership would supposedly include Ukraine, Hungary, Poland, the Czech Republic, Slovakia, Romania, Bulgaria, the Baltic states, Belarus, Moldova, and possibly Georgia. For a more extensive discussion of this Ukrainian security initiative, see Roman Solchanyk, "Ukraine's Search for Security," *RFE/RL Research Report* 2, no. 21 (1993): 1–6. Although plans for an east central European security organization have not been pursued, some of these countries see membership in NATO as a possible bulwark against Russia. Alexei Pushkov, "Building a New NATO at Russia's Expense," *Moscow News*, September 24, 1993.

32. For recent statements by officials of these countries on NATO membership, see *FBIS-SOV-96-179*, September 13, 1996, 65, for Latvia; *FBIS-SOV-96-175*, September 9, 1996, 84–85, for Lithuania; *FBIS-SOV-96-179*, September 13, 1996, 64, for Estonia; and Ustina Markus, "Belarus, Ukraine Take Opposite Views," *Transition* 2, no. 23 (1996): 22.

33. See, for example, "The Situation in Russia: Briefing of the Commission on Security and Cooperation in Europe," in *Implementation of the Helsinki Accords* (Washington, D.C.: Commission on Security and Cooperation in Europe, 1993), 5. The results of the policy of "Baltic exceptionalism" have been quite conspicuous. The conclusion of Russian-Latvian and Russian-Estonian treaties on the withdrawal of Russian troops from the territory of the two republics is in sharp contrast to the unregulated presence of Russia's Fourteenth Army in less "fortunate" Moldova. See Dzintra Bungs, "Russia Agrees to Withdraw Troops from Latvia," *RFE/RL Research Report* 3 no. 22 (1994): 1–19; Stephen Foye, "Estonia-Russia Agreement: Russian Perspective," *RFE/RL Daily Report*, July 27, 1994; and Socor, "Moldova to 'Compromise' on Russian Troops."

34. Porter and Saivetz, "The Once and Future Empire," 89.

35. Quoted in Crow, "Russia Seeks Leadership in Regional Peacekeeping," 28–32.

36. Suzanne Crow, "Russia Asserts Its Strategic Agenda," *RFE/RL Research Report* 2, no. 50 (1993): 1–8.

37. Peter Shearman, "Defining the National Interest: Russian Foreign Policy and Domestic Politics," in *The Foreign Policy of the Russian Federation*, ed. Roger E. Kanet and Alexander V. Kozhemiakin (London: Macmillan, 1997), 14.

38. Igor Torbakov, "The 'Statists' and the Ideology of Russian Imperial Nationalism," *RFE/RL Research Report* 1, no. 49 (1992): 10–16.

39. Alexander Kozhemiakin, "Democratization and Foreign Policy Change: The Case of the Russian Federation," *Review of International Studies* 23, no. 1 (1997): 49–74.

40. Quoted in Lena Jonson, "The Foreign Policy Debate in Russia: In Search of a National Interest," *Nationalities Papers* 22, no. 1 (1994): 190.

41. Besides a more assertive stance on the "near abroad," other changes in Russian foreign policy include the improvement of relations with Iraq; repeated attempts to protect Russia's "historical ally," Serbia, from international sanctions; and explicit criticism of what is perceived as the tendency of the United States to dictate its own terms in the international arena. Crow, "Russia Seeks Leadership in Regional Peacekeeping," 28–32.

42. For Primakov's views on Russian foreign policy, see *Izvestiya*, March 6, 1996.

43. Scott Parrish, "Chaos in Foreign-Policy Decision-Making," *Transition* 2, no. 10 (1996): 33.

Conclusion

Roger E. Kanet

As Charles W. Kegley Jr. and Gregory Raymond have pointed out, the end of the cold war was received and interpreted very differently by different analysts.[1] For those they call "optimists," such as Francis Fukuyama, the revolutionary changes associated with the collapse of communism in Europe represented "the end of mankind's evolution and the universalization of Western liberal democracy as the final form of government."[2] The global wave of democratization, the new superpower arms accords, the reinvigorated role of the United Nations, and the continued movement toward expanded world trade were all seen as encouraging developments toward a more cooperative and peaceful world. Others, however, have viewed the end of the cold war as a resumption of the historical process of power politics conducted by multiple actors now that two superpowers no longer dominate the world environment. Instead of introducing an era in which political, economic, ideological, and military rivalry no longer exist, the post–cold war period could mean "increased instability, unpredictability, and violence in international affairs."[3] The possibilities of renewed great-power conflict, nuclear proliferation, mounting protectionism and trade wars, nationalist revolt and civil war, and other dangers to global peace emerge in the post–cold war environment.

The essays in this volume treat one aspect of this set of problems that continue to beset the world—local and regional conflict, including warfare and the growing regionalization of international security. Although the world continues to be organized on the assumption that states—defined as sovereign entities that exercise effective control or supervision over the people, institutions, and activities in a given territory—are the key independent actors, increasingly this assumption does not match reality. As we have seen in these essays, in a large number of presumed states these conditions simply do not hold. In some, significant portions of the population—for religious, ethnic, ideological, or other reasons—do not accept as legitimate the constitutional arrangements under which they live. In addition, governments, even those of the so-called powers, are increasingly incapable of controlling much of the economic activity that occurs in their country. Despite these facts—and many others that also indicate the erosion of states as sovereign international actors—the world continues to be organized on the assumption that sovereign states are the most important units.

The essays address precisely the types of problems the world faces because of the weakness of existing political units, their incompatibility with the aspirations of large numbers of people, and the absence of alternative institutions that might deal with this predicament. Whether it is Catholics in Northern Ireland, Orthodox Serbs in Bosnia-Herzegovina, or other minority communities contesting a political order they find illegitimate, the issue concerns challenging the legitimacy of the state in heterogeneous societies and the ways in which these societies might be organized to reduce the pressures for conflict. Given the implications of the breakdown or implosion of state structures and the outbreak of military conflict for the regional or international community, a question arises about the responsibility and ability of third parties to help resolve conflict.

Although in the final years of the cold war progress was made in containing, even resolving, some regional conflicts—as in Angola, El Salvador, and Cambodia—the experience of the first years after the end of the superpower confrontation has not been encouraging about the ability of the international community to deal effectively with regional conflict in the future. The recent experience of such international organizations as the United Nations has been mixed, at best, in responding to regional conflicts. In Bosnia-Herzegovina thousands of murders and rapes and the destruction of a centuries-old multiethnic society occurred before the world community acted. Even now it is not clear that conflict will not break out again or that the world community has either the ability or the will to bring to a resolution the ethnic conflict that has torn apart the region. In Rwanda, Burundi, and eastern Zaire the mass murder of entire communities has still failed to attract more than token involvement of the major powers. Similar conflict situations exist in other world regions—from Somalia to Afghanistan, from Albania to Tajikistan. In none of these cases of local or regional conflict are external actors likely to be willing or able to play an important role in dampening the conflict and resolving the problems that contribute to it.

The conditions that apparently must be met for an international intervention to succeed in mediating conflict and strengthening the prospects for peace greatly limit the range of conflicts in which the international community is likely to become involved.[4] So long as the parties to the conflict are engaged in military actions and have not yet decided that some type of compromise solution is preferable to continued warfare, outside actors are not likely to become involved. As Paul Diehl has shown, of the three U.N. operations that he examined the most successful one was in Cambodia, where peacekeeping forces were deployed after a peace agreement had been reached. Moreover, such regional organizations as the European Union and the Organization for Security and Cooperation in Europe have been largely unsuccessful in marshaling effective support for efforts to constrain and mediate regional conflict. This has proven to be the case in Bosnia-Herzegovina, and more recently these organizations have been unable to take a leadership role in other emerging conflicts in the Balkans. Finally, when a self-proclaimed or presumed peacekeeper is an important contributor to regional conflict, as in the case of Russia, the prospects for peaceful resolution of differences remain very limited.

The future of peacekeeping at the regional level is unclear. Yet as the contributors to the present volume indicate and many other analysts have also argued, the successful containment and resolution of regional conflict are increasing important to the global community. If large portions of the world are not to be destined for a Hobbesian future, the international community must discover ways to respond to people's legitimate demands for security—defined in physical, economic, political, and cultural terms. Ways must be found that will reduce animosities and create environments that will permit disparate communities to live, interact, and resolve their differences peacefully. Progress has been made in this direction for Western Europe. It is important for the future of the human race that comparable progress in resolving conflict occur throughout much of the rest of the world.

Notes

1. Charles W. Kegley Jr. and Gregory Raymond, *A Multipolar Peace? Great-Power Politics in the Twenty-First Century* (New York: St. Martin's, 1994), 8.

2. Francis Fukuyama, "The End of History?" *National Interest,* no. 16 (1989): 3.

3. Samuel P. Huntington, "No Exit: The Errors of Endism," *National Interest,* no. 17 (1989): 6. For a selection of the writings that point to the potential threats in the current international environment, see Samuel P. Huntington Jr., "The Clash of Civilizations," *Foreign Affairs* 72, no. 3 (1993): 22–49; Michael T. Klare, "The Next Great Arms Race," *Foreign Affairs* 72, no. 3 (1993): 136–52; Stephen John Stedman, "The New Interventionists," *Foreign Affairs* 72, no. 1 (1993): 1–16; Stanley Kober, "Revolutions Gone Bad," *Foreign Policy,* no. 91 (1993): 63–83; and Lester

C. Thorow, *Head to Head: Coming Economic Battles among Japan, Europe, and America* (New York: William Morrow, 1991). Paul Kennedy, *Preparing for the Twenty-First Century* (New York: Random House, 1993), also lays out with great clarity the central problems facing contemporary society and the difficulty in responding to them.

4. Edward A. Kolodziej, "Thinking about Coping: Actors, Resources, Roles, and Strategies," in *Coping with Conflict after the Cold War,* ed. Edward A. Kolodziej and Roger E. Kanet (Baltimore: Johns Hopkins University Press, 1996), 363–93, deals explicitly with the problem of surmounting constraints on the ability of the international community to respond to regional conflict.

Contributors

Stephen P. Cohen is a cofounder and current director of the Program in Arms Control, Disarmament, and International Security and a professor of political science and history at the University of Illinois at Urbana-Champaign. Cohen, an expert on South Asian security and nuclear proliferation issues, spent 1985–87 as a member of the U.S. State Department policy planning staff and 1992–93 as a scholar-in-residence at the Ford Foundation in New Delhi. He is the author of *The Indian Army* and *The Pakistan Army* and the coeditor of *Nuclear Proliferation in South Asia; South Asia after the Cold War;* and *Brasstacks and Beyond.*

Paul F. Diehl is a professor of political science and a member of the Program in Arms Control, Disarmament, and International Security at the University of Illinois at Urbana-Champaign. He is the author of *International Peacekeeping*, coauthor of *Territorial Changes and International Conflict,* and editor of *The Politics of Global Governance; Reconstructing Realpolitik; Measuring the Correlates of War;* and *Through the Straits of Armageddon*, as well as the author of over sixty articles on peace and security affairs.

Roger E. Kanet is a professor and dean of the Graduate School of International Studies of the University of Miami. He is emeritus professor of political science and a former member of the Russian and East European Center and the Program in Arms Control, Disarmament, and International Security at the University of Illinois at Urbana-Champaign, where he also served as director of International Programs and Studies and associate vice chancellor for academic affairs from 1989 to 1997. He is the editor of *The Soviet Union, Eastern Europe and the Developing States;* coeditor of three books with Edward A. Kolodziej, the most recent of which is *Coping with Conflict* *after the Cold War;* and coeditor, with A. V. Kozhemiakin, of *The Foreign Policy of the Russian Federation.*

William F. Kelleher is an assistant professor of anthropology and member of both the Unit for Criticism and Interpretive Theory and the Program in Arms Control, Disarmament, and International Security at the University of Illinois at Urbana-Champaign. He is currently completing a book on culture, class, colonial legacies, and political conflict in Northern Ireland.

Edward A. Kolodziej is the cofounder and the first director of the Program in Arms Control, Disarmament, and International Security and a professor of political science at the University of Illinois at Urbana-Champaign. He is the author of numerous books and articles on international politics and security, including *French International Policy under de Gaulle and Pompidou* and *Making and Marketing Arms;* he has coedited three books with Roger E. Kanet, the most recent of which is *Coping with Conflict after the Cold War.*

Alexander V. Kozhemiakin is a graduate of the Moscow State Institute of International Relations of the Russian Ministry of International Relations and received his Ph.D. in political science from the University of Illinois at Urbana-Champaign. He completed a post-doctoral fellowship at the Olin Institute for Strategic Studies of Harvard University and is currently an assistant professor of political science at Georgia State University. His publications include the coedited volume *The Foreign Policy of the Russian Federation* and articles in scholarly journals.

Chetan Kumar received his Ph.D. in political science and has served as a research assistant in the Program in Arms Control, Disarmament, and International Security at the University of Illinois at Urbana-Champaign. He is currently with the International Peace Academy. His research interests include the role of technology in conflict resolution, international politics, and environmental security, and the security roles of international organizations. He is coauthor of articles on international intervention and coeditor of *South Asia Approaches the Millennium.*

Carol Skalnik Leff is an assistant professor of political science and an executive committee member of the Russian and East European Center and the Program in Arms Control, Disarmament, and International Security at the University of Illinois at Urbana-Champaign. Her research interests are East European domestic and international politics, problems of nationalism, and postcommunist transitions. She is the author of *National Conflict in Czechoslovakia*.

Robert J. McKim is an associate professor of religious studies and philosophy and an executive committee member of the Program in Arms Control, Disarmament, and International Security at the University of Illinois at Urbana-Champaign. He is coeditor of *The Morality of Nationalism* and has published numerous articles on ethics, history of philosophy, and philosophy of religion. He is currently finishing a book on the significance of religious diversity to religious belief.

Gerardo L. Munck is an associate professor of political science, an affiliate of the Center for Latin American and Caribbean Studies, and a member of the Program in Arms Control, Disarmament, and International Security at the University of Illinois at Urbana-Champaign. He is the author of *Authoritarianism and Democratization* and numerous articles on transitions to democracy in Latin America and on social movement theory.

Paul W. Schroeder is a professor emeritus of history and political science and a member of the Program in Arms Control, Disarmament, and International Security at the University of Illinois at Urbana-Champaign. He specializes in the history of European and world international politics since the eighteenth century and has published numerous articles and books on the history of international politics from the Metternich era through World War II, including *Metternich's Diplomacy at Its Zenith* and *The Transformation of European Politics, 1763–1848*.

Marvin G. Weinbaum is a professor of political science; the director of the South and West Asian Studies Program; and a member of the Program in Arms Control, Disarmament, and International Security at the University of Illinois at Urbana-Champaign. He is a trustee of both the American Institute of Pakistan Studies and American Institute of Indian Studies. Weinbaum is the author of four books, including *Pakistan and Afghanistan,* and over fifty essays on political development and political economy and is the coeditor, with Chetan Kumar, of *South Asia Approaches the Millennium.*

Index

Israeli-Arab conflict. *See* Arab-Israeli conflict

Italy: conflict with Yugoslavia over Trieste, 19; intervention in Mozambique, 189–90n.10; intervention in Somalia, 156, 160

Jamiat-i-Islami, 89
Japan: and Northeast Asian security, 30–32; relations with India, 101; relations with U.S., 31–32; support for Arab-Israeli peace process, 29
Jefferson, Thomas, 151–52
Jericho: Palestinian self-rule in, 29
Jinnah, Mohammed Ali, 114, 121
Joint Declaration, Irish-British (1993), 48, 52, 53, 75–76
Jordan: political instability in, 30; and regional balance of power, 24

Kabila, Laurent, 12
Kant, Immanuel, 136
Karadzic, Radovan, 15
Kashmir: Indian-Pakistani conflict over, 36–37, 87, 88, 92–93, 96, 99, 101, 103, 105, 108, 118, 120–21, 128; relations with China, 120
Kautilya, 111
Kazakhstan, 100
Kegley, Charles W., Jr., 241
Khan, Ayub, 115
Khmer Rouge, 169, 171, 178–79, 182, 183–84, 185, 186
Kissinger, Henry, 211
Koch, Koen, 216, 219
Kolesnikov, Mikhail, 237n.13
Kolodziej, Edward A., 3
Konrad Adenauer Foundation, 208
Korea. *See* North Korea; South Korea
Kothari, Rajni, 112
Kozyrev, Andrei, 226, 231, 235, 236n.8
Kravchuk, Leonid, 228
Kurdish civil war, 12
Kuwait: Iraqi attack on, 2, 26, 96; relations with Pakistan, 95; Western intervention in, 14
Kyrgyzstan, 100

Latin America: democratic transitions in, 200; regional security in, 33–34
Latvia, 233. *See also* Baltic states
Lebed, Lt. Gen. Aleksandr, 231
liberal institutionalism, 136–37

Libya: isolation of, 26
Lithuania, 233. *See also* Baltic states
Lloyd, David, 52, 53
Lois, Gen. Bruno, 156
Lough, John, 227
Louis XIV, king of France, 140, 148

Maastricht Treaty, 19
Macedonia: independence movement in, 19; NATO intervention in, 164; OSCE intervention in, 217; U.N. peacekeeping operations in, 162
Mahdi, Ali, 157
Major, John, 48, 75
Malaysia: ethnic conflicts in, 33; relations with Pakistan, 101
Maldives: Indian intervention in, 189–90n.10
Margalit, Avishai, 68, 71, 72, 75
Masoud, Ahmad Shah, 89
Mayall, James, 195, 198
Meri, Lennart, 214
Middle East: security system in, 24–30, **25;** superpower impact on conflict in, 1–2
Milosevic, Slobodan, 12
Mindanao: ethnic conflict on, 33
Mitchell, George, 44, 49
Mladic, Gen. Ratko, 15
Mobutu Sese Seko, 12
modernization theory, 58
Moldova, 205, 217, 230–31
Monroe Doctrine, 34
Morrison, Bruce, 52
Mozambique: Italian intervention in, 189–90n.10; post–cold war situation in, 1
mujahidin, 89, 90, 97, 98, 100
multiculturalism: in Northern Ireland, 61; virtues of, 70
Muslim fundamentalism, 26, 27, 28, 30. *See also* Islam
Mussolini, Benito, 152n.5, 211

Nagorno-Karabakh, 217, 228
Napoleon Bonaparte, 147
National Commission for the Consolidation of Peace (COPAZ), 183, 184
nationalism: Irish, 65–86; Serbian, 12, 206
national liberation movements. *See* independence movements
NATO. *See* North Atlantic Treaty Organization
Nazarbayev, Nursultan, 228
Nehru, Jawaharlal, 114, 115, 116, 120